MANAGING THEIR OWN AFFAIRS

MANAGING THEIR OWN AFFAIRS

The Australian Deaf Community in the 1920s and 1930s

Breda Carty

GALLAUDET UNIVERSITY PRESS

Washington, DC

Gallaudet University Press
Washington, DC 20002
http://gupress.gallaudet.edu

Library of Congress Cataloging-in-Publication Data

Names: Carty, Breda, author.
Title: Managing their own affairs : the Australian deaf community in the 1920s
   and 1930s / Breda Carty.
Description: Washington, DC : Gallaudet University Press, [2017] | Includes
   bibliographical references and index.
Identifiers: LCCN 2017040273 | ISBN 9781944838102 (hard cover : alk. paper) |
   ISBN 9781944838119 (e-book)
Subjects: LCSH: Deaf—Australia—History—20th century. |
   Deaf—Services for—Australia—History—20th century. |
   Deaf—Australia—Social conditions—20th century.
Classification: LCC HV2943 .C37 2017 | DDC 362.4/2576099409042--dc23
LC record available at https://lccn.loc.gov/2017040273

∞ This paper meets the requirements of ANSI/NISO Z39.48-1992
(Permanence of Paper).

Cover photo courtesy of the Deaf Society, Parramatta, NSW, Australia.

CONTENTS

ACKNOWLEDGMENTS

I AM GRATEFUL to Gallaudet University Press for their long-standing support for deaf history, and in particular to Ivey Wallace and Doug Roemer for their careful editing and their patience with unfamiliar Australian institutions and terminology.

Some of the information in chapters 3, 4, and 6 has previously been published in the collection *In Our Own Hands: Essays in Deaf History 1780–1970*, edited by Brian H. Greenwald and Joseph J. Murray for Gallaudet University Press in 2016.

This book started life as a PhD dissertation, and I am enormously grateful to my supervisors, Professor Mark Finnane and the late Professor Des Power of Griffith University, for their patience, encouragement and scholarly guidance.

I am indebted to the helpful staff in many libraries and archives—especially those at the Mitchell Library, the National Library of Australia, the State Library of Victoria, the John Oxley Library, the Public Records Office of Victoria, the Queensland State Archives, and the RNID Library in London. John Hay of the British Deaf History Society also helped me find my way around British records.

The Deaf Societies of Australia are important in this history, although they may not always appear in the most positive light. The modern incarnations of these oganizations are much more community-minded, and have all been very generous in sharing their archives and information. I thank the staff at the Deaf Society (New South Wales), Vicdeaf, Deaf Services Queensland, Deaf Can:Do (South Australia), and the Western Australian Deaf Society for their hospitality and assistance. I also thank Ken Donnell for his timely discovery of some long-lost records in Queensland.

John W. Flynn's collection of historical documents in the State Library of Victoria has been invaluable to my research. I am grateful for the time he spent helping me make use of his collection and for sharing with me his knowledge of Australian Deaf history and some of its key personalities. John Flynn, Brian Reynolds, Cameron Davie, and Adam Schembri also provided helpful comments on an earlier version of this book.

I thank Michael Uniacke for sharing tape recordings of interviews he conducted in the 1980s, for assistance with locating photographs, and for giving some of the people and events in this book another life in his fiction writing. I was fortunate to be able to interview Joe Conley, and the late Jeff Armstrong, Cliff Ellwood, Dorothy Griffiths, Jim O'Gorman, Fred Sandon, Caroline Spranklin, Ken Weber, and Edena Winn, and I thank them for sharing their memories with me. I am also grateful to Robert Adam, Colin Allen, Della Bampton, the late Betty Bonser, Peter Bonser, Merril Cook, Shane Hickey, Susannah Macready, Joe Murray, Carole Noonan, Jean St. Clair, and Darlene Thornton, who all helped with identifying and copying sources and many other large and small tasks.

My family has been a constant source of support. Thanks above all to my husband Cameron Davie and our son Rowan, for all the love, cooking, and technical wizardry and for keeping me living in the present rather than disappearing into the past.

And finally, I would like to thank the Australian Deaf community for being such a resilient, creative and sustaining presence in the lives of many generations of people.

LIST OF ABBREVIATIONS

AAAD	Australian Association for the Advancement of the Deaf
AAD	Australian Association of the Deaf
AFADS	Australian Federation of Adult Deaf Societies
ADDA	Australasian Deaf and Dumb Association
ADDSNSW	Adult Deaf and Dumb Society of New South Wales
ADDSV	Adult Deaf and Dumb Society of Victoria
BDA	British Deaf Association
BDDA	British Deaf and Dumb Association
JWF	John W. Flynn [Collection of papers]
MHR	Member of the House of Representatives
MLA	Member of the Legislative Assembly
NCDD	National Council of the Deaf and Dumb
NSW	New South Wales
NSWADDC	New South Wales Association of Deaf and Dumb Citizens
PROV	Public Record Office of Victoria
QADDM	Queensland Adult Deaf and Dumb Mission
QDDCRA	Queensland Deaf and Dumb Citizens Reformed Association
QLD or Qld	Queensland
SA	South Australia
VDDI	Victorian Deaf and Dumb Institution
VDS	Victorian Deaf Society [Collection of papers]
VIC or Vic	Victoria
WA	Western Australia

NOTE ON TERMINOLOGY

Deaf

I have used *Deaf* when referring to deaf people collectively and to entities, such as *Deaf community*, *Deaf culture*, *Deaf autonomy*, and other similar terms. I have used the lower-case *deaf* elsewhere.

I have also, of course, followed the use of *deaf* and *Deaf* in source material quoted. The use of the upper-case *Deaf* is not a recent phenomenon and has occurred prolifically in historical sources. It seems that writers (both deaf and hearing) in late nineteenth- and early twentieth-century Britain and Australia regularly used *Deaf* or *Deaf and Dumb* to refer to deaf people collectively, but rarely when referring to them as individuals.

Australian Terms

Premier: State leader (the equivalent of a U.S. state governor).
Constitution/Memorandum and Articles of Association: Bylaws of an organization.
Chief Secretary (formerly Colonial Secretary): Senior government official in some Australian states during the twentieth century. The role was known as the Home Secretary in Queensland.

1

Introduction

ON THE EVENING of May 8, 1929, police were called to a disturbance at the premises of the Adult Deaf and Dumb Society of New South Wales in Sydney. Deaf people were protesting the dismissal of welfare officer Herbert Hersee, the Society's most senior employee. During the course of the evening, the police were obliged to call for reinforcements in their efforts to quell the unusual gathering. The next day, the event was reported in the *Sydney Morning Herald* as a "demonstration" and an "angry meeting."

This event was one of many expressions of discontent and attempts to challenge the established deaf welfare organizations in Australia during the late 1920s and 30s. During this period, deaf Australians, like deaf people in a number of other countries, challenged the "charity" model of most of the schools and service organizations that served them, and they took significant steps toward autonomy and citizenship. The gains they made were temporary, however, and they disappeared during the war years and post-war period. Not until later in the twentieth century did deaf adults again assert their right to more representation and autonomy in their social and political organizations. The efforts of the earlier wave of activists in the first part of the twentieth century had been largely forgotten by then; however, these attempts to "manage their own affairs" were a significant expression of deaf people's aspirations. They reflected similar aspirations in other minorities within Australia and also paralleled deaf people's activities in other Western countries.

During this period, deaf people were very active, both in establishing new organizations that served their needs and in resisting the controls imposed on them by some of the older organizations. These efforts reflected some of the broader social movements of the time and demonstrated parallels with other Australian minority groups, such as Aborigines and women, in their articulation of themselves as citizens,

1

their search for advancement and equal rights, and their challenges to a charity model of service provision. Deaf communities became the sites of power struggles between some hearing administrators and a growing number of deaf people and hearing supporters who wished to have more control over their institutions and more equality with hearing people—aspirations that they often described as "managing their own affairs."

Many of the people involved were charismatic and ambitious individuals, some of whom had migrated to Australia from Britain or Ireland, bringing with them well-developed beliefs about how Deaf communities should be organized, and in some cases, unrealized personal ambitions that impacted their activities in Australia. Inevitably, many of the personalities and ideologies clashed, and the organizations they established were affected by these clashes.

The International Context

The historical development of Deaf communities and their sign languages is emerging in increasing detail around the world.[1] The work of historians has shown that by the close of the nineteenth century, when this study begins, education for deaf children was well established in Europe, North America, Australia, and many other regions. Deaf communities using signed languages were clearly defined and active in many countries. During the final few decades of the nineteenth century, growing numbers of deaf individuals had significant roles in forming community groups and national organizations, and establishing, administering, and teaching in schools for deaf children. However, these developments were being countered in many countries by a swing toward methods of educating deaf children that focused on teaching oral communication to the exclusion of signed languages, sharply reducing the numbers of deaf teachers in classrooms; and encouraging the spread of eugenic beliefs that sometimes mitigated against Deaf communities and deaf intermarriage.[2]

Most modern studies of Deaf history focus on deaf people's agency and creativity in seeking community, developing and nurturing signed languages, and forming identities and cultural worldviews that value deaf people and their contributions to the world—a theoretical framework that is now referred to as *Deaf gain*.[3] This has often run counter to wider social attitudes and has necessitated attempts to explain that deafness is not necessarily the tragedy that many believe it to be. As early as 1779, a deaf Frenchman, Pierre Desloges, felt obliged to write, "Nature has not been as cruel to us as is commonly assumed."[4] This was an early and succinct statement of one of the central values of Deaf communities, which have consistently rejected pity on account of their deafness, although they will claim it for those deaf people who are isolated, stigmatized, and language-less. This lack of self-pity has not always sat comfortably with the attitudes of hearing benefactors, who have frequently been motivated by pity, and who have regularly relied on evoking the sympathy of supporters.

Even when deaf people's impetus to come together is approved by others, tensions have often developed between deaf people who desire to build communities and establish institutions and those hearing people who wish to do it for them. Owen Wrigley has suggested that these tensions should be the real focus of Deaf history. He poses the question, "Isn't Deaf history really about the small land wars at the margins of society and self-identity, exactly where the Hearing administrations of the Deaf through these institutions don't quite succeed in controlling or suppressing Deafness?"[5]

Many of the events explored in this book are the "small land wars" that emerged in the Australian Deaf community in the early twentieth century, and they find parallels in other countries' Deaf community histories.

Great Britain

British institutions for deaf people were particularly influential in colonial Australia. Most early European immigrants to Australia were British or Irish, including deaf people and those who knew and worked with them. British varieties of sign language formed the origins of Australian Sign Language (with a minority developing Irish-Australian Sign Language), and British educational and social institutions for deaf people were imported to Australia virtually intact during the nineteenth century.[6] British philosophies of social and charitable service provision also informed the attitudes and culture of the developing colonial society in Australia.

Deaf adults in Britain had begun to gather for social activities and religious worship from the 1820s onwards, usually led by hearing people with evangelical or education connections. Over the next few decades, these gatherings evolved into charitable organizations variously called *missions, institutes, benevolent societies,* or *associations,* many of them set up by the Institution for Providing Employment, Relief, and Religious Instruction for the Deaf and Dumb. The missions held regular religious services and became centers for the social lives and leisure activities of deaf people around the country. Each mission usually had a leader who was known as a *missioner*. Most of these missioners were hearing, but some were deaf. The missioner's role was to "provide care and welfare for the deaf people in their areas, which included finding work and apprenticeships . . . . They also acted as advocates and advisors to deaf people . . . as well as providing interpreting between sign language and spoken language for deaf and hearing people."[7] Missioners could become quite powerful within their local Deaf communities and could entrench dependency among deaf people. According to Paddy Ladd, the missioner " . . . facilitated and controlled Deaf people's access to the society which surrounded them, but was also the gatekeeper for that society's representatives."[8] Ladd has described the power struggles that sometimes ensued between deaf members and missioners.

These missions, with their close connections to the established Protestant churches, were the model for early Australian Deaf societies, and the role of missioner or superintendent was also imported to Australian organizations. Britain and Australia both differed from the more secular organizations for adult deaf people that were developing in the United States.

The late nineteenth century also saw the establishment and consolidation of national organizations for deaf people in some countries, reflecting the growth of Deaf communities that made it possible for them to meet and debate issues on a national level. In the United States, the National Association of the Deaf was formed in 1880, with one of the reasons for its formation being the desire of deaf people to "attain the ability to intelligently administer [their] affairs."[9] The British Deaf and Dumb Association began in 1890 for similar reasons, although usually hearing people held the leadership roles.[10]

Transnational relationships between Deaf communities also began to develop during the nineteenth and early twentieth centuries. Deaf people in Europe and North America traveled more frequently across the Atlantic, with the explicit purpose of gathering with other deaf people.[11] International congresses and gatherings were held with increasing regularity, such as the International Congress of the Deaf and Dumb in Paris in 1889 and the World's Congress of the Deaf in Chicago in 1893 (an offshoot of the World's Fair), and drew enthusiastic crowds. Such meetings provided opportunities for deaf people to observe and discuss how those in other environments dealt with their common experiences, how different kinds of education systems worked, and how Deaf communities fostered the growth of signed languages. These gatherings also provided forums for deaf people to debate and respond to the issues that affected their lives.

From the late nineteenth century onwards, many Deaf organizations began producing their own newspapers, which were distributed widely. These newspapers helped to bring together national Deaf communities, and many were also sent to Deaf communities in other countries, increasing deaf people's awareness of each other and making it more possible for them to influence each other.[12] British and American deaf newspapers of the late nineteenth and early twentieth centuries were usually available in Australian Deaf missions and societies, and often included news from Australia. Newspapers facilitated further transnational contact between deaf individuals and groups, such as letter-writing. One letter-writing group, the Cosmopolitan Correspondence Club, was initiated in Australia and included deaf people in France, Scotland, Wales, Canada, and the United States.[13]

The Australian Background

Australia was colonized by the British in 1788 and was initially a penal colony. Little is known about the position of deaf people in Aboriginal societies prior to European arrival, although linguists report that signed communication has always been used within some Aboriginal language groups for specific purposes, such as communicating during mourning periods or while hunting.[14]

A number of deaf people were included in the convict transports to Australia, beginning with Elizabeth Steel. She was sentenced in London's Old Bailey in October 1787 to seven years transportation, for stealing a watch while engaged in prostitution. Her trial had proceeded, however, only after a special session "to enquire whether she stood mute wilfully and of malice, or by the visitation of God."[15] Once the jury was satisfied that she was actually deaf, she was tried and convicted, and arrived at Sydney Cove on the *Lady Juliana* in June 1790. From there, she was taken to Norfolk Island, where she served out her sentence. She returned to Sydney at the expiration of her sentence in 1794, but died soon afterwards.[16] Other deaf convicts were John Fitzgerald, who arrived in 1819, and James Smith, who arrived in 1827. Both of these men had interpreters at their trials at the Old Bailey, so they were sign language users.[17] They would each have been alone within a rough frontier community, negotiating barracks, chain gangs, pleas for leniency, and eventual freedom within the new colony.

Other British deaf people came to Australia as free settlers. An example was John Carmichael, who arrived in Sydney from Scotland in October 1825. He was a twenty-one-year-old engraver.[18] The fact that he was "deaf and dumb" was remarked on in newspaper references to his work and by government officials who commissioned work from him.[19] His use of English in some of his surviving correspondence with the colonial secretary also exhibits mistakes typical of a moderately educated deaf person.[20] Carmichael completed a wide range of engraving work during his career in New South Wales, including maps, charts, stamps, and illustrations for tourist guides. He self-published a collection of six engravings (from his own drawings) in 1829, *Select Views of Sydney, New South Wales*. He was considered by the postmaster general to be "the most competent engraver in Sydney."[21]

Carmichael had attended the Edinburgh Institute for the Deaf and Dumb as a child and was a fluent signer. Fellow students have left accounts of him entertaining his schoolmates with signed stories about cock fighting and horse racing, describing him as "proud of being . . . great in our eyes" when he came to school with new stories to sign.[22] Carmichael displayed considerable independence and assertiveness in maintaining his career as an artist and engraver. He died in 1857.

Henry Hallett was a small child when he arrived in Adelaide on the *Africaine* in 1836.[23] He would have been similar to many other deaf children who came to Australia with their families who were seeking a new life. Hallett's story is known to Deaf people today largely because he was the first of many generations of Deaf Halletts, some of whom still live in Adelaide. Henry's father John was part owner of the *Africaine* and became a successful pastoralist in South Australia.[24]

The Beginnings of Education

Some deaf children in colonial Australia, such as Henry Hallett, were sent back to Britain for their education. Others had to wait until the first schools began to appear in the major population centers. The first two schools for the deaf were both established by British deaf men. Thomas Pattison was born in Scotland in 1805 and attended the Edinburgh Institute for the Deaf and Dumb at the same time as John Carmichael. Pattison spent some years at his former school as a monitor and also worked as a coach painter; he was secretary and treasurer of the Edinburgh Deaf and Dumb Benevolent Society for 23 years. He emigrated to Sydney in 1858 to join his brother there.[25]

Pattison soon met the Lentz family, which had three adult deaf daughters, and through them became aware of other deaf children in Sydney. Some unsuccessful attempts had previously been made to establish classes for deaf children by an English migrant named Sherrington Gilder, but Pattison was to meet with more success.[26] With support from the Lentz family, he began classes for deaf children in Sydney on October 22, 1860, the first in Australia. These classes soon evolved into a small school, with deaf children slowly trickling in from around the colony. Pattison was principal of the school, with two of the hearing Lentz daughters working as assistant teachers. This would not have been unusual in the British education system, which was Pattison's model. There were many deaf teachers in Britain, including some who

Thomas Pattison.
Royal Institute for Deaf and Blind Children, Australia.

established and led new schools for the deaf, such as Matthew Burns.[27] However, Pattison's career in the school he began was not to be a long one—he was dismissed by the school's board of management in 1866 for reasons that remain unclear.[28]

Pattison's school, later known as the New South Wales Institution for the Deaf and Dumb and the Blind, began education for deaf children in Australia, and it was a significant beginning in other ways too. He used the British "combined method" in this school, communicating with his pupils through British signs and fingerspelling. Pattison's school, together with the school begun soon afterwards in Melbourne, established British signing dialects as the prototype of the sign language that was to develop in Australia. These schools also established manual communication as the method of instruction in Australian schools for the deaf. Even though oralist influences soon began appearing in individual classes and teachers, Australian schools for deaf children had a long signing tradition that was not seriously challenged until after World War II.

The school that Pattison established, like most large schools for the deaf, also served to bring together the widely scattered deaf children of New South Wales. It provided opportunities for them to learn a sign language and develop the strong social and cultural links that helped to consolidate the beginnings of the Deaf community there.

Pattison's school was Australia's first by only three weeks. Another deaf man, Frederick John Rose, opened a similar school in Melbourne in November 1860. Rose's career lasted longer, and his life is better documented.[29] He was born in Oxford in 1831 and attended the Old Kent Road Asylum for the Deaf and Dumb in London. He emigrated to Melbourne in 1852 with his brother, part of the huge influx of migrants who came in search of gold in the 1850s.

In February 1859, some correspondence in the Melbourne newspaper *The Argus* led to Rose discovering a new calling. Two letters in the newspaper signed by "G" and "Widow" claimed that more than 50 deaf and dumb children were living in Victoria, with no educational provision for them. The writer appealed for the establishment of some form of schooling for her deaf daughter, otherwise she would be "put to the peril and danger of a sea voyage to get her educated in Old England, but should such an institution arise here, I would enrol myself a life subscriber."[30] This letter-writer was Sarah Lewis, and she was referring to her eight-year-old stepdaughter Lucy. Rose replied to these letters a few days later, writing,

I would beg to state that I am deaf and dumb, and have received a good education in the asylum in the Old Kent-road, London, where I was for five and a half years; and, knowing the great necessity that exists for the instruction of the deaf and dumb, who, unless some little knowledge be imparted to them, cannot tell good from evil, I should feel most happy to further the views of your correspondents in establishing an asylum for the instruction of those who may be unfortunately deaf and dumb; or, if one were established, I should have no objection to render any assistance in my power in the way of instruction for a fair remuneration.[31]

Following this, Rose made contact with Lewis, advertised for other interested parents of deaf children, and made plans for the establishment of a school. He and his new wife, Elizabeth Manning Telfer (also deaf), opened the school in their rented home in Prahran, Melbourne, on November 12, 1860, just three weeks after Thomas Pattison had opened his in Sydney. The school was called the Victorian Deaf and Dumb Institution.[32]

Although Rose also worked under a committee of hearing men, he seems to have fared much better than Pattison and had a long and well-regarded career at the school, as both principal teacher and superintendent. His teaching was favorably mentioned in a number of government inspections of the school. He not only taught the pupils, but also trained many of the teaching staff, including several deaf teachers. Some of these deaf teachers were recruited from Europe, such as Miss Frances Lorigan, who had been educated at the Claremont Deaf and Dumb Institution in Dublin before being appointed in 1864.[33] Other deaf teachers were recruited from among the students and became pupil teachers, in accordance with common practice in all schools at that time. David Piper was an example of such a pupil-teacher.[34]

After Rose retired from the school in 1892, he lost his savings during the Depression of the early 1890s. He applied to the school for a pension, but the board refused and instead offered him a position as collector. So, Rose found himself at the end of his career traveling around the suburbs of Melbourne, soliciting public subscriptions for the school he had headed for so many years. It was another twenty years before the Victorian Parliament succumbed to repeated requests from the Deaf community and granted Rose a pension, supplemented by both the school and the Adult Deaf and Dumb Society of Victoria.

Frederick John Rose.
Deaf Children Australia.

Although F. J. Rose was commemorated for many years in the
Victorian Deaf community with an annual "Rose Day," after the 1930s,
he shared the fate of Pattison in joining the largely forgotten generations of deaf teachers, whose contributions were lost for a time and
are only recently being rediscovered. Like Jean Massieu, Laurent Clerc,
John Creasy, George Banton, and countless others, their work was over-
shadowed and marginalized by the professionalization of teaching and
the ascendancy of oralism.[35] In this respect, Australian Deaf history falls
neatly into line with that of other countries in the western world.

Several other schools for the deaf were established around Australia
during the late nineteenth century. The schools interacted with each
other and the Deaf communities in a variety of ways. When the New
South Wales Institution for the Deaf and Dumb and the Blind and the
Victorian Deaf and Dumb Institution (VDDI) became well established,
deaf children from further afield were sent to them, including some
children from other states that did not yet have schools for the deaf. For

example, a number of Tasmanian and South Australian deaf children went to VDDI in Melbourne, and some Queensland deaf children were sent to the New South Wales Institution. When the South Australian Institution for the Blind and Deaf and Dumb opened in 1874, some of their teaching staff were recruited from VDDI, most notably Samuel Johnson, who became principal of the South Australian Institution in 1885.[36] VDDI also provided the first staff for the Western Australian Deaf and Dumb Institution when it opened in 1896. Prior to this, many deaf children from Perth had been sent to the South Australian school.

The Queensland Blind, Deaf and Dumb Institution opened in 1893. Its first teachers, Miss Sharp and Thomas R. Semmens, were also recruited from VDDI. Most of the Queensland deaf children who had been traveling to Sydney for their education subsequently transferred to the Queensland Blind, Deaf and Dumb Institution, as had happened with Western Australian children returning to Perth from the South Australian Institution for the Blind and Deaf and Dumb. The Tasmanian Blind, Deaf and Dumb Institution opened in 1901.

These schools precipitated much movement among deaf children and those who worked with them, and the results of that may be evident in modern dialects of Australian Sign Language (Auslan). Pattison, like Carmichael, would have brought a northern (or Scottish) dialect of British Sign Language with him and used it in his work with deaf school children and other deaf associates in Sydney. Rose would have used a southern, or English, dialect and would not only have introduced it to his pupils, but also passed it on to the many teachers he trained. Although other deaf adults from varying parts of Britain and Ireland also migrated to different Australian cities and brought with them their dialects or sign systems, there are today two dominant dialects of Auslan—northern and southern—so the deaf students who moved around likely brought the signs they had learned with them.[37]

The Catholic Church also established schools for deaf children, beginning with Rosary Convent at Waratah near Newcastle in 1875.[38] Two other Catholic schools—St. Gabriel's School for Deaf Boys at Castle Hill in Sydney and St. Mary's School for the Deaf at Portsea near Melbourne—were established in the twentieth century. These schools were begun by Dominican nuns and Christian Brothers from "parent" schools in Ireland. One of the first teachers at the Waratah school was an Irish deaf nun, Sister Gabriel Hogan. Irish Sign Language was used as the medium of instruction and socialization in these schools until the 1950s, evolving into Australian-Irish Sign Language (AISL) and creating a language minority within the Australian Deaf community.[39] Graduates of these schools continued to use AISL among themselves and with their families, although they also learned the British-influenced Auslan and used that for their interactions with the broader Deaf community.[40]

Despite the efforts put into the establishment and development of these schools, education for deaf children did not become compulsory until the early decades of the twentieth century, after lengthy advocacy by the schools, Deaf societies, and Deaf communities.[41] All of the schools described above (apart from the Catholic schools) later came under the control of their respective state governments and were the major education centers for deaf children in those states until the middle of the twentieth century.

The schools played several important roles in the Deaf community during the late nineteenth century, in addition to their primary function of educating young deaf people and preparing them for work and citizenship in the wider community. They all brought together scattered populations of deaf children, were the primary centers for enculturating these children and transmitting sign language, and played key roles in building the social networks that formed the basis of Deaf communities around Australia. Each school had additional unique influences on their local Deaf communities. In Melbourne, deaf school staff such as Rose took leadership roles in the establishment of the Deaf Society in Victoria; in South Australia and Queensland, hearing teachers played key roles in organizing deaf people and beginning the missions; and in Sydney, the school provided a meeting place for the local Deaf community for many years.

The influence of the schools was facilitated by late nineteenth-century social and education systems, which allowed deaf people to take important roles in schools and missions without some of the obstacles that were to arise in the twentieth century—for example, the widely used pupil-teacher system of the nineteenth century was an accessible and culturally appropriate way for deaf people to become teachers.

Establishment of the Missions and Societies

Once the schools were established and the Deaf communities in each state began to coalesce, the demand for organizations and services for adult deaf people emerged. The British missions provided ready models for Australian deaf people, and their expectations and needs were shaped by those of their British counterparts—a meeting place, a center for religious worship, regular social and sporting activities, and some activities for the "uplift" and continuing education of the community. An implicit function of the missions was also to keep deaf people off the streets and out of undesirable places.[42]

The histories of the Australian missions and societies are relatively well documented. The Adult Deaf and Dumb Society of Victoria was the first to be established in 1884. (It was originally called the Victorian Society for Promoting the Spiritual and Temporal Welfare of the Deaf and Dumb, and then the Adult Deaf and Dumb Mission from 1886, before changing to the Adult Deaf and Dumb Society of Victoria early in the twentieth century.)[43] The people who were active in its establishment included deaf men, such as Rose, brothers John, Adam, and William Muir, Matthew Miller, and David Piper. The British influence on these men was obvious, as Rose and two of the Muir brothers had been educated in England and Scotland. The next state to establish a mission was South Australia in 1891. The superintendent of the South Australian Institution for the Blind and Deaf and Dumb was Samuel Johnson, a hearing Irishman, and he also took a key role in the beginnings of the Mission in that state—the South Australian Adult Deaf and Dumb Mission—as he had in Victoria previously. For many years, he was superintendent of both the school and the mission, but relied on several deaf and hearing men to do most of the work in building up the mission. One of these deaf men was Eugene Salas, who worked under Johnson as missioner from 1892 until his death in 1915.[44]

New South Wales (NSW) did not establish a formal Deaf Society until 1913; however, there were church services and regular meetings for adult deaf people for many years before that, usually associated with the NSW Institution for the Deaf and Dumb and the Blind (the school that Pattison had started). Once again, deaf people were very active in these developments. The most prominent was Fletcher Booth, a long-term resident of New South Wales and one of the early pupils at the institution. Booth was an untiring advocate and involved in many different stages of Deaf community development over his long life—from the early years of unofficial gatherings in borrowed spaces, to the beginnings of the Deaf Society, and later as part of the radical breakaway from the society that he had helped to establish.[45] From 1891 onwards, Booth was given a stipend from the school board to work "for the uplift of the Adult Deaf."[46] The NSW Deaf community was supported by Samuel Watson, the superintendent of the institution, and several other hearing men, some of whom had deaf relatives. Watson helped to secure some additional land adjoining the school site, and a building was constructed there in 1902 for the use of the adult Deaf community.[47] Although they did not have a Deaf Society, the NSW Deaf community was organized and active by the early twentieth century.

The Queensland Adult Deaf and Dumb Mission began in 1903, after several years of meetings and religious study groups convened by a hearing teacher of the deaf, Thomas Semmens, and an Irish deaf woman, Martha Overend Wilson. Wilson continued to organize the groups on her own after Semmens withdrew due to illness. She was one of the leaders of the group of deaf and hearing people who later met to organize the new Mission, and she continued to play a primary role in the development of the Mission and in later events.[48] Although other deaf women were active during these years, none had such a prominent or visible role as Wilson. The Queensland Mission, like the one in South Australia, employed a deaf missioner (later superintendent), Samuel Showell.[49] The Deaf societies of Western Australia and Tasmania were formed in the late 1920s.

Most of the early Deaf societies used the services of local ministers who were sympathetic to deaf people or had deaf relatives, who were former or serving teachers of the deaf, or deaf people themselves. Victoria was the first state to recruit a hearing missioner from Britain—Ernest Abraham, whose far-reaching influence on Australia's Deaf community will be described in later chapters.

Although some deaf people had explicit leadership roles in the new missions and Deaf societies, many more worked for them in other capacities, such as caretakers, domestic staff, and collectors. In an era when such organizations depended almost entirely on public donations or "subscriptions," the role of collector was critical to the Deaf schools and Deaf societies, as well as to almost all other charity organizations. Collectors canvassed specific areas of the state served by their organization, visiting homes and businesses and collecting subscriptions from the public. They were paid a percentage of the amount they collected. It was the money raised by collectors that made possible the payment of teachers' and missioners' salaries, the purchase of land, and the construction of schools and mission buildings in most Australian states. The majority of collectors for the schools and missions were deaf, and it was usually a sought-after occupation. Because collectors were in regular contact with the area they canvassed, they were the most likely to know the whereabouts of isolated deaf people and families with deaf children. They were often relied upon to help recruit pupils for the schools and new members for the Deaf societies and missions. Collectors also became the public face of their organizations, and they were expected to be well dressed and of "good character." Their access to the public sometimes gave them the opportunity to pursue agendas that competed with those of the missions, and this will be described in later chapters.

While the Deaf societies and missions were becoming established, deaf people were also building the infrastructure for other networks, particularly sport. The Victorian Deaf Cricket Club was established in 1881, and other states followed suit. An interstate (or "intercolonial" as it was before 1901) cricket match was first held in Adelaide in 1894 between Victoria and South Australia; another one between New South Wales and Victoria was held in Melbourne the following year, and interstate competitions continued regularly, expanding to include other sports.[50] These interstate excursions drew other deaf people as well, not just the cricketers, and from the outset, they provided the opportunity for meetings, conferences, and social gatherings.

A small conference held during the 1895 gathering in Melbourne was reported on in several issues of *The British Deaf-Mute* and revealed some of the emerging issues for Australian deaf people.[51] The conference chairman was F. J. Rose, who stressed the need for regular national gatherings in order to "enhance the social sphere, elevation of culture, higher polish and asserted independence" of Australian Deaf communities. Other deaf people addressed the conference on education for the deaf (David Piper of Melbourne), the superiority of deaf collectors over hearing collectors (G. Gibson of Adelaide), the advantages of mutual improvement societies (W. H. Bostock of Adelaide) and "self-development" (Fletcher Booth of Sydney), and the perceived risks of intermarriage among deaf people (Eugene Salas of Adelaide). This last paper reflected the European and American preoccupations with deaf intermarriage at that time and the spread of these eugenic ideas in Australia.[52] Deaf people seem to have been predominant in the organizing and presentation of this conference, indicating their growing independence and visibility within their organizations.

The Australian Deaf community at the beginning of the twentieth century appeared to be optimistic and energetic—poised to manage their own affairs.

2

Things as We Deaf See Them

Mr Ernest J. D. Abraham . . . appears to have spent a good share of his time in instituting, organising, establishing, founding, manufacturing, and managing.
—JOSEPH HEPWORTH, "CHRISTMAS AT THE HOME OF THE B.D.M."

THE ADULT DEAF and Dumb Society of Victoria recruited a new missioner from England in 1901—Ernest Josiah Douglas Abraham. He was to have a crucial role in its development and that of many of the Deaf societies, missions, and other deaf-related organizations that began around Australia during the next four decades. Abraham is a legendary figure in Australian Deaf history, and to a lesser extent in British Deaf history. His name is still recognizable in the shared culture and experience of Australian deaf people, partly because he bequeathed a cricket shield that was contested by Australian state deaf teams for many decades during the twentieth century.[1]

Ernest Abraham (1867–1940) was already well known in the British Deaf community by the time he came to Australia. His maternal aunt was deaf, and his mother's second (common-law) marriage was to a deaf man, John Jennings, who informally adopted Ernest and paid for his education. Jennings worked as a missioner and had founded the South London Gospel Mission to the Deaf and Dumb, and Ernest helped him in this role and took over (although he would have been only seventeen) when Jennings died in 1884.[2] A fluent and charismatic signer, the young Abraham also organized several other clubs and activities for deaf people in London, including a YMCA, a dramatics club, and a "Golden Society of Love."[3] In 1887, he was put in charge of the Bolton, Bury, Rochdale, and District Adult Deaf and Dumb Society

John E. Muir (left) and Ernest Abraham in his office at the Adult Deaf and
Dumb Society of Victoria.
Victorian Deaf Society Collection, State Library of Victoria.

in Lancashire (at first a subsidiary of the Manchester Society, but independent since 1892), and had also begun editing a national paper, *The
British Deaf-Mute*. He demonstrated a talent for "instituting, organising,
establishing, founding, manufacturing, and managing," as well as a gift
for self-promotion.[4] Another missioner for deaf people in London at the
time, the Rev. F. W. G. Gilby, commented in his unpublished memoirs,
"[Abraham] was a born advertiser, eaten up with the modern spirit."[5]

Evidently Abraham did not wish to confine his career to provincial
English towns. He attended the International Conference on Education
of the Deaf in Chicago in 1893 as the "Reverend" E. J. D. Abraham, and
presented a paper called "A Plan for the Permanent Employment of
the Deaf in the Higher Trades and Professions."[6] *The British Deaf-Mute*,
which he edited, found its way around the world and helped to establish his profile, because it always ran complimentary articles about his
work in Bolton, Bury, and Rochdale.

> Mr. Abraham had been instrumental in making the little town
> of Bolton famous in all parts of the world . . . . Should any of
> the Bolton deaf find themselves in America or Australia, he felt
> confident they would only need to mention that they came from

Bolton, when they would receive a hearty welcome from all sections of the deaf community.[7]

Abraham had made more than one application for positions in Australia before his successful appointment as missioner to the Adult Deaf and Dumb Society of Victoria in 1901. He had applied for the same position in 1892, and also for the position of superintendent at the Victorian Deaf and Dumb Institution (VDDI) around the same time, but was not successful until his 1901 application.[8]

A number of commentators have agreed that Abraham "ghosted" most of the laudatory articles that appeared about him in various print sources over the years.[9] The following article, from a magazine he edited in Australia, is a good example of both his style and of the image he strove to create for himself.

The name of E. J. D. Abraham was at that time (1901) a household word in all communities of the deaf and dumb throughout the world. Some of us (the deaf of Victoria) had known him through his writings, for years.

But what of the man as we actually know him? Well, when we saw the slim, quiet, smiling little man that stepped from the S. S. Austral we were for the moment puzzled. Can this be the man we had in our mind? We had known him for years, for always it had seemed, as an exceptionally strong man, who had fiercely and fearlessly battled in the cause of the deaf, often standing almost alone against great opposition, and yet coming out victorious. We had seen, too, many portraits of him, each of which gave him the appearance of a tall and physically powerful man with set iron features, yet there he stood, a lithe, nervous, almost bashful little man, undoubtedly E. J. D. Abraham, but not the one we had expected. Napoleon Bonaparte naturally flashed across our mind, and we have since had more than one opportunity of recognising the irresistible power behind the slim figure and laughing eyes. He works, attends to the most minute details, and in his company you have to work too. A perfect slave driver and sweater when anything has to be done, but he always takes the giant's share of the work, and will begin hours before anyone and leave off hours after, and that perhaps is the secret of his success. Though shattered, somewhat, in health he did not pause to think of it; love of work in the cause of the deaf clung to him.[10]

His adroit combination of self-deprecation and self-promotion, and his ability to weave Victorian melodrama through his appeals for support, usually made good copy. He was also a talented public speaker and organizer of "entertainments." These skills made him an excellent publicist and fundraiser, which, in turn, fed his preoccupation with "instituting, organising, establishing, founding, manufacturing, and managing." However, he always chafed under restrictive management, preferring that "his committee [give] him a free hand."[11] His move to Australia was most likely a search for more freedom and space to pursue his ambitious plans, although he usually claimed that he had moved for health reasons. He became bolder in admitting his aims the longer he stayed.

> There came to Victoria in 1901, a man, broken in health, but with a paradise for deaf mutes conceived, planned out and erected in his mind, and brick by brick, that "palace in the air" has been brought down to mother Earth, until now, after the space of eleven years, it needs only the coping stone to complete the greatest provision that has ever been attempted for the welfare of the deaf.[12]

Abraham dazzled the Deaf community in Melbourne, and soon the rest of Australia, with his energy and ideas, with his fluent signing and rapid immersion in the community. He quickly became the national expert on the affairs of deaf people.

A National Gathering

Abraham's organizational hand was evident early. One of the first major events he planned was a large national gathering of deaf people two years after his arrival. Although there had been interstate sporting meetings and conferences since 1894, the Australian Deaf and Dumb Congress that Abraham planned for Melbourne during the Christmas and New Year period of 1903–1904 was grander and more complex in its scope, and it attracted the patronage of luminaries such as the State Premier and an archbishop, as well as extensive and detailed media coverage. Abraham and his deaf organizers included in the event cricket competitions, church services, "conversaziones," grand banquets, garden parties, an exhibition of handicrafts, and a program of presentations by deaf and hearing people.

The Melbourne newspapers *The Age* and *The Argus* ran daily articles on the congress, and newspapers in other states also carried reports. Most of these commentators were struck not only by the unusual experience of relying on sign language interpreters to understand the proceedings, but also by the cheerfulness and desire for independence exhibited by the deaf participants. More than one reporter commented with surprise on the fact that they did not seem to feel sorry for themselves. An Adelaide reporter marvelled at the "complete absence of maudlin sentimentalism," and a Melbourne reporter commended the "really wonderful spirit of cheerfulness," remarking that "[t]he double affliction of the deaf mutes is borne with a cheerful resignation, which impels admiration."[13]

There were presentations on "School Life of the Deaf," "The Law and the Deaf," "Social Status of the Deaf," "The Family Life of the Deaf," "The Capabilities of the Deaf," and "The Past, Present and Future of the Deaf," as well as general debate and a presidential address by Abraham. The congress also drew newspaper correspondence about the education of deaf children, with a lively exchange of letters arguing the relative benefits of oral and manual methods of teaching. Samuel Showell, the deaf missioner of the recently formed Queensland Adult Deaf and Dumb Mission, made an eloquent defense of the use of sign language in education.

> As regards the rival systems of oral and manual, let the deaf and dumb themselves decide. . . . Signs to a large extent are natural to the untaught deaf mute, and can only be eradicated by a severity perilously bordering on cruelty. That the oral system is held in utter detestation by the majority of deaf mutes, and that if compelled to learn it they make little or no use of it, must be patent to all fair-minded people who have seen much of the deaf and dumb.[14]

But this educational debate was not as contentious an issue in Australia as it was in other western countries at the time, and the congress is more interesting as a portrait of the adult Deaf community at the beginning of a period of rapid development.

Abraham was mentioned often by the reporters, both for his interpreting and his addresses on behalf of deaf people's ideals and aspirations. The Adelaide *Register* reported him saying, "They did not ask for favours or privileges; all they asked for was justice. They asked for the opportunities and advantages which were already enjoyed by their speaking and hearing fellow-countrymen."[15] Although this stance was commended, it was also considered idealistic and unworldly. The editor of that paper wrote a prescient piece, identifying some of the conflicts that were to surface over the following decades.

> One may admire the splendid spirit of self-reliance exhibited by the mutes, and the fine courage of the Congress in requesting fair play for the afflicted; but it is doubtful whether Mr. Abraham is over-endowed with worldly prudence. In this age, which glories in humanitarianism, it is much easier to extract a charity dole than to obtain justice. Mankind prefers to act so as to be considered generous, rather than to make reparation which brings no credit but such as is associated with a stigma. What a satire upon a society in which so many other normal members are leaning against Government posts nursing "tired feelings," fostered by enervating politics, is the fact that the deaf and dumb should be heard eloquently preaching the gospel of self-help and manly independence![16]

Although this editorial underestimated Abraham, who was to demonstrate plenty of "worldly prudence," it identified an ongoing source of conflict in the administration of Deaf societies and schools, and indeed those of many other disadvantaged groups in Australian society—whether they should appeal to public sympathy in order to raise funds for their services and risk the "stigma" of charity, or aim to be self-sufficient and independent and risk being penniless. For at least the next few decades, most steered a middle path, using the rhetoric of independence but the organizational and fundraising practices of charity.

The events of the congress and the fortuitous variety of media commentaries it elicited (thanks to Abraham's skill as a publicist) provide a snapshot of the evolving Deaf community in Australia, its key personalities, its aspirations and beliefs, and the way it was regarded by wider society. Deaf people then, as always, were willing to travel long distances and endure considerable discomfort in order to meet and fraternize with each other; social and sporting events were well established in their communities, and deaf people and their sympathizers were then, as they have usually been, dismissive of oral philosophies in education and alarmed by their spread. Indeed, one of the resolutions of the congress was that Australian Deaf people join those in "Great Britain, America, Germany and France, in protesting against the use of the pure oral system in the instruction of the deaf."[17] Australian Sign Language was established as the preferred language of the community, although it was not yet defined as a language and would have been different in significant ways to Auslan today. Many deaf people, such as Frederick Rose and Samuel Showell, were already respected figures in their communities, and Abraham's far-reaching control and confrontational manner were already in evidence. It is also interesting to see that, with astute management, prominent political and religious figures were willing to patronize the Deaf community, and media interest seemed to be genuine and relatively well informed.

The Australasian Deaf and Dumb Association

One of the most significant outcomes of the congress was a resolution: "That an Australian Association of the Deaf and Dumb be formed on the lines of the British Deaf and Dumb Association, and the American National Association of Deaf Mutes."[18] The organization that grew

Mr. Abraham and Mr. Rose.

Frederick Rose (left) and Ernest Abraham.
From *The Gesture*, April-June 1908, p. 15.
The Deaf Society.

from this resolution was called the Australasian Deaf and Dumb Association (ADDA). It eventually had branches in Victoria, Queensland, New South Wales, and South Australia, with almost all members being deaf. Despite the name "Australasia" in the title, there is no evidence of any branch in New Zealand.[19] Abraham was president of the Victorian branch, which was always the most active of the state branches, and also president of the general board of the association.

The "Objects" of the association, adopted in 1911, were the following:

(a) To unite the deaf and dumb and all interested in their welfare.
(b) To organise congresses from time to time in different parts of Australasia, for the discussion of matters in relation to the deaf.
(c) To advance and protect the interests, to elevate the social status, and as far as possible to secure higher education, better employment, etc., for the deaf.
(d) To afford to the education departments, members of Parliament, school authorities, the press, etc., information as to the condition, education and opinions of the deaf.
(e) To gather and preserve all facts, statistics and opinions relating to the deaf, and to promote by every legitimate means the diffusion of the same by means of public meetings, the press, or other publications, etc., as shall be thought advisable by the Boards of Management.
(f) To promote the establishment of organisations for the welfare of the adult deaf in States at present neglected.[20]

Little information survives about the activities of the ADDA, except in Victoria, where it was regularly reported on in the Deaf Society's newsletters. The Victorian branch concentrated most of its efforts on advocating for the education of deaf children to be made compulsory (which was achieved in 1910) and on persuading the Victorian government and the VDDI to contribute to a pension for Rose (which they also achieved). They contributed to Object (f) by sending Abraham to Sydney to assist with the formation of the Deaf Society in that state (see below), and they did hold one more congress in 1911, again in Melbourne.

The 1911 congress was similar to the one in 1903–04. The ADDA adopted its rules, logo, (an eye superimposed on a hand), and the motto "Ad Educandum et Elevandum" (For Education and Advancement). Among the topics discussed were the desirability of adopting a uniform system of signs and fingerspelling throughout Australia and reducing regional variations (presented by John Muir); the importance of higher education and access to trades and professions (Martha Overend Wilson); the desirability of giving positions in deaf schools, missions and societies to deaf people where possible; the problem of deaf beggars and hearing people pretending to be deaf in order to beg (Matthew Miller); and the pure oral system as used in New Zealand (T. Williamson of New Zealand). The congress resolved to approach the New Zealand government and ask it to be more flexible in its method of educating deaf children.[21]

The subjects addressed by these presenters (all of them deaf) reflect similar concerns in Deaf communities in Great Britain and the United States in the early twentieth century.[22] As the Australian Deaf community became established and organized, it faced the same kinds of aspirations and obstacles as these older communities.

The ADDA seems to have had a harmonious relationship with most Deaf missions and societies. The only evidence that it was seen as a potential forum for change by deaf people who were dissatisfied with their mission was in South Australia, where there were a number of clashes between the South Australian Adult Deaf and Dumb Mission and the community during the early years of the twentieth century.[23] In 1902, a deaf immigrant to Adelaide was diagnosed with tuberculosis and sent to the sanatorium for treatment and isolation. The Deaf community challenged the Mission's refusal to support him and raised the money for the deaf man's expenses among themselves, attracting attention from the daily newspaper, the *Advertiser,* for their "true nobility of character" and embarrassing the Mission.[24]

In 1905, the South Australian Mission Committee established a separate Finance Committee, consisting only of hearing members, and this committee took over most of the administrative matters of the Mission, effectively disenfranchising the deaf members of the Mission Committee. The most significant clash occurred when Eugene Salas, the deaf missioner, fell ill with tuberculosis and was taken to the sanatorium in 1910. The Finance Committee immediately replaced him with a new hearing missioner and gave Salas's wife and children notice to leave their house. The Deaf community was incensed and organized a boycott of the Mission until Salas was promised his job back after his recovery.[25]

In this environment, the ADDA was seen for a time as a way for deaf people to be more autonomous. They pointedly rejected the application of the hearing superintendent of the Mission, Samuel Johnson, to join the ADDA, identifying it as an area where deaf people were in control.[26]

Abraham's National Role

Ernest Abraham's status and influence were not confined to Melbourne. Other states were eager to enlist his support, and he was usually more than willing to respond. An early example was his visit to the Queensland capital Brisbane in November and December 1904. The organizers of the recently formed Queensland Mission invited him to help launch their new Mission and raise public interest. Abraham obligingly made the journey (still a sea voyage during the early decades of the twentieth century) and conducted a number of public lectures and "entertainments" that attracted thousands of attendees and raised enough funds to give the new Mission a healthy opening balance in its building fund.[27]

Several years later, the Deaf community in New South Wales also sought his help. They were becoming frustrated with the lack of an organized Deaf society, when even the smaller states of Queensland and South Australia were boasting established societies, like that in Victoria. They were continuing to meet in the facilities of the school for the deaf and blind, in a purpose-built center adjoining the New South Wales Institution for the Deaf and Dumb and the Blind. However, this building was now too small for them and was owned by the school rather than the adult Deaf community; and the school would not allow them to have separate collectors, fearing that their own revenue would be reduced. After an initial unsuccessful attempt to set up on their own in 1912, the next year they invited Abraham to come to Sydney and help them begin a formal Deaf society. They remembered Abraham's assistance to the fledgling Queensland Mission and were aware of his impressive achievements in Melbourne.

Abraham jumped at the chance to demonstrate his talents for "instituting, organising, establishing, founding, manufacturing, and managing" once again. He visited Sydney in his role as president of the ADDA, not in his capacity as superintendent of the Victorian Society. This allowed him to promote the ADDA; however, it also meant that he did not seek permission from the committee of the Victorian Society for his trip, as they would probably have put restrictions on what he was able to do in Sydney.[28] As president of the ADDA, he had the free hand he relished.

Abraham spent at least two weeks in Sydney, meeting with influential people and raising support and funds. He was able to gain the sympathy of the lord mayor, who agreed to preside at a public meeting in the Town Hall. The school's committee fought against the move, met with the mayor themselves, and wrote to the newspapers. But Abraham and the Sydney supporters managed to counter their moves, reply to their letters, and sway the public. The meeting at the Town Hall on October 20, 1913, resolved to form a Deaf society, and a committee was appointed and permission secured to begin appeals for public funding. Abraham had reason to be very pleased with himself, and the Sydney Deaf community was full of praise and gratitude.[29]

John Patrick Bourke

In the closing years of the First World War, a recently deafened man appeared in the Melbourne Deaf community—John Patrick Bourke. He was to become not only an important participant in the troubled times ahead, but also one of the chief chroniclers of these events. In the 1930s, he self-published several short books and pamphlets about his experiences with the Deaf Society and the Deaf community in Victoria, and also self-published a magazine briefly in the early 1940s.[30] He was a prolific letter-writer and made use of his voluminous correspondence files in his books. Bourke's material is an invaluable resource, and he seems almost to have anticipated the role of the future social historian. He wrote the following in the Preface to one of his books:

> The Reader, if he has heard anything about the adult deaf and their society, has done so per medium of the Superintendent's [Abraham's] voice and seen it through his eyes. I have found it necessary therefore, to take the public behind the scene and show it things as we deaf see them.[31]

Bourke was not writing as an idle hobby—his writing was fired by anger and urgency. He was bitterly dissatisfied with his treatment by the Deaf Society, and his work is permeated with a desire to expose what he saw as injustice and corruption. He developed a particular hatred of Abraham, and it would be easy at times to dismiss his writings as a stream of vituperation and his observations as unreliable. But he took great care to substantiate most of his allegations, and details can often be confirmed from other sources, such as Deaf Society minute books and letters in newspapers. He considered the work he was doing a moral responsibility. Writing in a radical magazine for deaf people in the 1930s, he described what he saw as his and other deaf people's responsibility.

We deaf are writing the history of our Societies, and it is our
duty to get at the truth of what happened and to give a moral
judgment on events and persons and pass it on for the good of
posterity.[32]

Bourke's writing is a rich source of information, a forensic commentary
on events of the time as well as his own involvement in them. He made
extensive use of Abraham's letters and notes to him (carefully repro-
ducing Abraham's occasional spelling mistakes and marking them
with a "sic"). He defended this once by quoting from an Emil Ludwig
biography of Napoleon.

> For in truth a man always explains himself better than anyone else
> can do it for him; even when he is mistaken, or when he is lying,
> he reveals himself to those who come afterwards, to those who
> know the truth.[33]

Bourke's description of his own background and his introduction to
the world of deaf people is presented in the first chapter of *The Story of
a Deaf Drudge*.

> I lost my hearing when I was about twenty years of age. I was a
> Junior teacher at the time. My deafness making teaching impossi-
> ble, and not wishing to be a burden on a married sister, I set out to
> fight the battle of life for myself, untrained, without a home, with
> one or two friends to help, and with about £5 in my pocket.
>   It did not take me long to find out that the world did not want
> the untrained deaf. I became a drudge and the prey of those who
> wanted cheap labour. In the process I drifted from one dead-end
> job to the other trying to find someone with humanity enough to
> give me a chance to make a home for myself and settle down. It
> has been a hopeless quest.
>   In 1918 my eyes became very bad. I lost my employment (I was
> working on a dairy farm on 30/- a week), and on account of my
> eyes I could not seek other work.
>   When I had no more money to pay my board, I sought help
> from the Charity Organisation Society. It promised to bring my
> case under the notice of the Society for Helping Persons of Educa-
> tion. Instead of doing so, it turned my case over to Abraham. As a
> result, I had a letter from him inviting me to come to the farm for
> a rest and a holiday.
>   On the principle that beggars cannot be choosers I had to go.[34]

Deaf Society files indicated that Bourke had been born in Adelaide in 1884, and was living in India when illness (allegedly malaria) caused him to become deaf.[35] As someone who had grown to adulthood as a hearing person and been educated in hearing schools, Bourke would have been different from most of the other deaf people he later came to associate with. He would have been able to speak like a hearing person (although as he grew older, his speech may have become less distinct); his understanding and use of sign language probably never reached native fluency (although he has been described as being able to sign, fingerspell, and communicate effectively with deaf people); and his education would have been more extensive than that of most other deaf people.[36] His work as a "junior teacher," his writing skills, and the many quotes and literary references in his work show that he was comparatively well educated and widely read. This seems to be confirmed by the fact that the Charity Organisation Society almost referred him to the Society for Helping Persons of Education for assistance, rather than to the Adult Deaf and Dumb Society.

Another effect of his education as a hearing person may have been that he escaped the set of beliefs that deaf people could acquire through growing up in the deaf education and welfare systems in the nineteenth and twentieth centuries—a belief that hearing people were all-powerful and all-knowing; that their legal, religious, and government systems were mysterious and sacrosanct; and that deaf people were inferior and dependent, without a proper language.[37] Bourke referred obliquely to this set of beliefs.

> Societies need hearing Superintendents who are experts in the language of the deaf and dumb, in order to bridge the gulf that stands between the hearing and the deaf worlds and to act as interpreters between the hearing and the deaf and dumb.
>
> It is a noted feature of the character of the deaf and dumb that they become very dependent on these Superintendents who can interpret their signs to the bystanders. They look to such men in all their difficulties, lean upon them in their troubles, rally round, love, and follow them blindly right or wrong.[38]

His late arrival to the Deaf community may have given Bourke clearer eyes to see the Deaf societies with all their strengths and weaknesses, and to point out and protest about things that other deaf people may have been more likely to take for granted or not to question. As well as being widely read and highly literate, he obviously maintained an interest in current affairs and the political events of the day, as he often referred to these in his writings. He was able to compare the practices used in the Deaf Society to those used by other institutions, large and small, and thus bring a broad perspective to his experiences within the Deaf world.

On the other hand, Bourke's status as a former hearing person would have stigmatized him somewhat within the Deaf community. He would always have been seen as something of an outsider, and there would have been areas of the Deaf experience and worldview that he would not have fully understood. The particular circumstances of Bourke's becoming deaf, and his education, placed him outside of the "elite" of the Deaf community. In early and mid-twentieth century Australia, this elite traditionally included those who excelled in the Deaf school system, had a skilled trade, held roles in Deaf community organizations, and (preferably) blood or marriage connections to a deaf family that extended over several generations. People like Bourke, with their very different backgrounds, could be assimilated and accepted, and sometimes became very astute observers and advocates within the Deaf community, but they often remained slightly awkward outsiders. Around this time, men who had been deafened during the First World War sometimes gravitated to the Deaf community too, as there were few other support services for them (e.g., Alf Taylor, who was involved in the NSW Deaf community and is mentioned elsewhere in this book). They might today be called *hybrids*—those who develop an identity forged from two usually separate cultural experiences.[39]

Influences on Bourke

Bourke's sources of inspiration compare to those of many other aspiring social reformers of the time. He often referred to Dickens and compared Abraham to Dickensian figures such as Squeers, the abusive schoolmaster in *Nicholas Nickleby*, Christopher Casby, the patriarch in *Little Dorrit*, and Bumble, the workhouse master in *Oliver Twist*. As well as Dickens, Bourke also cited Elizabeth Fry and John Howard's writings about prisoners, Lord Shaftesbury's work on behalf of factory children and the insane, and William Lloyd Garrison's writings about slavery in the United States.[40]

Another influence on Bourke's writing was Arnold Hill Payne's *King Silence*, a polemical novel published in England in 1918.[41] Payne's deaf father was headmaster of a deaf school in Wales, and his hearing mother was matron there.[42] His novel was an unrelenting critique of the oral method of teaching deaf children and a plea for the use of sign language in education at a time when this was very unfashionable. But it also included many scathing indictments of the ways in which unscrupulous hearing people abused deaf people (obviously based on Payne's experiences with his parents and their deaf pupils), and this was what drew Bourke to it. Bourke often quoted from *King Silence*, although its portrayal of deaf people as uncomplaining victims was not always compatible with his calls for activism.

> The deaf set out with a cheery smile and no word of complaint along an uphill road of life strewn with hard boulders of isolation, misunderstanding, unfairness, and often tyranny. The hustling hurrying sons of Sound elbow them aside, shameless by taking many a mean advantage of them, and noisily squabbling over the good things of life as they go. The deaf glance wistfully at them as, at best, the hearing pass them by on the other side, or, worse, give them a kick or a cuff to hasten them out of the way.[43]

Although Bourke may not have entirely identified with the passive deaf people described here, he certainly endorsed the depiction of many hearing people as "hustling, hurrying sons of Sound." He used a quote from *King Silence* on the title page of his book *The Story of a Deaf Drudge*, which helped to set the tone for that book's bitter account of his experience of "drudgery" under Abraham: "Added to which was the fact that John was deaf, and therefore was obviously intended to be a hewer of wood and a drawer of water for his inferiors."[44]

Bourke's writings are comparable to those of Albert Ballin, a deaf writer who was active in the United States at about the same time, although there is no evidence of any direct influence. Ballin published a book in 1931 called *The Deaf Mute Howls*, protesting against the dominance of hearing directors of deaf-related institutions and the injustices and inadequacies of deaf education.[45] Although Ballin's writing is leavened with more humor, his underlying premise was similar to Bourke's: "All [the deaf-mute] asks for, nay, **demands**, as his birthright, is to be respected and treated as an equal and be given an equal chance in this life."[46] And Ballin's justification for his writing could also have applied to Bourke over the years.

> Long, loud and cantankerous is the howl raised by the deaf-mute! It has to be if he wishes to be heard and listened to. He ought to keep it up incessantly until the wrongs inflicted on him will have been righted and done away with forever.[47]

Bourke and the Adult Deaf and Dumb Society of Victoria

Bourke's employment history with the Deaf Society can be pieced together from his own accounts and from Society records, although each gives a rather different picture of the man. According to Deaf Society records, Bourke was a "lonely fellow" and an incorrigible complainer, frequently ill and with a tendency to weep over "trivial affairs."[48] He had three periods of employment with the Society. The first was from June 1918 until November 1920, when he lived at the Society's farm and home in Blackburn on the rural outskirts of Melbourne (a residence and flower farm for "aged, infirm and feeble-minded" deaf people, and also those in need of temporary accommodation or employment).[49] Bourke lived and worked there as a poultry farmer and general farm hand. He resigned from this position. The second period (which Bourke does not mention) was when he was given a position as a collector. He "only lasted three weeks, his failure to succeed reducing him to tears." The third and final period was from April 1924 to April 1925, when he worked as a gardener and caretaker at the Society's new headquarters at Jolimont. He was dismissed from this position, allegedly because he continually purchased supplies without permission. In addition to these official positions, he was given unemployment relief and temporary accommodation in the Blackburn home during some additional periods.

Bourke's own version is given in his book, *The Story of a Deaf Drudge*, and also is mentioned in many of his other writings. His account confirms the details in the Society's records, apart from omitting his illfated attempt at collecting. But, as any autobiography does, his writing also gives us much more insight into his motivations and aspirations. For example, Bourke makes it very clear how strongly he aspired to "a living wage and a chance to make a home and settle down."[50] The fact that he had grown up with the education and expectations of a hearing person evidently made him unwilling to accept that he should be denied this basic opportunity because he was deaf. For most of 1918 to 1925, his feelings toward Abraham vacillated between gratefulness that Abraham seemed to be giving him a "chance," and outrage when Abraham continually overworked and underpaid him, keeping him dangling with promises of future pay rises.

Bourke regularly described how Abraham was able to manipulate him by making use of his aspirations and desires. Abraham did not merely dispense relief and give or take away jobs. He made a point of finding out what kind of people his charges were, of understanding their hopes and fears. This made it easier for him to manage them and keep them psychologically dependent on him. For example, early in Bourke's first period of employment at the farm,

> [Abraham] noticed my nervousness and asked if I was a nervous man. I said "No, but that I had worked hard all my life and yet could find no one who could see any good in me and give me a chance in life." He told me not to worry, but to stick to him, that he was my friend and he would see that I got my chance.[51]

Such assurances served (successfully) to make Bourke feel overwhelming gratitude to his "benefactor" and tolerate a level of abuse that he may not otherwise have accepted. Abraham would remember and re-use such information—for example, when Bourke began his later position as a gardener at Jolimont Square, Abraham wrote him a note, saying, "You now have the opportunity for which you have craved for years. The future is with yourself."[52] He then proceeded to demand long hours of work from Bourke at a low rate of pay.

Bourke recognized this strategy in retrospect and described how effective it was: "I was to come completely under his spell. He set out to be very nice to me."[53] It worked even when he was warned about Abraham by other deaf people.

> The deaf overseer, who had worked under Abraham for fifteen years at the farm, warned me not to work for him. He told me that Abraham would make me all sorts of promises which he would never keep, but at this time (1918) I was completely under Abraham's spell and no one could make me believe a word against him.[54]

Bourke described his work at the farm in painstaking detail. He was given responsibility for poultry farming (work that he loved) but was also expected to do the work of a general farmhand. He was paid a meager salary in addition to his board and lodging; however, Abraham continually assured him that if he could show that "poultry paid," the Society's board would be convinced of the value of the scheme, and his wages would increase—£200 a year was promised.[55] Bourke poured his energy and resources into the job, frequently paying for materials he needed out of his own pocket, because, he claimed, "I had a devil of a time trying to get anything out of Abraham. He would exasperate me by ignoring my requests for stock, materials, etc."[56] Whenever Bourke protested about his low wages, Abraham would promise to bring up his case again before the board and later tell him that he had not been successful. Bourke claimed he was later informed by a deaf member of the board that Abraham had never actually presented his case to the board at all.[57]

Abraham was able to use Bourke's passion for poultry farming as another way of manipulating him. He would threaten that the poultry scheme might be disbanded.

> He could see by this time that I was in love with my job and he played on my emotions accordingly. He said that his Board did not believe that poultry paid; that if he asked them for an increase in wages for me they would close down the poultry scheme and dismiss me.[58]

Alternatively, he would flatter Bourke by offering him public praise. Two years after Bourke had commenced, Abraham wrote an enthusiastic report about "Our Poultry Experiment" in the Society's newsletter, congratulating Bourke and referring to him as "our poultry expert."[59] Bourke later expostulated,

A group of residents and staff at the Blackburn Farm and Home, 1917–1918. Victorian Deaf Society Collection, State Library of Victoria.

When he wrote that he was giving me 15/- a week. An expert on
15/- a week! He showed me that paragraph himself, and I admit I
was pleased and flattered. I thanked and shook hands with him.[60]

Eventually, however, Bourke could no longer accept the conditions and
low pay, and he resigned when he found another job at "double the
wages" he was receiving on the farm. He found it difficult to leave the
regular company of other deaf people and the poultry work he was so
attached to. He wrote that "it was good to work with, amongst and for
those handicapped like oneself. . . . I felt mean and as if I were deserting
my post, and apologised to Abraham for leaving him."[61]

Despite the disappointments of his job at the farm, Bourke had not
yet lost faith in the Society, and specified that he left bearing no grudges
against Abraham or his board.[62]

The Decline of the Australasian Deaf and Dumb Association

The ADDA survived during the 1920s only in Victoria and (to a
lesser extent) Queensland. Its meetings were occasionally reported
in the *Monthly Letter* of the Adult Deaf and Dumb Society of Victoria,
although it seems not to have been very active. One of the few tradi-
tions that the Victorian branch maintained during the 1920s was the
celebration of "Rose Day," which commemorated F. J. Rose's establishment of the school for deaf children. In 1925 it was reported,

This year [Rose Day] was held at the Adult Deaf Centre, Jolimont
Square, on the 12th of November, and the chief feature was an
exhibition of photographs bearing upon the Education of the Deaf
and occurrences pertaining to the Deaf generally. Mr. Abraham
presided and there was a good attendance.[63]

The remaining state branches of the ADDA seem not to have been
happy with its gradual decline and tried on one or two occasions to
revive it. One such occasion was a meeting of representatives of the
Deaf societies from Victoria, New South Wales, South Australia, and
Queensland in Sydney in October 1922. The delegates had a lengthy
discussion about whether the ADDA should be revived or abandoned
in favor of a new organization that represented Deaf societies, rather
than the Deaf community. The meeting was attended by some people
who became key players in later developments, and the record of the

meeting reveals not only the issues under discussion, but also much about the personalities of these people and the underlying tensions between some of them.[64] Some comments at this early meeting show attitudes that remained consistent over many years; others said some very surprising things in light of their later activities.

Robert Luff (the deaf president of the Victorian branch) described the ADDA as having "the flower of the Deaf Community on its Committees." Luff's terminology looked forward to some of the more radical organizations formed in the late 1920s and 1930s (in which he was to be a participant). He talked often about "rights" and claimed that the ADDA was working to "try to secure [deaf people's] just claims to citizenship." He described the members as having "pledged themselves to keep their eyes open for any injustice or oppression that may be placed upon the Deaf at large, and make every effort to alleviate such." He stressed that "[i]ts operations will not clash with the operation of the Adult Deaf & Dumb Societies, because these Societies work for the Deaf, but this Association will assert their rights."

Luff also repudiated the notion of charity, especially in relation to education. One of the Victorian branch's proudest achievements was helping to fight for compulsory education for deaf children (which was won in 1912): "[W]e opened our eyes to see the injustice the Government were doing in placing us Deaf and Dumb under charity, when with the normal people free education was a right."

Samuel Showell, the deaf missioner from Queensland, supported Luff's comments and urged New South Wales and South Australia to revive their membership and support the ADDA. Abraham did most of the talking, as he so often did. He was a passionate supporter of the continuation of the ADDA and could not conceal his impatience with the sceptics from South Australia and New South Wales, who questioned its value and "benefits from subscriptions." He remarked,

> [T]he Victorian Branch set to work and did achieve success as I have just pointed out. . . . South Australia simply formed themselves into a Branch and did nothing. Did they expect the Victorian Deaf to go over there and work for them?

Perhaps the most surprising contribution was from Fletcher Booth, who had been a prominent leader in the New South Wales Deaf community for more than 30 years. He spoke against the ADDA, objecting, in part, to the extent of the Victorians' control of the organization. "The rules were made by Victorians alone," he noted, and New South Wales members "never advised their adoption." However, he also warned that having a branch of the ADDA in each state would mean "two Societies in each State and would cause friction, and it is possible if any deaf and dumb have a grievance against the Society, they might make a breakaway." He compared this with the breakaways happening in the Labor movement (trade unions), which he said caused "trouble, trouble, trouble." But most intriguingly of all, this long-serving and outspoken deaf man, who would later be one of the biggest defenders of breakaways and of deaf people managing their own affairs, said,

> I am sorry to say that the Deaf and Dumb have very little business faculty, and we can trust the hearing Board to look after the interests of the Deaf and Dumb. They have greater influence with the Public than the deaf and dumb. The best way is to leave our troubles and disputes and grievances to the hearing Board of Management, they will look after us very well.

Booth's contribution was welcomed by Alfred Lonsdale, a hearing member of the board of the Adult Deaf and Dumb Society of New South Wales, who was to become another key person in the events that followed. Lonsdale had joined the board only two years previously. He was active as a lay preacher in the Methodist Church, but had no prior connection with deaf people.[65] Lonsdale rephrased Booth's words in his own way, revealing much about his attitudes and motives for becoming involved in the Deaf Society.

> I agree with Mr. Booth. I am a hearing man, and I think that if you will get a few hearing people into the control of your Society, you will get very much better results. We sympathise with these deaf chaps here, because we love them, but we think that they have not got just that ability to control the Association as it should be controlled.

This claim that deaf people were not capable of controlling their organizations was very important. After almost fifty years of deaf activism and involvement, Lonsdale declared in a national forum that they were not capable of controlling their organizations and needed hearing people to do it for them. Significantly, Lonsdale was not challenged on this point by anyone present and even appeared to have support from Booth. In a way, he had casually pointed to a change in the balance of power between deaf and hearing people that was to be central to the conflicts that were to follow.

One of Lonsdale's objections to the constitution (or bylaws) of the ADDA was that it admitted as members only "[h]earing persons who have spent three years of actual work among the Deaf," and this rule excluded him, and some other hearing people he respected, from membership. However, his main objection seems to have been that such an independent organization could be a potential thorn in the side of the societies. He favored instead

an Association or a Federal Body of the Societies. Every Deaf mute has the right and privilege of becoming a member of the Society. There is nothing to debar or stop him and they have the right of electing their officers. Why should we create another Society? Everything will be done by us for the advancement of the Deaf and Dumb. I believe that is the right way.

Lonsdale warned, "The Australasian Deaf and Dumb Association might become very powerful and be able to overthrow the Societies' management." Despite his low opinion of the abilities of deaf people, this warning suggests that he feared the idea of deaf people gathering *en masse* without the explicit control of hearing people.

Abraham seemed to find this meeting very difficult. He desperately wanted the support of New South Wales and South Australia in order to revive the ADDA, but he could not help bristling at their criticisms. He found himself in the role of defender of the deaf people who originally framed the rules of the ADDA, and he did this quite eloquently. In reply to Lonsdale's complaint that he and others were debarred from becoming members of the ADDA and that hearing people were needed to "control the Association as it should be controlled," Abraham expostulated,

Well, that is pretty rough on me. It was the New South Wales Society that invited the Australian Deaf and Dumb Association to send its President over there and found the Society, and . . . now New South Wales turns them down. It is beautiful. However, I can see the point Mr Lonsdale is driving at. That article [admitting only hearing people who had worked with deaf people for at least three years] was at the time strongly opposed by me, but I was convinced in the end that it was self-defence. That is, had they not put that clause in, the Board of Management of the Australasian Deaf and Dumb Association in its infancy might have been swamped with hearing and speaking gentlemen, in full sympathy perhaps with the Deaf and Dumb, but not with the knowledge to enable them to do that which was best as the Deaf, and the deaf themselves, thought for themselves. They had the feeling that their opinions would be swamped by outsiders, and it was a very natural feeling too.

By the end of the meeting, Abraham seems to have bowed to the arguments of Lonsdale and a Mr. Cox (superintendent of the South Australian Mission). Although Abraham still held out for retaining the ADDA, he assured the meeting that he supported the inclusion of hearing people as members. The meeting concluded by carrying the following resolution (proposed by Lonsdale and seconded by a Mr. Martin of South Australia) that effectively postponed any decision.

> That the State Societies of the Deaf and Dumb recommend to consider and obtain data with a view to: (a) Re-forming the Australasian Deaf and Dumb Association or (b) The creation of a Federal Body of State Societies, and to report on this and any other matters relating to the Deaf, to a Conference to be held in 1923.

No conference seems to have been held in 1923, but the issues of national associations and the power relationships between deaf and hearing people certainly did not go away. The views expressed by various individuals at this meeting were, in some cases, almost prophetic of their later actions (especially Lonsdale's), and in others (e.g., Booth's) indicative of some strong influences that were later able to change their views. Abraham demonstrated here his chameleon-like ability to be both an eloquent champion of deaf people's views and a firm supporter of the hearing people whom he perceived as holding power. Lonsdale also demonstrated his uncanny ability to get his own way—toward the end of the meeting, almost everyone expressed their agreement with his views about including hearing people in a national body and safeguarding the role of the Deaf societies.

* * *

In contrast with the activity of its earlier years, the ADDA during the 1920s stagnated and declined. Its membership was aging, and its successful projects, such as making education for deaf children free and compulsory in some states and securing a pension for F. J. Rose, were receding into the past. It hosted no more national gatherings after the 1911 event. The dominance of Victoria in national affairs was no longer as readily accepted by the other states. As with other such organizations that come to an end, it had obviously ceased to meet the needs of its community. The Australian Deaf community and its institutions were changing, and the time was ripe for new leaders and new organizations to emerge.

New leaders and organizations did begin to appear during the late 1920s. Some of these leaders were deaf, either younger more radical people, such as William Crush and John Bourke in Victoria, or re-politicized older people, such as Fletcher Booth in New South Wales and Martha Overend Wilson in Queensland. Two hearing men also emerged as significant leaders, both professionally, as welfare workers committed to a higher level of independence among deaf people, and more indirectly, exerting strong and radical influences on the deaf people they knew and worked with (see chapter 3 and 4).

The "Banned Baby" Incident

The Adult Deaf and Dumb Society of Victoria received a burst of bad publicity in February 1923, when a Melbourne newspaper ran a series of articles highly critical of their treatment of some former employees.[66] The employees in question were a young married couple who had interviewed for the position of joint caretakers at the Society's headquarters on Flinders Street. They were appointed to the position, but before they could commence work (although after the man had resigned from his previous position), Abraham withdrew the offer, because he found out that the woman was pregnant. He advised them that they would not be able to accommodate a child at the center "from a health point of view." Although he claimed to have made this clear in the interview, the couple said he had not. Having lost their former work, and unable to find another position, they were experiencing great difficulties, and their newborn baby was in poor health.[67] The Herald's exposé attracted an avalanche of public condemnation of the Deaf Society and offers of support for the young couple.[68] Abraham refused to comment to The Herald on the incident, saying that it was a matter for his management committee.[69]

Bourke was moved to defend Abraham and the Deaf Society. He wrote a letter that was published in The Herald, defending Abraham and his board, although he expressed his sympathy for the unfortunate couple. As he later explained,

> I was still under Abraham's influence at the time and it stung and hurt me to hear the way people were speaking about him. Also the rememberance [sic] of his pretended kindness revived in my memory. It was a very dark hour for him, and I was the first to

come forward and plead that there might be some extenuating circumstances behind his and his Board's action.[70]

He wrote in his letter that he had "received much kindness from Mr. Abraham," and concluded, "Our committee consists of shrewd business men, and they know better than we deaf people what should be done."[71] The last part of Bourke's letter is very similar to the comments of Fletcher Booth the year before, when he said, "we can trust the hearing Board to look after the interests of the Deaf and Dumb."[72] These comments, from two deaf people who were to take leading roles in later developments, are an interesting measure of how much the Deaf community's opinion was to change during the 1920s.

Bourke was taken aback when some deaf people became "very upset" about his letter to *The Herald* in defence of Abraham. They "believed that Abraham had written it and got me to sign it and send it to the 'Herald.'"[73] Although he was surprised by this at the time, he was later to become very familiar with this tactic of Abraham's. The fact that people were "upset" indicates that, by this time, there were numbers of deaf people in Melbourne who no longer supported Abraham and were aware of the way he manipulated public opinion and the Deaf community.

This is supported by an intriguing anecdote from one of Abraham's later successors, Ernest Reynolds. In an interview in the early 1980s, Reynolds recalled a group of disenchanted older deaf people in 1920s Victoria. The following anecdote took place at the Flinders Street headquarters of the Deaf Society before its move in 1925, when Reynolds himself was a boy accompanying his deaf parents to the Society.

> There was a [group] in Victoria headed by a lot of the older deaf. . . . They were a little more highly intelligent than the average deaf. . . . I was only a boy of about 10 or 11 [when] I was, if you could put it this way, honorary interpreter for the [group].
>
> [At] Flinders Street Mission . . . we used to sit up at the back and my Mum or Dad or both would take me in there and the older deaf would sit round and I had to tell them what was being said by the speaker which Mr. Abraham was interpreting the other end of the hall.
>
> Q: What, they refused to watch Abraham?
>
> A: That is correct, that is correct and I was only 10 or 11 . . . and Mr. Abraham came up, he was my Godfather, and he came up and he said Ernest what are you doing, and I remember this as if it was

yesterday, and I said I'm telling the deaf here and he turned round to the deaf and he says why and they said you don't tell us what should be told us . . .[74]

In saying to Abraham, "[Y]ou don't tell us what should be told us," these deaf people were challenging both Abraham's authority and the accuracy of his interpreting. The anecdote suggests that some of them no longer trusted Abraham, and that they sometimes publicly challenged him as a group, not just as individuals.

A "Drudge" Again

John Bourke's final period of employment with the Deaf Society was from April 1924 to April 1925. The Society had recently sold its Flinders Street headquarters and acquired a new property at Jolimont Square, with extensive grounds. Bourke himself asked Abraham for the position of gardener, and Abraham agreed. The ensuing year, according to Bourke, was another round of broken promises. These ranged from having to "batch" for himself (cook and clean, although he had furnished quarters) for a period of seven months instead of the few days initially agreed to; filling the caretaker's role for up to three nights a week in addition to his work in the garden; and Abraham's failure to pay Bourke a portion of the profits from the produce he raised, despite a written undertaking to do so.[75]

Once again, Bourke ordered and paid for many items on his own initiative. He claimed that this was because his requests for necessary items were ignored, refused, or delayed, and he wanted to proceed with the job, so that he could impress Abraham and others with his abilities. He gave the following example of one of these independent purchases (which he always claimed back from the Society):

> I had asked him for a pair of scales to weigh broad beans when I sold them to tenants and friends. This is his answer:
> "As to scales. I suggest you buy a lb. of beans and take what you receive as a guide to your own sales."
> I had more sense than to follow such a silly suggestion, so I bought a pair of scales myself.[76]

Deaf society records indicated that Bourke's unauthorized purchases amounted to almost £15.0.0 during that year and included fowls and timber. They stated that this was the "chief reason for his dismissal."[77]

Midway through his term of employment, new caretakers were employed and, as agreed, Bourke moved into lodgings off-site. His salary of 35 shillings was increased, but only up to £2.15.0, instead of the "living wage" of £3.16.0, which he had hoped for (the Australian minimum wage in 1924, established by the Commonwealth Court of Conciliation and Arbitration, was £4.5.6).[78] Bourke was deeply disappointed and tried unsuccessfully to argue his case with Abraham.

During this period of employment, the relationship between Bourke and Abraham deteriorated rapidly. Abraham had less compunction about criticizing Bourke's work and dismissing his complaints outright instead of pretending that he would consult the board. He wrote irritably to Bourke, "Whatever I have tried to do for you has produced its batch of bitter, complaining letters. In fact you are always grousing and I am weary of such epistles."[79] Bourke, for his part, began to develop the manic hatred of Abraham that was to remain with him until Abraham's death. Although Bourke does not record the incident, Deaf Society records allege that toward the end of his employment there, "whenever the Principal was in his office Bourke spent the whole of the day mowing a small piece of lawn in front."[80] Bourke mentioned elsewhere that Abraham hated noise and had nagged him about his cough, so his behavior with the lawnmower suggests the furious revenge of a man using one of the few weapons (noise) that he could control and that had no power to harm him.[81]

Toward the end of this period of employment, Bourke began to make threats. He later wrote,

> I turned on the brute, and in spluttering and stuttering wrath I told him that I would take my case to the Government and let the public judge between us.
> He said, sneeringly, in deaf signs, "Good! Good!"[82]

The Deaf Society's version was that he "repeatedly threatened that if he was dismissed he would spend the rest of his time in trying to ruin the Principal and the Society."[83] Notwithstanding this, he was dismissed in April 1925. Later that year, he managed to find a similar position elsewhere and held it for many years afterwards.[84] His summed up his employment under Abraham as follows:

> As his employee, I owe him nothing but four year's [sic] of drudgery. I always got better treatment and better pay from others than I did from him. I did not know what a curse deafness could be until I worked under him.[85]

Bourke's subsequent attempts to "take his case to the Government" illustrated many of the issues that were to become important in the Australian Deaf community over the next decade—deaf people's right to be treated as citizens, to maintain some autonomy in the management of their own affairs, and to seek recognition of the corruption and abuse that arose in some of the organizations that controlled deaf people.

The National Scene

By the mid-1920s, most Deaf societies in Australia were comfortably established and had increasing numbers of prominent public figures—all hearing men—on their boards of management. They included E. R. Peacock in Victoria, who had been a consul to Czechoslovakia and owned a large printing firm; Digby Denham in Queensland, who had been Premier of the state from 1911 to 1915; philanthropist J. H. Angas in South Australia; and William Brooks in New South Wales, who was a member of the state parliament.[86] Most of the Deaf societies were actively consolidating and expanding their property and services.

In Queensland, Samuel Showell resigned as superintendent of the Queensland Adult Deaf and Dumb Mission in 1925, and Martha Over-end Wilson took over temporarily as acting superintendent. Although Wilson was also deaf, the Mission's annual report in 1926 stated unequivocally that in appointing a new superintendent, "preference should be given to one not handicapped as Mr. Showell has been in this respect," and "applications have been invited from hearing persons qualified to fill the vacancy."[87] Showell and Wilson were to be the last deaf superintendents of any Deaf Society in Australia during the twentieth century.

In NSW, the Deaf Society acquired a new building at 5 Elizabeth Street in central Sydney in 1927, and the board was beginning to consider employing more experienced and qualified welfare staff. Along with the Queensland Mission, they looked to Britain to fill this need.

Abraham's Continuing Influence

During the 1920s, Ernest Abraham maintained his position as the leading figure in the Australian Deaf world. Although things were becoming complicated for him within his own Deaf Society, these internal rumblings had not yet affected his status as the nation's "chief expert" on deaf people. In 1926, he celebrated the twenty-fifth anniversary of his arrival in Melbourne, and a huge celebration was held at the center, at which he was presented with a gold watch and chain inscribed to "Our Chief."[88] His anniversary also elicited effusive newspaper articles in the Melbourne newspapers, most of which suggest Abraham's guiding pen. An article in *The Argus* reaffirmed, "[The Society] is what the deaf mutes claim to be 'their world,' and Mr. Abraham is its 'uncrowned king.'"[89]

An example of his influential standing in the Deaf societies and general Deaf communities of Queensland and New South Wales is described in a detailed report in *Our Monthly Letter* in 1926, describing a "rest" holiday he took—a sea voyage to Brisbane and Sydney.[90] It began with an extract from an article in the Brisbane *Telegraph*, which described Abraham as "the chief expert in Australia in matters pertaining to the Deaf and Dumb," as well as "a very interesting and original personality." His earlier visits in support of the Queensland Deaf Mission were described, and his preaching, including his use of "flowing and emphatic gesture," was admired. The article concluded,

> Mr. Abraham praised the work done in the mission, and he criticised too, but criticism from a man with such intimate knowledge of every wide avenue and every blind alley of deaf mission work, and every twist and turn of deaf mute character, could not fail to be well received and to carry weight.[91]

The references to "every blind alley of deaf mission work" and "every twist and turn of deaf mute character" reflect the more somber and cynical view of deaf people that Abraham seemed to be developing during the 1920s.

A more detailed article followed in the same issue of *Our Monthly Letter*, describing his many rounds of visits to the Deaf Mission in Queensland and its various projects, the Deaf Society in New South Wales, and the schools for the deaf in both states. His days were an endless round of visits, meetings, lunches, dinners, escorted motorcar trips to scenic spots, church services where he preached, and "welcome socials," where he was greeted by crowds of deaf people. The names of those who entertained him were all recorded. As well as his meetings with the churchmen, barristers, and accountants who made up the Deaf Society boards of the time, he was taken out to lunch at "Brisbane's most fashionable cafe 'Rowe's'" by Martha Overend Wilson and another deaf woman. He also had several meetings with Alfred Lonsdale in Sydney. Although their relationship was usually guarded, on this visit,

they spent considerable time together and praised each other in public.[92] Lonsdale welcomed Abraham at a social, referring to him as "the
Father of the Deaf and Dumb of Australia"; and Abraham told Sydney
deaf people "how fortunate they were in having . . . Mr Lonsdale . . .
conducting their services and attending to their every need, he knew of
no other committee man devoting so much valuable time to the cause
of the deaf."[93]

Although Abraham continued to be the dominant personality on the
national scene, his status began to decline a little during this time. The
ADDA over which he had presided was largely defunct. The domestic
problems he was experiencing with Bourke and others, although not
yet widely known, seemed to sap some of his energy and enthusiasm.
A number of other influential Deaf Society leaders made their appearance during the 1920s, although none of them seriously challenged him
until later. Lonsdale in Sydney, although never a popular and charismatic leader in the way that Abraham was, gradually began to accu-
mulate power and influence, and always remained stolidly unawed by
Abraham. Two other hearing superintendents arrived from Britain later
in the 1920s—Herbert Hersee in New South Wales and John M'Caig
Paul in Queensland—and as we shall see, these men did indeed challenge Abraham's control. Abraham's image was imperceptibly shifting
from that of an energetic young crusader with bold new ideas, to that of
an aging patriarch unwilling to cede his entrenched control.

Bourke and the Deaf Community

At about the same time that Bourke was struggling through his last
period of employment with the Deaf Society, he began to participate
more actively in other organizations within the Deaf community. In
1924, he was elected to the Deaf Committee, and the following year, he
appeared on the committee of the Men's Guild.[94] His actual involvement
in general community life is rather difficult to gauge. He never seems
to be listed in the social pages of *Our Monthly Letter*, winning prizes at
the socials, playing for the sports teams, or sending cheery greetings to
his friends while away on holidays (although it is possible that he was
always unlucky, had two left feet, and could never afford holidays). But
he was certainly familiar with the social side of Deaf community life.

Happiness is a noted feature of the character of the deaf when they
are assembled together. Nature, as if in remorse for her injustice

to them, has made the deaf mute a great talker . . . . On social evenings round the card table at their headquarters they frequently
growl at one another for holding up the game to talk. We (the
author included) have too much to say at times. In fact, they have
a special sign for the loquacious deaf mute.[95]

Most Deaf societies had Deaf committees (sometimes called *Deaf general
committees*) up until the 1980s, with generally similar compositions and
roles. These committees were also a feature of British missions and Deaf
societies at the time—usually called *social club committees*—and Paddy
Ladd has provided an insightful ethnographic study of their roles
within Deaf communities and missions. In Britain, with its clearer class
structure, the social club committees were usually composed of middle-
or upper-class deaf people. Although membership in these committees
was prestigious, they had little actual power. Ladd describes the "two-
tier administrative structure" of a hearing board of management and
a deaf social club committee as "the essential colonialist structure."[96]
In Australia, the Deaf committees were composed almost entirely of
elected deaf people (usually men during the '20s and '30s), along with
two or three representatives of the boards of the state Deaf societies,
and had responsibility for day-to-day matters, such as "the arrangements for Divine worship, classes, meetings, and social gatherings held
at the Centre."[97] As in Britain, membership of the Deaf Committee was
usually a highly regarded role in the community.

   Bourke left an acerbic description of the workings of the Victorian
Deaf Committee during Abraham's time. It was made up of ten deaf
people, a hearing member of the board (appointed, not elected), and
Abraham. Abraham was always chairman.[98] Abraham wrote the constitution, or "Rules of the Deaf Committee," and was usually able to make
sure that the Deaf Committee was stacked with deaf employees of the
Society, deaf people on unemployment relief (which he controlled),
and others under his influence, because most of these people could be
counted on not to oppose his wishes.

   As Chairman of all committee meetings he arranges the Agenda,
   cajoles and flatters those under his influence, sneers at and insults
   the strong members if they dare to speak their minds to him,
   frowns down the employees if they oppose his wishes, and tries
   to mould everyone's thoughts to his own way of thinking and get
   them to vote in the way he wants them to.[99]

Although Abraham may initially have wanted Bourke on the Deaf Committee, because he was an employee of the Society, the acrimonious conclusion to Bourke's employment and his opposition to Abraham and the Society would soon have made him a liability. So Abraham made use of another of Bourke's problematic attributes to remove him from the Committee. Bourke was a Catholic at a time when Australian society was very sectarian, and Catholics were excluded from many public roles.[100] This had already caused some tensions between him and Abraham. Bourke described how Abraham had challenged his involvement in a "denominational Deaf and Dumb Association" while he was working at the Deaf Society and on the Deaf Committee. Abraham (although he was not an ordained minister) conducted Protestant church services at the Deaf center every Sunday, and he told Bourke that Deaf Committee members were expected to participate fully in these services. He alternately cajoled Bourke, telling him that "he and I were pals and here I was breaking our friendship and drifting away from the Society," and threatened him.

> He played on my emotions; took advantage of my helplessness and difficulty in securing other work; my love for my job; bullied and browbeat me; threatened that I would lose my job and my place on the Committee, and had me whimpering.
> He is a slow-torturing devil![101]

But Bourke refused to "put aside all [his] principles and act the hypocrite for the sake of a job at thirty-five shillings a week." So, after he had been dismissed from his position as gardener, Abraham used his religion to work him out of the Deaf Committee. At the final meeting for the year, just before the election for a new Deaf Committee, Abraham

> called members [sic] attention to a supposed rule of the Society which read that only members of the Protestant persuasion were eligible to stand for election to the deaf committee.
> He brought under notice the fact that I [Bourke] belonged to a different denomination to the rest of the members, and asked the meeting to decide whether I had the right to be a member of the Committee.[102]

According to Bourke, only one member of the Committee stood up for him, two supported Abraham, and all the others said nothing. No decision was made at this meeting, but the damage was done, and Bourke was defeated at the election for the next year's Deaf Committee—"his

[Abraham's] dirty work had had its effect."[103] He was not reelected (or did not stand) at the next year's annual meeting of the Men's Guild either, possibly for the same reason.[104] Using religious sectarianism in this way would have been an effective political tactic, and as Bourke wrote later, Abraham also "[threw] my religion in my face in order to hurt my feelings." It provided yet another reason for his implacable hatred of Abraham.

Bourke's Campaign Against Abraham

Bourke's condemnation of Abraham did not stem only from resentment at his own treatment. He described many other transgressions that he believed merited exposure and public condemnation. These included Abraham's physical brutality to some inmates of the Blackburn farm and home, his heavy demands on them for domestic and farm labor, and the meager allowances he gave them out of their pensions.[105] He also despised Abraham's hypocrisy in calling himself a "chaplain" and leading church services for deaf people, while at the same time demonstrating what he saw as immoral behavior. Not only did Abraham regularly "gather us round him at Blackburn and tell us risqué stories,"[106] he was a notorious womanizer. Abraham's sexual exploits with women (especially deaf women) were legendary. He was reputed to seduce young deaf women when they became engaged, to "prepare" them for marriage, and to have numerous illegitimate children in the Deaf community. One informant, interviewed in the 1980s, matter-of-factly described deaf men in the 1930s asking each other, "Is that child yours or Mr. A.'s?"[107] Bourke wrote that his "taking liberties with the deaf girls" was "the thing that the deaf are most resentful against Abraham for."[108] Another informant claimed that a deaf man committed suicide because of Abraham's affair with his wife.[109]

Bourke claimed to have made a sworn declaration about Abraham's behavior with deaf women to the speaker of the Victorian Parliament, and he wrote that others had complained to the board of the Society, who "merely pooh-poohed the idea and answered, 'Nonsense, he is an old man.'"[110]

Another charge that Bourke made against Abraham was that he co-opted and corrupted some of the ablest and most intelligent deaf people in the community.[111] He described the case of James Johnston in particular, giving him the pseudonym of "P. Clay" in his writings.[112] Johnston was, according to Bourke, originally "a man of fine principle

with natural good qualities and noble instincts and ideals." Not only
was he a leader and an active worker in community organizations as
a young man, he also saw through Abraham and boldly challenged
him—"he used to thrill us all by the outspoken way he opposed Abraham and stood up for our rights."[113]

Abraham gave Johnston the job of assistant missioner at the Society
in 1923, a job that he was to hold for more than twenty years. According
to Bourke, he then "turned [Johnston's] head" and used the security of
his job to coerce Johnston into doing much of his "dirty work." This
included taking action against deaf people whom Abraham deemed to
be troublemakers. Abraham's astute co-option of Johnston and others
helped to consolidate his role and protect him from disaffected deaf
people in the community.

James M. Johnston.
Victorian Deaf Society Collection, State Library of Victoria.

Bourke considered that Johnston was "ashamed to do many of the things that Abraham forces him to do," but that he eventually saw little point in resisting.

> He came to see, however, that Abraham was all powerful [in] the Society and that the deaf were quite helpless to do anything against him. Except that some of the deaf grumbled at Abraham's trickery and deception, nobody seemed to be able to put a stop to it all. In the end he took the atmosphere of lies, deceit and treachery that Abraham had created in the Society as a matter of course. To throw up his job for the sake of decency was too great a sacrifice to make when nobody seemed to care whether Abraham was bad or not. He saw that Abraham beat everybody in the end and that nobody could shift him, so [Johnston] just floated with the tide.[114]

Because Bourke was one of the troublemakers whom Johnston had to act against on occasion, his attitude to Johnston may have been influenced by this. He may also have felt personally hurt by the way Abraham set Johnston above people like himself. Johnston was working at the Jolimont Center during Bourke's stint as gardener there in 1924–25, and they would initially have their lunch together, but Abraham "told [Johnston] that he degraded himself by having his lunch with me."[115] However, Bourke always refrained from being too critical of Johnston, probably because he knew all too well what the security of a good job meant to a deaf man. He even conceded, "I often wonder whether I would have gone the same way if Abraham had paid me a living wage and left me alone when I worked for him."[116]

Bourke carried through on his threats to "take his case to the Government" and to try and arouse public concern for deaf people. In the years following his dismissal from the Deaf Society, he regularly wrote letters to the Melbourne newspapers and to various government officials. Most of his dealings with government bodies will be dealt with in later chapters.

Taking on Abraham and the Society in this way would have made Bourke's position within the Deaf community more precarious. Putting his name to public criticisms would have made further opportunities to participate in organizations like the Deaf Committee unlikely, and, although he continued to have some deaf friends and allies, these people would probably have been taking risks in being seen to be too closely associated with him. Like Johnston, many deaf people probably felt that Bourke had no chance of defeating Abraham and was making life unnecessarily hard for himself. Others would have remained too much in awe of Abraham (or too frightened of him) to see any value in Bourke's campaign. Bourke acknowledged these community attitudes in his writings, perhaps nowhere more poignantly than when he tried to explain his campaign by quoting Brutus's speech in Shakespeare's *Julius Caesar.*

> Romans, countrymen, and lovers! Hear me for my cause, and be silent, that you may hear: . . . [C]ensure me in your wisdom, and awake your senses, that you may the better judge. If there be any in this assembly, any dear friend of Caesar's, to him I say, that Brutus' love to Caesar was no less than his. If then that friend demand why Brutus rose against Caesar, this is my answer.[117]

It is doubtful whether such literary allusions would have worked for many of Bourke's readers, although they help his quixotic image for later generations!

In a letter to *The Herald* on January 18, 1926, Bourke called for more "public interest in the afflicted deaf and dumb at the Blackburn Home." One of the deaf-blind men there had been in the hospital for a month, but had had no visits from Abraham (although it was Johnston's duty to visit deaf people in the hospital—and he had done so—he had been away on holiday for some weeks, so the responsibility fell to Abraham). Bourke visited the man regularly and claimed the man told him he had had no visitors for a week. He concluded his letter by saying, "The Deaf of Victoria need a new leader."[118]

Bourke's letter was met with an indignant reply in *The Herald* the next day signed by James Johnston. This letter asserted that Johnston himself and "a large number of deaf mutes" had been to visit the man in question, and declared that the invalid would be "the last man to complain."[119] Bourke insisted, however, that this letter had been written by Abraham, and that he had made Johnston sign it, saying, "It is a well-known fact that Abraham writes all the letters that appear in the Press about the adult deaf. When he answers complaints he seldom puts his name to them, but gets one of his . . . dupes . . . to sign them."[120]

Bourke's letter and the reply were reprinted in the Deaf Society's magazine *Our Monthly Letter* with an accompanying article called "Now—Lest We Forget," which attempted to marginalize Bourke and his complaints and rally support from the faithful.

Now there is a younger generation growing up who have found all their ways made smooth for them and perhaps it would be well if only in thought they should be taken back over the stony road of the older generation when the only clubs for the Deaf were convenient lamp-posts and public house bar-parlours. Also, at that period the Blind-deaf, Mentals and Poor Deaf had no one to care for them. Therefore, it is up to us in every way to honor and respect men like F. J. Rose and E. J. D. Abraham who have blazed the trail for practically everything the Deaf of Victoria now enjoy and are ever likely to enjoy. So stand firm, boys and girls, don't let their work and the work of our pioneer deaf men and women be lightly thought of or damaged by outsiders, keep the flag flying for Our Colours must never be lowered![121]

Abraham obviously felt that Bourke's letter-writing merited a message to the community that such activity was not acceptable. Bourke was thus dismissed as an "outsider" and as part of an ungrateful younger generation. But Abraham's approach to dissidents was multifaceted and creative—he did not merely rebut Bourke's arguments in public, he also continued to work on Bourke himself.

He . . . does not like the deaf to be out of friends with him. If he thinks you are important enough, he will go to a great deal of trouble to get you back on to his side again. He will do it all in a very sly, crafty and cunning way. You need to be very strong-willed to resist him, for he is very persevering and persistent . . . .
. . . I had not the moral courage to hold him off. He . . . forced me to make friends with him against my will and inclination. He still had me under his influence, but I had lost all respect for him.[122]

Bourke continued his campaign. Another of his letters was published in *The Age* (Melbourne's most respected newspaper) in May that year, criticizing Abraham for the way he was treating the deaf-blind men at the farm. Bourke claimed that these men, especially one young man who could have benefited from industrial training, were kept at the farm for "propaganda" purposes, and that the youngest one was allowed to "sit for eight years in despair and idleness on a dole of two shillings a week. (Yes, two shillings!)"[123]

Bourke's activities were having an effect. The minutes of the Society's general board meeting in July 1926 recorded that the secretary of the Charities Board, Mr. Love, had summoned Abraham and several of the board members "to meet him in conference relating to the complaint made by Mr Burke [sic], that this Society was receiving pensions and not giving adequate pocket money to the inmates." The chairman of the board pleaded ignorance—"if we had not been complying with the regulations, we failed to do so because of a lack of knowledge." Further investigations revealed that the Society was not "a proclaimed Institution under the Pensions Act" as it was not subsidized by the government. It was therefore not obliged to follow the requirements of the act and provide inmates with a minimum of four shillings out of the £1-per-week pension they collected for each of them.[124] Although no wrongdoing was proved, it can hardly have helped the Deaf Society's image to be under investigation for such a matter.

* * *

Bourke stayed away from the social gatherings at the Deaf Society for some months after writing these letters, lacking the "moral courage" to go there. When he returned, Abraham was full of charm. "He asked where had I been all this time, and said he was glad to see me back. I told him that I was glad too, and that I could not keep away any longer. He shook me effusively by the hand."[125] Bourke was still vulnerable to Abraham's power, not quite able to stand up to him in the flesh, even though he was aware of his motives.

> He got talking about my letters to the papers and as I was still a bit overawed by him I muttered something to the effect that I had not meant to attack him, that all I was concerned about was the welfare of the deaf. He ended up by asking me, "Do you want a job?" I told him I was in work.[126]

Abraham had seen that Bourke could indeed cause trouble for him, and needed some delicate handling. He knew how desperately Bourke aspired to a decent job and used that to bribe him, not only face to face, but also through other people. Bourke admitted that

> some time later an unemployed mate told me that Abraham was going to get us both splendid positions through his Rotary Club mates. The temptation was too much for me and I told Abraham I would be grateful if he would get me a position.[127]

Abraham used Bourke's temporary weakening to flatter him further and try to entice him back to the fold. He wrote a letter to Bourke soon afterwards saying,

In the very short conversation we had you told me that your only
motive for recent acts on your part . . . was your interest in the
deaf and desire to help them.

Now as that has been my only motive <u>for living</u> for the past 40
years and more, why cannot you come and join forces with me? I
would welcome your assistance with open arms.

. . . It is not possible for one to <u>always</u> do the right thing, any-
way I have always tried and I believe have accomplished more for
the Deaf and Dumb than any living man—And that is no boast.
Come along and let us have a heart to heart talk.[128]

Bourke claimed that he managed to resist this "humbug," although
Abraham kept the job promise dangling for some time. Around this
time, Bourke described his vengeful approach to the Deaf Society as
changing into a broader interest in the "welfare and future" of deaf
people. This, he claimed, was prompted by visits to the Institute for
the Blind, where the young deaf-blind man from the farm had been
transferred after a new manager took over the Blackburn home. He
was most impressed by the workshop there that had enabled the deaf-
blind man to learn a trade (weaving) and earn around £2.7.0 a week.
He was struck by the contrast between the Institute for the Blind and
the farm and home at Blackburn—"The whole place was a hive of
industry and a heartening and soul-stirring contrast to the dismal,
dreary degrading and useless lives these blind men and myself had
lead under Abraham."[129] He began to turn more attention to proposals
for improving the lives of deaf people, although his writing never lost
its strong vein of criticism of Abraham and the Deaf Society.

Bourke had two letters published in *The Age* in May the following
year, proposing that a vocational training scheme was the only solution
to the "hard and hopeless lives which the untrained deaf were leading."[130] Abraham sent him a cautious note after the first letter, saying,
"I appreciate very much your letter in the "Age" of the 6th. It is just the
thing. I would like to see the deaf keep that ball a'rolling." Abraham
assured him that he hoped to establish a Vocational Training Institute
for the Deaf, but that it would be "very up-hill work and it will be
necessary for the better educated deaf to stand by me and help, to a
man."[131] But Bourke was finding it easier to resist such flattery, and his
success at getting letters published in the newspapers (especially the
prestigious *The Age*) was emboldening him.

His next target was Abraham's appropriation of the mislead-
ing title of *principal*, which confused many people and constantly
annoyed the school administrators at the Victorian Deaf and Dumb
Institution. Because both the school and the Deaf Society competed
for public funds, and it was considered easier to rouse people's sympathy for children, Abraham tried to give the impression that the
Society catered to children as well as adults. Using the title of principal was one of his strategies for doing this. In response to a mention in the *The Age* of Abraham as principal, Bourke wrote a letter
explaining the differences between the school and the Society, pointing out that Abraham's title should be superintendent. He could not
resist adding, "We deaf, ourselves, have no voice whatever in the
policy of [the] Society," and he seemed to plead for the support of
the *The Age* in his campaign: "If we can secure a policy of utility,
usefulness and uplift we shall owe the 'Age' a debt of gratitude for
allowing us to reach 'the great heart of humanity,' for there alone lies
our salvation."[132]

A reply appeared in *The Age* the very next day, signed by J. M.
Johnston, "Deaf Vice-Chairman of the Deaf Committee of Management." The letter sidestepped the issue of Abraham's title, going
straight to Bourke's allegation that deaf people had "no voice" in the
affairs of the society. This, the reply said, was "not quite accurate." It
asserted instead that "the deaf have a powerful voice in the management of all deaf mute affairs connected with the Society," and that "the
whole of the actual work amongst the deaf is under the control of a
Committee of eleven deaf mutes and one hearing man (the principal)
elected by the deaf and dumb members annually."[133] (This, of course,
referred to the Deaf Committee, giving it powers that it had never
possessed.) Bourke wrote bitterly that he and "all the deaf" knew that
Abraham had written the letter. He "charged [Johnston] with signing
that letter at Abraham's urging. He has never denied it."[134] This letter
was a great blow to Bourke. "I had got the ear of a great newspaper,"
he said, "and Abraham had . . . [taken] advantage of his position . . . to
discredit me with the 'Age.' The letter put an end, as I thought, to all
my hopes of reaching the public conscience."[135]

Abraham wrote again to Bourke the next day, using every tactic he
could think of—a dazzling job offer, an enticement to join a prestigious
committee, a pretension that he and Bourke were on the same side, a
declaration of honesty.

Dear Bourke.

Thanks for your letter to "Age." Such help is appreciated. A few slight erras (sic) but they give opportunity for further letters which is (sic) in its way helpful to the Cause. I'm very tired and this is my last effort of an unusually heavy day.

Before writing again may I suggest you come to the Centre and consult the Records of the past twenty-five years. Leave nothing open to debate. Absolute truth is my motto, and will win through and bring into existence that which we are all aiming at.

How would a job as 'folder' at one of the Newspaper offices suit you? Wages are £4.16.0. This is confidential and in haste and the child of a weary brain. I am proposing an 'Advisory Board' of the Deaf to consider plans of buildings, objectives etc. If you care to join that Board I will propose it.[136]

An outraged Bourke rejected every ploy. In his reply, he dismissed the invitation to look at the records with "I do not need to look at any records to know that you are incurably and contemptibly selfish." To the suggestion of a place on the putative advisory board he wrote, "I have no intention of holding an official position in the Society, and the deaf will not have me if I would." And to the enticing bribe of a good job, he replied unequivocally, "[W]ell you might get me a job at full wages! You have made me pay in ten years of bitter drudgery for believing in [obscured] honour and sincerity. Poor fool that I was. You go and buy someone else, I'm not for sale!"[137]

After this ringing rebuff, Abraham rarely attempted to win Bourke back into his camp, and Bourke no longer had any lingering susceptibility to his lures. He declared in 1939, "I have refused to speak to or have anything to do with him from that day (June, 1927) to this. He had tried often to get me on friendly terms with him. He has never succeeded, and he never will."[138] The gloves were off, and they were in open enmity.

* * *

The relationship between John Bourke and Ernest Abraham crystalized the tensions developing in the 1920s between the Deaf societies and some of the more autonomous and outspoken deaf people. The Deaf societies were settling comfortably into the role of benevolent charities, despite their beginnings when deaf people had collaborated in or led the efforts to establish them. Abraham represented both the "old days" of partnership with deaf people and the new order of hearing control. However, not all deaf people were willing to acquiesce to this new order. Bourke was in many ways an atypical deaf person; however, he articulated both deaf people's need for security (and the dependence that could result) and their desire for independence, with its associated fears and uncertainties in a world with little support. In doing so, he provided a consistent and valuable "view from below" that intersected with official records and provides us with a richer and more complex understanding of the time and place.

These events set the scene for the developments of the late 1920s and 1930s, when the conflicts between deaf people and those who wished to control them grew from isolated individual struggles toward larger, more organized movements. The first such movement occurred in New South Wales.

3

The Prerogative of Every Citizen

I think I have stated enough for anyone to be convinced of the capabilities of the Adult Deaf in organising, controlling, or managing their own affairs. IT IS NO LONGER A POSSIBILITY; IT IS AN ACCOMPLISHED FACT.
—"The Deaf A R E Managing their Own Affairs"
The Deaf Advocate (emphasis in original)

During the late 1920s, individual conflicts such as those described in chapter 2, began to develop, in some states, into organized movements. Despite the years of deaf people's involvement in setting up the missions and societies, the hearing businessmen they had invited on to their Deaf societies' boards were becoming entrenched and powerful. These men had their own ideas of how such organizations should be administered and how they should be represented to the community at large, and their ideas were a function of the society they lived in, where "charity" was the responsibility of the affluent and altruistic.[1] Funds and publicity became (or were seen to be) dependent on a particular image of deaf people being "looked after" by benevolent hearing people. This image was very different from the ideas held by most deaf people, and by the end of the 1920s, conflict was rife in the Deaf societies of New South Wales (NSW), Queensland, and Victoria. The forms these conflicts took, and the ways in which they were articulated by both sides, reveal much about the social construction of deaf people and their place in the world.

It would be overly simplistic to portray the conflicts as merely deaf against hearing. In the charged atmosphere of the time, with volatile events and personalities demanding responses, deaf people joined

58

forces against other deaf people, and hearing people attacked other hearing people. The primary conflict centered on how to conceptualize deaf people and the institutions that served them. One view saw deaf people as having their greatest opportunity for security and progress by working within the institutions that had already been established and by being loyal to the hearing people who now controlled those institutions. The other view rejected this path as denying the achievements and capabilities of deaf people and turning them into passive objects of charity, and instead saw deaf people as capable of independence and of "managing their own affairs." In Victoria, these differing views were exemplified by James Johnston and John Bourke; in New South Wales, they were to be embodied by many other people.

Deaf people were not the only marginalized group seeking greater equality and a voice in public affairs during the 1920s; nor were they the only ones to use the idea of "citizenship" as a way of articulating their aims. Australian women, who had gained the vote in 1902, continued to organize and educate each other. The Australian Federation of Women Voters, active during the 1920s, was originally called the Australian Federation of Societies for Equal Citizenship, and was committed to the goal of equal citizenship with men.[2] Members educated other women in the skills needed for good citizenship, such as running meetings, debating, public speaking, and using the media, and sought involvement in national and international organizations that embodied their aims, such as the League of Nations.[3] Aboriginal Australians were also beginning to organize and demand their rights as citizens, establishing organizations, such as the Australian Aboriginal Progressive Association in 1924 in NSW and the Australian Aborigines League in 1933 in Victoria.[4]

Herbert V. S. Hersee

In the state of New South Wales, the catalyst for much of the upheaval was the arrival of Herbert V. S. Hersee to begin work at the Adult Deaf and Dumb Society of New South Wales. He had been recruited from England by the Society to become their new superintendent-secretary and arrived in Sydney on the ship *Euripides* with his wife and two small children in April 1928.[5]

Hersee was quickly accepted by the Sydney Deaf community, and in a very short time he appeared to influence the aspirations and assertiveness of many of them, creating a significant body of people (hearing as well as deaf) who identified with the second view described before.

Hersee had been missioner to deaf people at Portsmouth in England since 1920.[6] He was a hearing son of deaf parents. His parents were prominent in the English Deaf community, and his father was a missioner for the Deaf in North London.[7] The younger Hersee was regularly mentioned in *The British Deaf Times* columns on the activities of various missions, with comments on his energy and wide contacts, and the significant increase in attendance and involvement that followed his appointment to the Portsmouth Mission. He is reported to have written in his first annual letter to the members of his Mission, "I found it necessary to drop a bomb, for you were all asleep."[8]

Hersee actively tried to broaden the experiences of the deaf people he worked with. He encouraged them to participate in other organizations, such as a local brotherhood, which had "upwards of 3,000 members, where each Sunday famous men in the world of science, letters, art, travel, journalism, and public affairs give addresses. These are interpreted by the Missioner, and the deaf are publicly welcomed at each meeting."[9] He also initiated a relationship with Toc H, a Christian service organization that had its origins in the First World War (the name *Toc H* is derived from Talbot House, a rest and recreation house for soldiers that operated in Flanders from 1915. It was usually called *T.H.*, which became Toc H in signallers' code).[10] Hersee had been a pilot during the war, so his ties with Toc H may have been personal as well as professional. It was an organization he was to call on again in Australia in more pressing circumstances. Hersee was also involved in the activities of the national Deaf organization, the British Deaf and Dumb Association (BDDA). In 1925, he took charge of organizing one of the BDDA's regular congresses, and he was a member of the Executive Committee in 1927–1928.[11]

Hersee seems to have been unusually outward-looking for his time and his profession. Rather than insulating deaf people from the dangers of wider society, he believed in providing access for them to the activities, philosophies, and practices of other organizations. At the same time, as a child of deaf parents, he knew and understood deaf people's language and participated actively in their complex social, sporting, and political networks. His approach contrasted with the practices of most British missions of the time as well as those of Australian missions and societies that focused more on creating a "home" and a safe place for deaf people. Hearing organizations were regarded as the territory of hearing missioners, if they were relevant at all. For example, Ernest Abraham regularly attended meetings and luncheons of the Rotary Club and the Masons in Melbourne, but these were his preserve alone, to be used for cultivating influence with influential hearing people and recruiting powerful board members. He never brought deaf people with him to such events—although his deaf chauffeur was always waiting patiently in the Austin outside.[12]

Trouble Looms

Hersee worked for the Society for little more than a year. The minutes of Executive Committee meetings recorded increasing tension between the hearing councillors and their new employee, and a particularly acrimonious relationship between Hersee and Alfred Lonsdale, who had been volunteering in the role of superintendent prior to Hersee's arrival. The minutes of a meeting in August 1928 (barely five months after Hersee's arrival) showed the first ominous rumblings of conflict: "Mr Hersee conveyed desire of deaf mutes for him to represent them on the Board but was informed that Mr Lonsdale acted in this capacity."[13] Incidentally, this meeting also recorded the Executive Committee's permission for Hersee to allow the local branch of Toch H [sic] to use the Society's hall—an indication that Hersee was seeking to establish the same kinds of relationships with wider community organizations that he had developed in England.[14]

Lonsdale's lack of signing skills and his inability to develop any sort of close relationship with deaf people were embarrassingly exposed by Hersee's instant rapport with the Deaf community and his ease of communication with them; however, Lonsdale was unwilling to relinquish the authority he had accumulated or to share his intimate knowledge of the daily workings of the Society. The relationship between Lonsdale and Hersee obviously caused some concern to the Executive Committee—they agreed in September 1928 that "it was necessary to define Mr Lonsdale's position as between the Executive Mr Hersee and the Deaf and Dumb."[15] They attempted to formalize Lonsdale's role by making him "executive officer" of the Council, the overarching management body for the Deaf Society that met only a few times a year. The Executive Committee met monthly and had the most direct responsibility for day-to-day management. However, this did not prevent disagreements from becoming increasingly frequent and explicit.[16] Hersee chafed under what he saw as the restrictive structure of the Society's administration, and he made it clear that he thought there was insufficient communication between the deaf people and the Executive Committee. He could not accept that he was not allowed to bridge this gap. The minutes of the Executive Committee meeting in October 1928 reported that

> the Executive's view of representation on the Council or Executive was explained to Mr Hersee, the view being held that as a paid official it was undesirable (even if eligible) for the Welfare Director or any other officer of the Society (other than honorary) to have a seat on the Council or Executive. Mr Hersee was asked accordingly to make it clear to the Deaf and Dumb that he was not available to represent them, but Mr Hersee replied that he thought he should have a seat on the Executive with or without a vote. In support of his contention he explained that such was the custom in England and he expected it here.[17]

Later that month, Hersee requested that "a member of the Council or Executive attend the general monthly meetings of the Deaf Committee." Of course, it was Lonsdale who "undertook to make arrangements."[18] Ella Doran, a young sign language interpreter who worked for the Society, recalled

> When I joined the society staff, [Lonsdale] told me that this meeting [with the Deaf Committee] was a waste of time and achieved nothing, but he needed me there to interpret and thought my presence might "keep them in line." At almost the same time, the committee were saying among themselves that my presence might get Mr Lonsdale to see their point of view. Naturally, I didn't tell either side what the other was saying.
>
> The deaf men did have some good ideas, which I did my best to help them develop because I knew that Mr Lonsdale would never pass on the decisions to the board.[19]

Philosophical differences about the role of the Executive Committee in relation to deaf people also became evident after the annual picnic in January 1929. A dispute arose at the next Executive Committee meeting over Hersee's request that they make up a financial loss in relation to the picnic (evidently incurred because Hersee had distributed free tickets to deaf people who could not afford to go to the picnic). The Committee refused to do this and asked for details of "such persons."[20]

The disputes between Hersee and the Executive Committee of the Society escalated during the early months of 1929. The minutes of meetings reported that Hersee "indicated that his activities were impeded by the conditions under which he was working," and that he "felt himself to be unduly restricted by the Executive."[21] He complained about Lonsdale's hostility and constant interference in his work. The president of the Executive Committee, the Hon. William Brooks, claimed that Hersee "wanted to decide matters himself, and merely report to the Executive and to have quite uncontrolled authority except in matters relative to the raising of money."[22] The members of the Executive Committee were also unimpressed with reports that Hersee was publicly discussing his relationship with the Executive Committee. This was reflected in a letter they received from the Deaf General Committee in March 1929, which queried a "report of the impending resignation of Mr Hersee." In this letter, three deaf members of the Deaf General Committee—Fletcher Booth, James Sinclair, and Ernest Quinnell—invoked Article 46 of the Society's constitution, summoning a special meeting of the full council of the Society.[23]

This meeting was duly held on April 8th. Hersee was not admitted to the meeting, although he was in the building, and the deaf people asked for him to be present as their interpreter.[24] Booth, Sinclair, and Quinnell presented in detail the concerns of many deaf people about the Executive Committee's treatment of Hersee, their fears that he would be dismissed, their dissatisfaction with Lonsdale's intrusive role, and their suspicions as to Lonsdale's motives. Quinnell also pointed to the lack of salaried deaf workers in the Society, and criticized the Executive Committee members for not employing any deaf workers in their own businesses.[25] The chairman dismissed their complaints as "based upon misconception," and emphasized the Council's position that an organization such as the Society must be firmly controlled by its Executive Committee, "with all the weight of our names." He declared that Hersee needed only to "do away with the feeling that he must run the show." He also sharply rebuked the deaf members for being "absolutely disloyal" and expressed his resentment about "the aspersions that had been cast upon the Executive by our friends."[26] At the conclusion of the meeting, Booth said ominously, "The Executive will have to regret very much for their attitude to the Deaf, also they will pay later on."[27]

Booth reported later, "The meeting has been declared 'the most disgraceful one in the history of the deaf,' as all protests and requests of the deaf were ignored."[28] Soon after the meeting, he wrote to the Executive

Committee, asking for three copies of the record of the special council meeting, but was informed in reply that "the notes could be perused at the President's office on making arrangements to do so."[29] It is unlikely that Booth found this arrangement very accessible, and he declared:

> The Executive's policy was apparently to keep information and knowledge away from the deaf: they did not want them to know what was being said at the meetings, and this despite the fact that the society was reared up by the deaf and dumb themselves after many years of hard work.[30]

Booth's statement pointed to the extent to which deaf people's anger resulted from a feeling of betrayal. This was the Society they had worked to create for themselves over so many years, and they felt it had now been commandeered by hearing people who excluded and patronized them.

There were other signs of dissatisfaction with the Society, such as the honorary secretary of the Deaf Tennis Club writing to ask permission for the club to withdraw from the Society.[31] These events indicate that the Deaf community was growing restless and had a new willingness to challenge the control of the hearing Executive Committee. Deaf people had clearly found an ally in Hersee and were becoming bolder in their support for him and their efforts to reshape the Society according to their wishes. Hersee obviously had considerable influence on the beliefs and actions of these deaf people—only seven years earlier, Booth had been on record as saying,

> we can trust the hearing Board to look after the interests of the Deaf and Dumb . . . . The best way is to leave our troubles and disputes and grievances to the hearing Board of Management, they will look after us very well.[32]

Booth no longer had faith in the good intentions of the hearing board and was ready to express his anger. The hearing Executive Committee, however, perceived Hersee to be the problem and did not appear to have given any serious acknowledgment to the mood of independence and rebellion that was growing among deaf members—to their cost, as they soon found out.

These events were taking place against the backdrop of economic, political, and social upheaval in Australian society. During the first months of 1929, as Australian industries became less competitive internationally during the economic downturn, government efforts to lower wages led to strikes by waterside workers, timber workers, and miners. There were frequent, and sometimes violent, demonstrations by unions, communists, and the unemployed. The conservative government was crumbling amid increasing anti-Empire sentiment, disillusionment with those in power was becoming widespread, and dole queues were growing longer.[33] Although there is no direct evidence of Hersee's or the Deaf community's response to these developments, it was a time when a dissatisfied minority group such as theirs could readily take inspiration from events happening around them.

Dismissal

Hersee prepared a letter for the Executive Committee of the Deaf Society in late April 1929, in which he succinctly pointed out the centrality of deaf people to the organization: "I hope you will recognise my only aim is to further the work of the Society, and particularly those of its members who are handicapped: without whose membership, of course, there would be no need for the Society, or for me to hold the position I do."[34] The Executive Committee was unmoved by this reminder of their reliance on deaf people. After further altercations, Hersee was asked to tender his resignation on Friday, May 3rd, due to "an impossible and intolerable situation [that] had been already brought about by Mr. Hersee's failure to conform to the requirements of the Executive."[35] He responded by asking that the matter be referred to the full Council of the Society, where deaf representatives would have some say in the matter, claiming "I feel sure that the majority of the Council are not in accord with the step taken by the Executive, and probably some of them are ignorant of it altogether."[36] This request was declined. Hersee refused to resign and was dismissed from his position late on Wednesday afternoon, May 8, 1929.[37]

Revolt

A meeting of deaf people had been scheduled at the Society that evening and was attended by more than 100 people. As news of Hersee's dismissal spread among them, the gathering was transformed into what was later described as a "demonstration" and a "riot."[38] The meeting was addressed by Fletcher Booth and other deaf people outraged at Hersee's dismissal. Newspaper reporters were soon on the scene and watched as Lonsdale's framed photograph was smashed and thrown in a urinal, and William Brooks' photograph was turned to face the wall. "Fists were flourished," *The Sydney Morning Herald* reporter wrote the next day, attempting to describe the unusual scene of rebellion, "Hats were thrown into the air. Those persons who were not entirely voiceless shrieked with excitement. Others stamped and clapped their hands. The noise could be heard out in the street."[39]

The caretaker summoned the police, but the lone constable who arrived found himself unexpectedly out of his depth when he loudly told the crowd to leave the hall. "Although nobody could hear him, everyone understood his mission," observed the *Herald* reporter. However, instead of a docile and obedient retreat, "someone wrote on the blackboard, 'We are a hundred to one,' and those present showed the constable that they intended to stand their ground."[40] The constable called for reinforcements, but the five additional police officers who arrived were no more effective, "and so the meeting continued until 10 o'clock, when it disbanded. The police thankfully left." In this altercation, the reporters were observing a classic deaf strategy of defiance— even when the shouted words and flailing gestures of the hearing are transparent, deaf people can choose to retain their privilege of "not hearing" when it gives them an advantage.

STRANGE DEMONSTRATION BY DEAF AND DUMB ADULTS.

Excited members of the Adult Deaf and Dumb Society leaving the premises in Elizabeth-street last night after the meeting at which angry scenes were witnessed.

The Sydney Morning Herald, May 9, 1929, p. 12.

The article that appeared in *The Sydney Morning Herald* the next day was accompanied on the following page by a photograph of a score of deaf people emerging from the building, smiling broadly, waving jubilantly at photographers and throwing their hats in the air. It is an image of people tasting the exhilaration of independence and equality, not one of meek and grateful recipients of charity.

At a special meeting of the Society's Executive Committee called the following day, no mention was made in the minutes of this "riot," nor of the embarrassing publicity it had engendered. Discussion focussed on interim measures for keeping the Society operating, and it was resolved to "close the building at 6 pm daily in the meantime: circulars to be sent out to all deaf members at once."[41] They did not anticipate the response to this decision—deaf people interpreted it as "locking them out." This decision sharply illustrated their differing perspectives with regard to the Society's premises. To the hearing councillors, concerned with property and propriety, this decision was most likely a practical one with an element of punishment thrown in; to deaf people, the Society was their meeting place, a "home" which they had worked for many years to create, and to be locked out was an outrage.[42]

Aftermath

Hersee fought back swiftly and effectively. He did not scruple to use the facilities and resources he had acquired during his employment with the Deaf Society, as well as his support from the Deaf community and his contacts with other organizations, such as Toc H. The Executive Committee of the Deaf Society claimed at their next meeting that a circular "had been sent out *in our addressed envelopes* to deaf members generally inviting them to a church service last Sunday at Toc H headquarters" (italics added).[43] Hersee's strategy was effective; although the Deaf Society held a church service that Sunday too, the attendance was abysmal. Ella Doran (the interpreter at the service), later recalled,

> Mr. Lonsdale was there, ready to lead, as he was a lay preacher in the Methodist Church. The congregation consisted solely of the caretaker, cleaners and collectors, with their wives and husbands. Every other member had gone to the place Mr Hersee had arranged.[44]

Toc H's support for Hersee and the Deaf community was prompt and generous. It was Toc H which sent out the letters inviting deaf people to the alternative church service on Sunday, May 12th (albeit in Deaf Society envelopes), and it was in Toc H's headquarters that this service was held. When deaf people found themselves locked out of the Society's building on the night of Friday, May 10th, they "formed a silent procession to the Headquarters of Toc H in Hamilton-street where they held a breakaway meeting under the Chairmanship of Mr. Hersee . . ."[45] It was there that the decision to form a new organization was made, with Hersee as superintendent and secretary. Gordon Winn, a former councillor and life member of the Deaf Society, who immediately switched his allegiance to the new organization, guaranteed Hersee's salary for three months, but did not have to pay it, as deaf people raised enough funds themselves.[46] Two days after his dismissal, Hersee was able to conduct a triumphant newspaper interview.

> "Many people when dismissed are ashamed of themselves," said Mr. Hersee, "and hang their heads in sorrow, but mine is up. The executive of the Adult Deaf and Dumb Society have so far refused to tell the public what I was dismissed for. I am not ashamed of the fact that my people were deaf and dumb, and I count the afflicted of Sydney among my personal friends."[47]

The breakaway group formed at the meeting on May 10th quickly established itself as a viable alternative and rival to the Deaf Society. Although initially called the New South Wales Society for the Adult Deaf and Dumb, within a few weeks it was named the New South Wales Association of Deaf and Dumb Citizens.[48] It was usually referred to as the "Association," as distinct from the "Society." Its new name not only avoided any legal injunction from the Society against the use of a similar name, but also signalled a clear departure from existing Deaf organizations in Australia. All of the Deaf societies had been established on the British "mission" model, which—even with extensive deaf involvement—was predicated on the need for deaf people to be supported and given succor by benevolent helpers. Identifying themselves as "citizens" was a rejection of this model. As citizens, deaf people declared that they had the same rights as everyone else to a free, public education (not yet guaranteed for deaf children in NSW), jobs at the basic wage, and the standard types of government support if needed. They were also declaring that they were capable of fulfilling the obligations of citizens, such as assistance to others and participation in the life of the broader community. Later commentators often affirmed and praised the way the Association fulfilled the "obligations of citizenship."[49]

The Reverend E. J. Davidson, Padre of Toc H and soon to be a vice president of the new Association, wrote soon afterwards,

> The Deaf and Dumb of this city of Sydney have passed through a troublous time. Through the failure of that fine sensitiveness which is the characteristic mark of gentlemen, they have been subjected to treatment worthy only of naughty children . . . the writer has no hesitation in appealing to all friends of the deaf and dumb to support them in this courageous attempt to secure that measure of self-determination which is surely the prerogative of any and every citizen, whether he can hear or not![50]

He said elsewhere in the article, "They do not need, nor do they want, our 'Charity.'" Davidson signalled the key themes that were to be articulated by the new Association. Deaf people were not children; they were capable of self-determination and managing their own affairs; and they rejected "charity" and claimed equality with hearing people and the rights of citizens.

If the Deaf Society was alarmed by these events, the minutes of Executive Committee meetings gave little indication of it. Although the hearing Executive Committee met more often (every few days during the week of Hersee's dismissal and every week for a while afterwards), the minutes reported the "formation of a new Society and Toc H's connection therewith" and "various newspaper reports" without comment. They did, however, approve legal action to "apply for an injunction against the use of a name similar to our own,"[51] and they sent letters and statements to the newspapers defending their position and playing down the upheaval. In a statement to *The Sydney Morning Herald* a week after the dismissal, Brooks said, "The work of the society is being carried on, and any dislocation that has temporarily arisen, will no doubt adjust itself in a very little time."[52]

The Society complained to the federal president and padre of Toc H, asking for "action to be taken to remove interference with this Society's work by the Sydney branch of Toc H," and also had meetings with Padre Davidson and a Mr. Warren from the Sydney branch. However, they were soon obliged to record that "Toc H . . . had decided to adhere to their previous attitude towards our Society."[53]

It is revealing that the members of the Society's Executive Committee, when searching for reasons for this upheaval, looked only to other hearing men for possible causes. They blamed Hersee for "insub-ordination" and Toc H for "interference," but they did not seem to acknowledge that deaf people's own outrage and resolve may have had anything to do with events. They made no attempt to meet or communicate with the deaf people who had left the Society, to find out the nature of their grievances. In all likelihood, they simply did not see deaf people as capable of making such decisions independently. Regardless of whether the Society had been "reared up by the deaf and dumb themselves after many years of hard work," these men now saw themselves as in charge.[54] They saw their role as contribut-ing to the socially endorsed work of charity for those less fortunate than themselves, and if their work was not appreciated, then the fault was with the recipients. The closest they came to acknowledging that deaf people had made things difficult for them was a dour note in the minutes of an Executive Committee meeting a few months after the breakaway—"The present financial depression and the ingratitude of a section of the Deaf made the work of charity peculiarly difficult at the moment."[55] In a classic example of paternalism, the anger and deter-mination of the deaf people who broke away from the Society were regarded simply as "ingratitude."

If it was hearing men that the Society blamed, it was to another hearing man that they turned for advice and assistance. Ernest Abra-ham, with impeccable timing, visited Sydney the week after Hersee's dismissal. This time, he sided with the board of the Society, not with the dissatisfied deaf rebels, as he had in 1913. The Society rallied him to their defense, and he met with the Executive Committee to discuss strategies for ensuring that the Society could retain its position and to suggest possible replacements for Hersee. He met a number of times with deaf people (it is not mentioned how many attended these meet-ings), and according to the Executive Committee, did "good work." The committee obviously recognized that Abraham had the charisma, eloquence, and authority that they lacked, and hoped that he might counter the magnetic pull of Hersee and his followers. Or, as some deaf writers later asked perceptively, "Was it . . . thought the deaf would be intimidated by Mr. Abraham's magic Victorian rod?"[56]

Abraham recommended the Reverend George Poynder (a former teacher of the deaf) as a replacement for Hersee and helped to expe-dite his appointment.[57] Other strategies that the Executive Commit-tee quickly adopted had Abraham's stamp on them too. One was the placement of weekly notices in all the newspapers, "warning the Public against giving money to Collectors who are unable to produce proper authority from the only Registered Adult Deaf and Dumb Society in this State."[58] Another strategy was the employment of a deaf man, Samuel Phillips, to "visit Deaf & Dumb with Mr Poynder," and later to "assist in the work generally."[59] Although this may at first appear to have been a practical move, showing a greater respect for the capabilities of deaf people, it is very similar to the strategies Abraham used in Victoria, employing deaf people, such as James Johnston, who, although holding responsible positions, were also used to protect Abraham from criticism, help him keep his ear to the ground, and carry out reprisals against troublesome deaf people when necessary.[60]

Gordon Winn later described these men (with whom he had sat on the board of the Deaf Society) in the pages of *The Deaf Advocate*.

How can our well intentioned Members of the hearing Boards of Control know anything of the minds or capabilities of the Deaf whose affairs they consider it their right and duty to direct. The majority of them can smile their deaf friends a gracious greeting on their rare occasions of meeting and hold up their thumbs and nod and smile as they would to a small grandchild and that is all they know of their mentality except for hearsay evidence from paid or unpaid superintendents whose interests it may be or whose mental tendency to regard the deaf as incapable. Truly the deaf need protection from their friends.[61]

The New Order

The Society's annual general meeting was held on August 23rd that year and was a grim indication of the new state of affairs. Fletcher Booth described it as follows:

The Annual Meeting of the Society was awaited with anxiety, in the hope that things would improve and reconciliation take place. About 200 deaf and dumb from the Association, accompanied by sympathising supporters, attended the Annual Meeting in August, 1929, and were surprised to find that the Executive of the Society already had the police patrolling the hall, even before the meeting commenced.

The meeting turned out to be an utter farce, as several speakers were rudely ordered by the President to sit down, with the assistance of the police; even a Press reporter was asked by the

Organising Secretary, Mrs. Gore Jones, not to report the speeches
of any but Executive members. I myself was described to a
reporter by an official of the Society as "mentally deficient."
The President could not, however, prevent Mr. G. R. Winn
from speaking, as he is a life member of the Society. Mr. Winn
moved an amendment to the Report, and in his speech he was
frequently applauded by the deaf for his remarks. The amendment of Mr. Winn was carried by a very large majority, but the
Chairman refused to accept the voting result, saying the deaf
were not financial members of the Society. This caused a scene
of demonstration and protest, as the deaf and dumb always
voted at their Annual Meetings for the last fifteen years, and as
a demonstration they got up and left the hall. While they were
doing this, and with only a very few people remaining, the
President declared the Report carried, and the Council elected
themselves for another year of office.[62]

Newspaper reports the following day were less restrained. Under
the headline, "Wild Meeting. Policemen Present," the *News* described
"rowdy scenes, which terminated in the wildest uproar," reporting that
"police officers watched the proceedings from the rear, and were frequently compelled to caution rowdy members."[63]

Winn's amendment was in response to an item in the Annual Report
praising Hersee's successor, Reverend Poynder, whose "knowledge of
their need" had "endeared himself to the Deaf and Dumb."[64] Winn's
amendment sought to replace the statement about Poynder with the
words, "The departure of Mr. H. V. S. Hersee during the year is a great
loss to the Association [sic], and it is hoped that he will be induced to
resume his former position."[65] Ernest Quinnell seconded the amendment, "on behalf of over 200 adult deaf and dumb," and Winn made a
lengthy speech in support of it. A member of the Society's board, Mr.
Skye, made an even more lengthy defence of the Society's action in
dismissing Hersee, but the majority of those present still voted for the
amendment. When the president insisted that only the small number
of financial members could vote (a clause in the constitution that had
never been invoked before), "disorder broke loose . . . the audience gesticulating wildly, and the din drowned all efforts of the Committee to
restore peace. Intervention of the police, however, somewhat relieved
the situation."[66] A similar report was carried in *The Daily Telegraph Pictorial*, which quoted a hearing supporter of Winn's amendment calling

out to the president, "You're fooling the deaf and dumb!" The man was "cautioned by a policeman." The article concluded by quoting Padre Davidson of Toc H, who called for a public inquiry, pointing out that the government was granting £2,500 a year to the Deaf Society, when they had only about 30 deaf followers compared to the breakaway Association's 200.[67]

Although it is astonishing to read of a charitable organization's annual general meeting being patrolled by the police, this happened in 1929 during a time of widespread unrest. Arranging a police presence to deter possible protests was probably a more routine precaution at that time. Newspaper reporters were used to describing scenes of "uproar," "disorder," and police intervention, and may have reverted to stock phrases to describe these scenes. They were, however, unused to deaf people being the source of such unrest, and their lack of experience with deaf people's use of sign language is reflected in their use of phrases, such as "gesticulating wildly," to describe deaf people's communication. This would also indicate that the interpreter at the meeting did not interpret everything that deaf people said. When reporters wrote that "a man jumped to his feet waving his hands in an effort to be understood" and in the next sentence quoted a hearing person's comments verbatim, they provide a useful reminder that most of what survives is the commentary of the hearing, and that the contributions of deaf participants have often been reduced to descriptions of people "gesticulating wildly."[68]

At the breakaway group's first annual meeting a year later, pointed reference was made to the contrast between the meeting of the new Association and the infamous 1929 annual meeting of the Deaf Society. The Reverend E. J. Davidson told the more than 400 people present,

> I cannot help feeling what a different spirit exists at this Annual Meeting to that at which I was unable, and not allowed, to speak at last year. Many of you will remember that at the old Adult Deaf and Dumb Society's Meeting several of us felt that there were matters concerned with the life and welfare of the Deaf and Dumb which needed the cool breezes of publicity. We were not given a hearing and we were not able to make ourselves heard. At this meeting with at least three times as many Deaf and Dumb present and a greater proportion of the hearing public, it is possible even now to hear a pin drop and to see and to realise the new spirit amongst the Deaf and Dumb of New South Wales.[69]

* * *

An opportunity for mediation in the dispute arose in September 1929, when the Premier of NSW, the Hon. T. R. Bavin, offered his assistance in resolving the impasse between the Society and the Association. Bavin happened to be a vice president of the Society's council (though he was not on the Executive Committee), and he was also a member of the council of Toc H. Bavin met with representatives of the Association in September and November that year, and they requested that he "convene a conference to accept a settlement," in consideration of the additional demands on public subscribers and the use of government money by the Society. However, when Bavin met with Brooks, the president of the Deaf Society, in December, Brooks was said to have "denied categorically" the statements of the Association, and "emphatically declined" any mediation in the dispute.[70]

On April 24, 1930, a public meeting of the Sydney Deaf community was convened by two deaf people, Isabel Winn and Cecil Green (Green was a returned soldier who had been deafened during the war). The meeting was not described or promoted as being for members of either the Association or the Society, but as a "publicly convened meeting of adult Deaf and Dumb."[71] It was held at the Adyar Hall and was attended by at least 130 deaf people (although the Society tried to bribe people away from it by offering free tickets to the circus).[72] The resolutions passed at the meeting were widely distributed to all Deaf-related organizations in NSW, government bodies and churches, and the press. They included a statement of no confidence in the council of the Adult Deaf and Dumb Society, a call for their resignation, and a condemnation of "the action of the President of the Adult Deaf and Dumb Society in denying [the Deaf and Dumb] their privileged right to vote at the last Annual Meeting of the Society after the Deaf and Dumb had possessed this privilege for an unbroken period of 15 years."

Other resolutions deplored the Deaf Society's attacks on Toc H and the "misrepresentations and deception to the Premier of this State and the General public by Mr. Brooks and his associates on the Council of the Adult Deaf and Dumb Society." In an unusual and pointed rejection of the charity philosophy, they also expressed "entire disapproval that the publicly subscribed funds of the Deaf and Dumb should be used for the purpose of private social functions to which the majority of the Deaf and Dumb are refused admission."[73] This referred to the regular charity fundraising events conducted by the Women's Committee of the Deaf Society, which were aimed exclusively at the wealthy and were regularly reported on in the society pages of the newspapers. Deaf people were never present at such functions, except for the occasional pretty little deaf girl who might be brought in to present a bouquet to a dignitary. The president of the Society's Women's Committee at this time was Lady Belinda Street, wife of the Chief Justice of NSW and mother-in-law of Jessie Street. Jessie Street was one of the most active and outspoken feminists of her time, who later became involved in the United Nations and the application of its Universal Declaration of Human Rights to Aboriginal people.[74] "Red Jessie's" mother-in-law remained supportive of the Society during the breakaway, and the organizing secretary wrote to the Executive Committee in March 1930 stating,

> Lady Street and the ladies of the Womens' Central Committee have asked me to convey . . . their great regret that Mr Hersee's conduct should have subjected them to such annoyance and unpleasantness. They expressed their absolute confidence in the action of the Executive in the dismissal of Mr Hersee and their sympathy with them in such a difficult position.[75]

The Executive Committee of the Society continued to dismiss all suggestions that deaf people should have any significant control of the Society, or even that this was what deaf people wanted. In a letter to the Minister for Education in July 1930, William Brooks repudiated further proposals for a conference with the breakaway Association and defended the Society's stance on the relative powers of deaf and hearing people.

> What is called the essential difference between the old Society and the new is on the question of complete self determination and control in what is described as their own affairs, by the Deaf. The policy of our Society from the commencement has been to allow the Deaf as much say and control in the internal and domestic affairs of the Society as is possible by Deaf Committees. It is however, a definite proceedure [sic], and has been ever since its formation, that the policy and finances of the Society must necessarily be under the control of an Executive and a Council. On the Executive no Deaf members are considered to be practicable. On the Council there are five deaf members. This arrangement has always worked admirably until the advent of Mr. Hersee, and is still so working.[76]

Brooks did not mention that the council met only a few times a year, whereas the Executive Committee met monthly (sometimes more frequently) and made almost all administrative and policy decisions for the Society. After claiming that the Society was run in the same way as other Deaf societies around Australia, in the "best interests of the deaf," by "men who are in a position to judge what is both desirable and expedient," Brooks concluded,

> The Deaf did not at any time demand full powers for themselves. Since the break-away, well over one hundred Deaf have returned to the old Society and many who have been interviewed deny that they ever made any demand for what is called self determination.[77]

Brooks' unwillingness to accord significance to the claims of dissatisfied deaf people was evident in his phrasing—"what is described as their own affairs" and "what is called self determination." The assurances of those deaf people who had returned to the Society were enough to confirm his belief in sticking with the practices he was familiar with.

The New South Wales Association for Deaf and Dumb Citizens

After one or two temporary offices (including a room in the Toc H headquarters) the Association leased rooms in McIlrath's Building on the corner of Pitt and Goulburn Streets in central Sydney from late 1930 onwards. Hersee was immediately employed as its superintendent-secretary. The Association provided the same services as the Society—welfare work (assistance with employment, domestic, legal, and financial problems), interpreting, church services, and (later) limited accommodation facilities. It also provided a meeting place and a rich variety of social activities, so important in binding a community together. Deaf people comprised 51% or more of its council, and Fletcher Booth soon became chairman (the chairman for the first year was Padre Davidson of Toc H). Most of the hearing people on the council had deaf relatives.[78] Rather than a shadowy "Executive" or "Finance Committee" making the decisions, this council had a Management Committee, composed entirely of deaf members. Membership was free to all deaf people—the declared policy was that, rather than a fee, "[t]he Council simply look for the good will and support of the Deaf in their efforts on their behalf."[79]

Fletcher Samuel Booth.
The Deaf Society.

The Association published two issues of a magazine called *Onward!* in August 1929 and January 1930; then from December 1930 until 1937, it regularly published a magazine called *The Deaf Advocate*.

The Association was occasionally challenged by the Deaf Society, but it managed to avoid legal problems by a mixture of adroit word-play and insouciance. For example, in April 1931 the Society's solicitors wrote to Fletcher Booth, who was chairman of the Association's council, objecting both to *The Deaf Advocate* (which they referred to as a "pamphlet") and to a circular distributed by the Association. The Society took exception to the *Advocate*'s claim to be "the Official Magazine of the New South Wales Deaf," and to the circular's statement "[t]hat this is the only Association of Deaf and Dumb in New South Wales." The solicitors scolded, "As you must be perfectly aware this is absolutely incorrect," and they claimed that "the circular and magazine is [sic] doing considerable damage to the Adult Deaf & Dumb Society of New South Wales." The letter concluded,

We are writing to you in order to give you the opportunity of
withdrawing the circular letter that you are issuing, and correct-
ing the error, and also of deleting the statement on the Magazine.
Unless you accede to our request and notify us accordingly, we
have received instructions to apply for an injunction against you,
but we trust that this will not be necessary, and we shall be glad to
hear from you at your earliest convenience.[80]

Following instructions from his council, Hersee sent a detailed reply
to this letter. Although gallantly acceding to the Society's requests,
he took obvious pleasure in using sophistry and sarcasm to claim the
moral high ground, with the result that he appeared to be humoring
the Society in granting their requests, rather than backing down from
a legal threat.

In regard to the circular, I wish to point out that the statement
complained of viz, "that this is the only Association of Deaf and
Dumb in New South Wales," is not intended to imply that there
are not other Associations interested in the welfare of the deaf and
dumb, but merely that this is the only Association the membership of which is constituted by the deaf and dumb themselves.

I may further state, that while my Association consider [sic]
that you have no ground for complaint, it does not contemplate
sending out further copies of this circular neither does it intend to
issue any further circulars containing the statement to which you
take exception.

I am to point out that the circular complained of was not
addressed to the general public, but only to the present members
of this Association. It is therefore difficult to see how such circular
could in any way cause your clients any injury.

In deference to your objection, we purpose describing our
magazine in the future as "The Official Magazine of the N.S.W.
Association of Deaf and Dumb Citizens."

I may add that it is our desire not to encroach in any way upon
your Society and to avoid anything that may lead to confusion
and we trust that the Adult Deaf and Dumb Society of N.S.W. will
reciprocate this attitude.

Without wishing to be critical, I am asked to draw your attention
to the statement in the April Number of "The Silent Messenger" in
which it is stated that "a team from the Society, representing New

South Wales, will visit Melbourne at Christmas time." Your clients
are requested not to state, in future, that the team in question is
one "representing N.S.W." seeing that it is only a team from their
Society.

I am to suggest finally that in the event of their being any further correspondence my Council hardly consider it necessary that
such correspondence should come from a solicitor.[81]

Despite these occasional skirmishes, the Society and the Association did
not attempt to legally challenge each other, and indeed they seemed to
have very little direct communication until changes in government legislation brought them into contact again a few years later.

The *Advocate* editors made inquiries into other deaf organizations
around the world, to demonstrate that their Association was "'in step'
with go ahead Deaf organizations" and that the Society was "out of
step." In June 1932, they reported on organizations such as the National
Association of the Deaf and the National Fraternal Society of the Deaf,
both in the United States, and the National Deaf Club in Britain, which
they claimed were all "managed by the deaf themselves" or "managed
by the deaf exclusively." Organizations such as the ones they examined
did indeed have similar ideals and used the same rhetoric. The National
Fraternal Society of The Deaf had asserted as early as 1904 that its work
could "give stronger evidence of the ability of the Deaf to manage their
own affairs, prove their independence and settle once and for all time
the 'object of charity' delusion."[82] The article in the *Advocate* concluded,

I think I have stated enough for anyone to be convinced of the
capabilities of the Adult Deaf in organising, controlling, or managing their own affairs. IT IS NO LONGER A POSSIBILITY; IT IS
AN ACCOMPLISHED FACT.[83]

On the Association's fourth anniversary in May 1933, they declared
their hope that they would "go on and on for ever." The *Advocate* printed
birthday greetings from Prime Minister Joseph Lyons; the premier of
NSW; the mayor of Sydney, John Love, the principal of the Western
Australian Deaf and Dumb Institution; Oliver Redman, the superintendent of the South Australian Mission; W. J. McCaskill, superintendent
of the Victorian Deaf and Dumb Institution, and many others.[84] Their
fourth annual general meeting was held the following month, attended
by more than 250 people. Their old friend Padre (now Canon) Davidson from Toc H was a guest, and he spoke about "this very, very happy

Association," and his wish that if there were a Committee of Deaf and Dumb in the afterlife, whether "up above" or "down below," he would like to join it—although he was not confident that "all Deaf and Dumb will be gathered together in the one place."[85] The relevance of that comment to the Sydney Deaf community of the time was probably not lost on his audience.

The War of Words

The battles between the Association and the Deaf Society were conducted on several fronts. Although the Society probably won the fight for public money and a high profile in the social pages of the newspapers, there can be little doubt that the Association won the war of words. Their regular broadsides about the Deaf Society still make revealing and entertaining reading.

Alfred Lonsdale was a particular target of the Association's writers. He was lampooned as "the Shadow" for his ubiquitous presence in the Society's building—"Visitors . . . are sure to have their passage obstructed by the shadow of Mr. A. L. Lonsdale; for the 'Shadow' is everywhere about the premises," and for his intimate involvement in every aspect of the Society's affairs.[86] He was deputy-chairman of the Society's council and a member of the Executive Committee; he also served as the honorary welfare officer and was chairman of the Deaf General Committee, chairman of the Church Committee, president of the Men's Club, president of the Tennis Club, and vice president of the Chess and Draughts Club.[87] The *Advocate* editors seized the opportunity to explain the concept of fascism to its readers in July 1932 by using the illustration of the hearing board of the Adult Deaf and Dumb Society.[88]

One of the deaf representatives on the council of the Deaf Society, James Sinclair, seems to have vacillated between the two organizations. Sinclair's re-election to the council of the Deaf Society by deaf members in 1932 was "not confirmed" by the Executive (possibly because he consorted with Association members), and the Executive neglected to inform him of the fact for several months.[89] Sinclair's experiences with the Deaf Society (together with Booth's and Quinnell's) are the most likely source for a satirical description in *The Deaf Advocate* of a council meeting of the Society from the point of view of a deaf representative, called "Good Bye to all That":

Attending your first "Council Meeting" you will be asked to approve of "Minutes" of which you know nothing! These, no doubt referring to a Meeting of the "Executive" at which you were not present, nor could you have been! or ever likely to be! The Chairman will note your bewildered look, and as if to make amends he will place the "Minute Book" in your hands for your own perusal—the other "hearing members" having it all off by heart they can get on with new business! Looking up from the book, you observe there is a general discussion on and knowing it is bad manners to read in company, you hasten to hand the book back—unread! The Minutes are then put and approved! Because, dear reader, for you to have objected in any way or form would have been considered impolite: nay, it might have spoilt the "harmony" of the Council Meeting, and as the Chairman remarked: "Harmony must be retained at all costs!—and what a cost! But you are forgiven! Many have been in the same position, to their sorrow! . . .

You are a Councillor, certainly: but, "thus far and no further!" Your position is to approve ONLY! Not to execute. That is reserved for themselves alone! . . .

Having finished the Council business you are politely requested to retire: (Whaffor?) So that the "Executive" can propound new Minutes for you to approve of at the next meeting![90]

When describing a new year's dance at the Association's hall at the end of 1933, *The Deaf Advocate* highlighted some politically inspired decorations referring to the headquarters of the Deaf Society at No. 5 Elizabeth Street.

A very sarcastic note was struck by a very large spider, which had spun a large web over a door, marked No. 5. Attached to the web was a notice to the effect that the web had been there for five years, and visitors were requested not to disturb it. We leave our readers to draw their own conclusions.[91]

The Association also took delight in pointing out the many ways in which the Deaf Society's magazine, the *Silent Messenger*, imitated their own publication *The Deaf Advocate*. In the August-September 1934 issue, the *Advocate* editor listed several column headings and editorial features that he claimed the *Silent Messenger* had copied from them, adding

One glaring omission in the "Silent Messenger" in comparison with "The Deaf Advocate" is the lack of a Personality Column.

We are very loath to think that this is because they have no personality worth recording.[92]

Choosing Allegiance

What were the real levels of support for the two organizations? The
breakaway Association had begun with 130 members on May 10, 1929;
however, there do not seem to be any comparable figures for the Deaf
Society's membership at the time of the breakaway.[93] Indications are
that, at least during the first couple of years, a significantly higher number of deaf people were supporters of the Association. This is suggested
by Ella Doran's description of the Society's deserted church services
after the breakaway and Padre Davidson's assertion in August 1929
that the Society had only about 30 followers compared to the Association's 200.[94] It has been claimed that deaf people "boycotted" the
Society; however, if there was a boycott, it was short lived and not universally observed.[95] Doran recalled that although the majority of deaf
people went to the Association at the beginning, some began to "drift
back" to the Deaf Society soon afterwards, especially young girls who
enjoyed her physical culture classes and men who wanted to play bil-
liards on the Society's three tables.[96]

The Deaf Society's president, William Brooks, claimed in July 1930
that "well over a hundred" deaf people had returned to their organization.[97] In December that year, the Society provided a Christmas dinner
at which "over 200 Deaf and Dumb assembled." This, they claimed,
was "the largest number of deaf that ever sat down to a Christmas dinner in Sydney, and the tables have never before been provided with
such quantity or quality of edibles."[98] This was, however, in the middle
of the Depression, and political allegiance may not have been the overriding reason for deaf people's attendance. The Association claimed
257 members in April 1932, and 190 attendees at their Christmas dinner
in December 1932, although it was probably not able to provide such
lavish meals or entertainments as the Society.[99]

As the Sydney Deaf community adjusted to their new circumstances,
regular club nights and special events tended to be well patronized at
both venues. To many deaf people, that is all they were—two alternate
venues. Not all deaf people understood, or were interested in, the political philosophies behind the two organizations, especially younger deaf
people who had just left school or moved to Sydney from elsewhere.
These deaf people did not have long memories of the Deaf community's

efforts to create the Society, and were primarily in search of friendship and entertainment. A series of interviews conducted with older members of the Sydney Deaf community in the 1980s captured some of the memories of people who would have been just entering the Deaf community in the late 1920s and early 30s. None of the interviewees volunteered information about the political background to the two organizations, but several remembered the conflicts between them and the disapproval directed at people who attended both. One man remembered,

> I went to the Society. There was another place called the Deaf Association. There were two Clubs. I went to one to have a look where my friends went. Then I would go to the other one. People called me "two-faced." They would whisper, "Bob Herman, there's Bob Herman. He goes to the other Club too." I never worried about that. I only wanted to see my friends, my mates so I would go to both of them.[100]

Another man confirmed that "there were two clubs. One called the Association for the Deaf and the NSW Society for the Deaf. Two different Clubs and I used to go to both of them . . . . They were in opposition. It would cause trouble if you went to one then next time go to the other one."[101]

In reality, deaf people probably chose their allegiance for a range of reasons—not only to the organization they supported ideologically, but also to the one their friends or spouses attended, the one that had better social functions, the one that provided the best opportunities for sporting participation (a consideration well exploited by the Deaf Society), and—as the Depression took hold—the one that could provide the most practical support or threatened the more dire consequences for lack of allegiance. Religious considerations also seemed to be significant, with indications that Catholic groups favored the Association, in contrast with the wealthy Protestant ethos of the Society.[102]

The Role of The Deaf Advocate

The Deaf Advocate is unique in the history of deaf-related newsletters and papers in Australia. Few other publications have adopted such an uncompromising ideology of deaf autonomy and capability, while so unequivocally and fearlessly opposing the dominant institutions within the Deaf world. Although it never avoided the responsibility of providing local news and information for the NSW Deaf community, it actively welcomed contributions from other states. It is not an exaggeration to say that *The Deaf Advocate* was a significant factor in the existence and survival of not only the NSW Association of Deaf and Dumb Citizens, but also of later organizations, such as the Queensland Deaf and Dumb Citizens Reformed Association and the Australian Association for the Advancement of the Deaf and some of its state branches. The *Advocate* provided a sympathetic channel for these organizations, especially during their shaky beginnings, to reach the Australian Deaf community and make their aims explicit. Because none of these organizations ever developed their own magazines, *The Deaf Advocate* became a de facto mouthpiece for them at times. Disaffected individuals who had no forum within their own states were able to publish their letters and articles freely in *The Deaf Advocate*—there were many contributions from J. P. Bourke and others from Victoria, and from John M'Caig Paul and other individuals from Queensland. Because of this, the *Advocate* often appears to be a national magazine rather than a local one. From the perspective of researchers many decades later, it is a goldmine of primary sources, the "view from below" par excellence.

The Deaf Advocate.
The Deaf Society.

Many personalities, events, and organizations that have all but vanished from the official record retain a voice in the pages of the *Advocate*.

The magazine began in December 1930 as a twelve-page duplicated paper. Its honorary joint editors, Fletcher Booth and Ernest Quinnell (both of whom were deaf) emphasized in this first issue that the magazine was to be "the official publication for all the Deaf and Dumb, published entirely by the Deaf and Dumb."[103] The first issue had no title, and the editors called for members and friends to propose a name. The following month, it appeared for the first time as *The Deaf Advocate*, with the subtitle "Integrity, Unity, Liberty." The cover declared that it was "The Official Magazine of the New South Wales Deaf, Published under the Auspices of the Association of Deaf and Dumb Citizens."[104] This was an obvious challenge to the Deaf Society and its newsletter *The Silent Messenger*.

The *Advocate* responded to Deaf people's need for "openness of information" by printing complete and unabridged texts of important letters or speeches, and therefore allowing Deaf readers to judge for themselves the authors' motives and the appropriateness of the responses.[105] This was recognized as a key strategy in deaf people's greater management role, as articulated in one of the early *Advocates*: "The Association has always stressed the point that the Deaf and Dumb should have complete knowledge of what goes on in the management of their own affairs."[106] For example, in June 1931, the *Advocate* printed the complete texts of the letter from the Society's solicitors threatening an injunction against the Association, and the Association's reply, introducing them with, "We publish same without comment and leave our readers to form their own opinion."[107]

There were many other examples of the *Advocate*'s policy of "openness of information." After the 1931–32 Cricket Carnival in Melbourne, from which the NSW Association's cricket team had been barred, the *Advocate* devoted seven pages to reprinting the entire correspondence between themselves and the Carnival organizers (principally James Johnston), relating their unsuccessful attempts to be represented in the carnival. The story is lively and absorbing, laced with jaunty and sarcastic commentary, pointing out "to what despicable ends some people will stoop even in the grand old game of cricket."[108]

At a time when deaf people were given so little information by those who ran the Deaf societies, this policy of openness was appreciated. An unnamed "Deaf Subscriber in Victoria" wrote in response to the Cricket Carnival article,

The correspondence on the Xmas Carnival was an eye opener to
many of us. It's a pity the light of day is not shed on many other
subjects as well. There would be less suspicion and a better understanding all round then . . . . With grateful thanks from the many
Victorians who have gained so much strength and courage from
the pages of the Advocate.[109]

Gordon Winn succinctly described the *Advocate*'s role and its ideological stance in several letters he wrote to the editors. In early 1932, he
declared, "Your paper is making articulate deaf aims and ambitions
and the deaf spirit of independence."[110] Later that year, he wrote again.

[*The Deaf Advocate*] doesn't merely record the harmless jottings in
regard to Mrs. So & So's baby having cut a tooth, but it expresses
the aims and ambitions of the deaf world, and it expresses them
in a way that demonstrates the character and intelligence that are
behind them, in the minds and hearts of the deaf community. The
deaf have become a thinking and articulate unit, capable of self
expression and this is a big attainment.[111]

The first issue of *The Deaf Advocate* in December 1930 had a circulation of 300. It remained a monthly newsletter until the beginning of
1934, when it became a bimonthly, professionally printed, 24-page
magazine. By the middle of 1934, it claimed a circulation of 4,000, a feat
that has rarely, if ever, been achieved by other deaf-related publications
in Australia.[112]

The breakaway and the establishment of the New South Wales Association of Deaf and Dumb Citizens in Sydney significantly impacted
the Deaf communities and Deaf societies in other Australian states.
Their relationships to the Sydney community suddenly became more
complicated, and a new kind of diplomacy was required when engaging in routine Deaf society business, such as organizing sporting
competitions. Those who rejected the societies' perceived charity and
paternalism and sought a way for deaf people to manage their own
affairs were becoming a distinctive movement, not merely a few radical individuals. The seeming success of the breakaway group provided
inspiration, or inflammation (depending on one's perspective), to
restless and disaffected groups and individuals in other states. A new
model for dealing with repression had suddenly arisen, and it was to
prove effective in at least one other state.

4

An Open and Official Breakaway

My deaf friends, it is of no use that you say you have proofs, evidence, first hand information, direct complaints. That according to the moral standards ruling among men of repute you are right. You are only the deaf and dumb, what is praiseworthy among hearing people as a desire for justice, honourable conduct, the upholding of moral standards, the maintenance of common rights IS IN YOU, A SUSPICIOUS NATURE.
—John Paul, "A Letter from Queensland"

EVENTS IN NSW exacerbated feelings of discontent and frustration in other Deaf communities, especially those in the states of Queensland and Victoria. In Queensland, the mood of unrest was soon to lead to the formation of another breakaway group. These events provided further affirmation of the belief emerging among many in the Australian Deaf communities of the 1920s and '30s that deaf people should manage their own affairs. In Queensland, the voice of revolt is more difficult to recover, because fewer records survive. Neither the Mission nor the breakaway group seems to have had a magazine or newsletter at this time. It was in the pages of the New South Wales Association of Deaf and Dumb Citizens' magazine *The Deaf Advocate* that Queenslanders left some of the most direct and detailed accounts of their breakaway.

John Paul

As in Sydney, the arrival of a British missioner was an important catalyst for the events that led to the Queensland breakaway. John M'Caig Paul, another hearing son of deaf parents, arrived in Brisbane in March

1927 to begin work at the Queensland Adult Deaf and Dumb Mission. His deaf father, James Paul, had established a mission for deaf people in Ayrshire, Scotland, in 1881, and worked there as missioner for many years. James Paul was also elected the first treasurer of the British Deaf and Dumb Association (BDDA) on its establishment in 1890.[1] His hearing son John spent most of his life working with deaf people. He came to Australia before the First World War, and spent the years 1914 to 1918 working as a missioner at the Adult Deaf and Dumb Society of Victoria, where he worked under Ernest Abraham.[2] Few indications remain of what their working relationship was like, although one commentator, Ernest Reynolds, referred to a "bust-up" between them at the end of Paul's tenure there.[3] Reynolds also recalled that Paul and Abraham "didn't see things eye to eye on many occasions," as Paul was "rather forthright in his expressions and belief," and Abraham did not take kindly to anyone who disagreed with him.[4] Paul returned to Scotland in 1918 when his father became ill and was later reported taking up the

John M'Caig Paul.
Deaf Services Queensland.

position of missioner and superintendent at the Aberdeen Deaf Mission
in 1921, where he was said to have rendered "excellent services."[5]

Some of John Paul's character is preserved in a collection of his surviving papers.[6] He had wide-ranging contacts with Deaf organizations
in several countries, a long-standing interest in studying and recording
sign language and preserving its integrity, and an idealism that found
expression in his writings for overseas journals as well as Australian
publications.[7] Paul wrote for American Deaf newspapers, sometimes
using the pen-names "Lone Coot" or "Ian O'Marnoc," and these writings are often more revealing of his character than the pieces he wrote
for Australian magazines, where he confined himself to commenting on
national and state events, often with some acerbity. One article written
in 1920 for the *Deaf Mutes Journal* in New York indicated how strongly
Paul was influenced by his father and other Scottish deaf pioneers, and
described how Gallaudet College in the United States was an international beacon inspiring him and his forebears.[8] Paul's approach to
working with deaf people is best summed up in a short greeting he sent
to an Australian organization in 1933.

> Every effort which has brought real benefits to the Deaf has been
> one which enlarged their freedom, increased their opportunities,
> called for their co-operation and raised their status. The same
> principles apply to the "hearing" world, so in a sentence it is "To
> treat the deaf as you treat the hearing."[9]

This approach was not destined to be a comfortable fit with the pater-
nalistic charity culture of Australian Deaf missions and societies in the
late 1920s.

Paul stayed in contact with the Victorian Deaf community during his
nine years working in Scotland. The newsletter of the Deaf Society, *Our
Monthly Letter*, carried occasional reports of him, such as a notice about
the birth of his son in September 1925 and a quote from a letter written
by him on the retirement of Mrs. Abraham from the position of Matron
in 1926.[10] On his voyage to Australia with his family to take up his new
position, he visited the Adult Deaf and Dumb Society of Victoria when
his ship docked in Melbourne en route to Brisbane. He was greeted with
a social presided over by Ernest Abraham, who "welcomed Mr. Paul
back to Australia wishing him success in his new sphere."[11] The sort of
success that Paul was to achieve was probably not what Abraham had
in mind.

Early Tensions

John Paul's experience working for the Queensland Mission was soon to become similar to Herbert Hersee's experience with the NSW Society. Initially welcomed and praised for his work, Paul's quick rapport with the Deaf community and his disapproval of some of the Mission's policies soon began to strain relations with the Management Committee.[12] The Queensland Mission's Management Committee was unusual in at least two ways: First, it included women as full members and had no separate "Ladies Committee" for charity fundraising until 1932; and, second, it always seemed to include an unusually high number of teachers of the deaf. Although teachers may have brought wide knowledge and experience to their position on the Committee, it seems that some also brought an unfortunate tendency to persist in seeing deaf people as children. The annual reports of the Mission sometimes referred to the deaf members as "girls," "boys," and "lads"; and the Queensland Mission had a greater focus than other Deaf societies on providing classes in skills such as cookery, dressmaking, and cabinet-making.[13] They considered that such intervention was particularly important for deaf people, referring to "lads who were only too apt to drift into idle and vicious ways, from the very nature of their infirmity."[14] Like teachers everywhere, they were mindful of the approval of parents—"the parents are deeply grateful for all the Mission has done and is still doing for their sons and daughters."[15] A man like Paul, reared by a generation of Scottish deaf people who struggled to be independent, and who believed in "treat[ing] the deaf as you treat the hearing," was not likely to be at ease with these attitudes.[16]

Paul survived in his position for four years, compared to Hersee's one year; however, the four years were marked by conflict and tension. That he lasted as long as he did may be attributed to the Management Committee's lack of unity and consistency during the late 1920s, which made it difficult to supervise and control their sometimes-recalcitrant superintendent. Paul also seems to have had a less mercurial temperament than Hersee, although he could be scathingly outspoken when he chose his course.

Paul and many others, both deaf and hearing, became increasingly dissatisfied with the management of the Mission. They complained that public money was not being spent wisely, and there was particular dissatisfaction with an industrial training scheme that was being run for the Mission at the Brisbane Polytechnic and the diversion of funds to the young deaf men in this scheme at the expense of others.[17] A depot established to sell the furniture produced through the industrial training scheme was also criticized as a waste of funds, particularly as it employed some of the young deaf men who had been through the training scheme. These men should, it was considered, have been able to find work in the general community, given the resources the Mission had expended on their training. Paul's objections to this system, and to the general attitude of the Mission, are set out in a memorandum sent to the Management Committee in February 1928. [18]

> The Deaf and Dumb are not mentally below par, and the Mission having given them a vocation, a start in life, they, like hearing persons must fight for themselves . . . . Up until quite recently the attitude of the Mission has been to regard the Adult Deaf and Dumb as just an ordinary citizen, more heavily handicapped in the race for a living than the hearing competitor; it is certainly our business to "level up" that handicap, but not to "molly coddle" the Mute, or rob the mute of his independence and manhood, and there is ample evidence that this attitude is in general agreement with leaders of the Deaf in other parts of the world . . . . There are certain pressing improvements needed in our Women's Department. It is not fair to tie up so large a portion of our resources in helping boys to learn a trade, and <u>thereafter continue them in work</u>.[19]

Martha Overend Wilson continued working at the Mission as Paul's assistant missioner, and they appear to have worked well together and shared a similar philosophy. A suggestion that Paul was influencing Wilson and changing some of her ideas was raised rather ominously by W. R. Kingwell, a committee member who was from the Brisbane Polytechnic, in a meeting in June 1928.

> Arising out of Miss Wilson's report . . . Mr. Kingwell said that the report did not show the real Miss Wilson but someone behind her. It was a sinister influence which was at work . . . . The same sinister influence he had seen in matters concerning himself and the same was behind the meetings of the Deaf. Miss Wilson gave an emphatic denial that any sinister influence actuated her or that anyone had influenced her.[20]

It appeared that the Committee was beginning to regret its appointment of Paul. It was decided that he not be allowed to attend the Cricket

Martha Overend Wilson.
The collection of Edena Winn.

Carnival and Conference of Superintendents in Hobart that Christmas, because he was "under a cloud."[21] Divisions within the Committee were hinted at in the minutes, and some of the longer-serving members, who had worked for years with Wilson and other deaf people, began to resign. E. J. T. Barton resigned in May 1928, and the Committee president the Hon. Digby Denham and Isaac Dickson resigned in April 1929. A sharp and peremptory tone became more evident in the minutes of meetings. Wilson, now that she was tainted with Paul's "sinister" influence, was treated dismissively—in response to a letter she sent the Management Committee in January 1929, it was agreed that she be written to, "instructing her that the Committee wish her to confine her attention to her duties as set out."[22]

A former member of the Committee, R. F. Tunley, was becoming an active opponent of the Mission, allying himself with the more dissatisfied deaf people in the community. The Mission Committee evidently considered that Tunley was one of the people "inflaming" deaf people and were distrustful of his acceptance by them; however, deaf people responded by saying that Tunley "had a right to speak as an old friend of the deaf but not as their representative."[23] Tunley spoke out at the Mission's 1930 annual general meeting, declaring to the public that "the Report they had read was not a true account of the affairs. He was sure they did not know what was going on."[24]

The breakaway and formation of the NSW Association of Deaf and Dumb Citizens in Sydney in 1929 obviously influenced the Deaf community in Queensland. This can be seen in an interesting resolution taken by the Queensland Deaf sports teams in early 1930, as reported by Paul.

> An inter state Deaf Athletic Carnival is to be held in Melbourne at Christmas. Our deaf have turned down an invitation to attend because doing so would be to participate in a boycott of one of the Deaf Societies [the NSW Association, whose cricket team was barred] which has the loyalty of many of their deaf friends.
>
> I am entirely in agreement with the action of the deaf.[25]

When *The Deaf Advocate* began publication in 1930, Queenslanders quickly began using it as a forum for their complaints about the Queensland Mission.

A New Constitution

A major source of anger toward the Mission was a new constitution that was prepared during 1930 and passed in 1931. The president of the Committee, C. A. Midson, later acknowledged that the decision to revise the constitution was taken, in part, to give the Mission more protection against "attacks" from disaffected members.[26] The original constitution had been very simple and only a page long, but the new one was extremely detailed. Whereas previously, those who had paid a subscription were automatically members, Clause 8 in the new constitution declared that "[t]he Council [usually referred to as the Committee] may elect any person who shall have subscribed."[27] Not only did the council now have the right to decide who could become members, they also had new powers to "prohibit from entering the Mission premises any person or persons who in the opinion of a majority of the said Council are a menace to the peace and happiness of the deaf and dumb and to the realisation of the objects of the Mission."[28] In case there should be any ambiguity about whose peace and happiness was at stake, the constitution also offered a "Definition of Adult Deaf and Dumb" (marred by an unfortunate typesetter's error), which declared,

"The term . . . shall mean persons over sixteen years of age who are: (a) Congenitally Dead [sic] (Deaf from Birth); (b) Such other cases of deafness as shall from time to time be determined."[29]

Meetings could no longer be held on the Mission premises without written permission from the honorary secretary of the council.[30] An explicit "loyalty" clause was inserted, declaring that "[t]he policy outlined by the Mission Council in office shall be loyally supported by all officers and servants of the Mission."[31] The issue of loyalty was raised many times by missions and Deaf societies during these troubled years, and the Queensland Mission had already found cause to rebuke both Paul and Wilson for questioning decisions and policies of the Committee.[32] The constitution also provided indirectly for the withholding of information from deaf people in a section of Clause 14 ironically called "Information for the Deaf." This declared, "For the benefit of the deaf and dumb the Honorary Secretary shall prepare from the minutes of each Council meeting those portions of the minutes which in his opinion are likely to be of interest to the deaf and dumb community."[33]

This constitution did not have an easy passage. In a rather strange development, the document "went missing" in November 1930, and the police were called in to investigate. After they had conducted a fruitless search, Paul eventually produced a draft copy, which had been in his office all along. His explanation was that he had rewritten the constitution in "proper order" from this draft and given the revised version to a deaf man to deliver to the Mission's solicitors, but it never arrived. The Committee was "gravely concerned" at Paul's action in not immediately revealing to the police that he had this draft copy. Paul refused to comment.[34] When the constitution was finally ready, the Mission allegedly "stuffed the rolls" in order to pass it. Paul later wrote, "[T]hose having financial interests can flood a voting roll through an irregular channel, taking in even a message boy . . . and endeavouring to insist on his voting on an elaborate constitution."[35] It was passed at a special meeting on May 8, 1931, by a motley collection of people, some of whom were described sarcastically in *The Deaf Advocate* as "[m]essage boys, their 'Bottle O,' their typists, their staff and relatives, deck hands on their ferry, and their sweethearts (not exceeding 3 each), the Charlady and her father in law, business associates and wives, their tradesman, the rat gang."[36] This vein of sarcasm was to be a highlight of the accounts of Queensland events in *The Deaf Advocate* during these years.

Paul's contract with the Mission was due to expire or be renewed at the end of January 1931. Unsurprisingly, the Committee decided that

his tenure would not be renewed. They requested their solicitors to prepare a letter for Paul, giving him three months' notice of the termination
of his employment, and at the same time, to prepare another letter with
which to re-engage him on a "month to month basis."[37] So, although
he continued to work for the Mission, Paul knew from the beginning
of 1931 that his position was precarious. There is no evidence that this
made him any more submissive, even though it was the middle of the
Depression—indeed, the contrary seemed to be true.

This was evident in his comments at a "surprise celebration" given
to him and his wife on the occasion of the fourth anniversary of their
arrival in Brisbane in March that year. At this event, he praised his
deaf friends and thanked them for their kindness and support, "under
the almost unbearable oppression thrust upon us without just cause or
reason."[38] Among the supporters who gathered to show their appreciation were two of the erstwhile Committee members, E. J. T. Barton
and Isaac Dickson, both of whom voiced their support for Paul and
their condemnation of the misguided new Committee. Dickson was
particularly explicit.

> [He] made a scathing exposure of the element in the Committee
> which had made Mr. Paul's life unbearable, called upon the Deaf
> to maintain the fine spirit they were showing in rallying round
> Mr. Paul and protect their freedom before they found they would
> have to go down on their knees and beg for even the right to meet
> in their own Institute: Mr. Paul had never had a chance and the
> deaf should show the subscribers they could organise to protect
> their liberties and keep the man they want.[39]

A long account of the celebration, quoting Paul and Dickson at length,
was published in *The Deaf Advocate* the following month, indicating
that Paul was making no particular effort to hide his feelings about the
Committee or to protect his position. The vigilant Kingwell tabled this
article at the next Committee meeting, however, at that time, they could
not take any action against Paul because of a new development—an
official inquiry into the Mission.[40]

A Government Inquiry

In early 1931, some hearing subscribers (allegedly at Paul's and
Tunley's instigation) successfully requested a government inquiry into
the affairs of the Queensland Mission.[41] This request was discussed at a

special meeting held on February 10th that some deaf members asked to attend. The meeting was moved to another location at the last minute, because of "reliable information" that deaf people planned to storm the meeting, release the main electrical switch to plunge the building into darkness, and then attack Mr. Holle (the Hon. Secretary).[42] The police were notified of this "information," and (it seems) were asked to patrol the next meeting of the Committee.[43] The climate of heightened distrust and suspicion was savagely satirized in a letter to the editor of *The Deaf Advocate* by "Benedict Arnold II," most likely written by John Paul or R. F. Tunley.[44]

> The Brisbane Deaf sent notice that a deputation of two would wait on the Committee to ask for information. After a display of officious shuffling, the Committee secretly changed the place of meeting so that it was not held at the Mission. The Superintendent, Assistant Superintendent and Deaf representatives were NOT INFORMED, but the office girl knew all about it.
>
> At the next meeting of Committee the deputation of two found the Institute patrolled by police in pairs and under survelliance [sic] of plain clothes officers. Why should our noble and intimate friends of the Committee be subjected [to] such awful risks? We demand that the Military be mobilised in future. For a deputation of three, bombers should fly round the Institute; for a deputation of four, the Fleet should come up the river and anchor just off the lawn. But the decks must be cleared for action and every man at his battle station. A deputation of more than four shall not be allowed as it would be a menace to life, property, currency, codlin moth, the sugar bounty, starting price betting, the climate, Cockattoo [sic] Island, conceit, evasiveness, lying.[45]

The inquiry into the administration of the Queensland Adult Deaf and Dumb Mission was conducted by W. Bradbury of the Home Secretary's Department. He consulted extensively with the Mission's Management Committee and staff, teachers at the Brisbane Polytechnic, and very little with deaf people themselves. Paul initially refused to give evidence unless he was allowed "the right to make a statement," but the Committee ordered him to appear, telling him that "they looked upon his action as a crass order of insubordination."[46] The deaf people who were summoned to give evidence (such as Alf Eaton) were those who were receiving relief payments from the Mission. (Deaf societies and missions had responsibility for distributing unemployment relief to deaf people during these years.) When those deaf people also tried to refuse, they were ordered to comply, or their "weekly allowance [would] be at once withdrawn."[47] But another deaf man, C. C. Garner, later claimed he "was not allowed to go in, though he had evidence to offer."[48] Garner was not receiving relief payments and so was less amenable to control by the Committee.

While Bradbury prepared his report, the Mission held their annual general meeting on May 29th, at which the mutinous feelings of the audience were very much in evidence. Eaton criticized the annual report for not giving credit to the work of Paul, his wife, and Martha Overend Wilson. Garner complained about the number of teachers on the Committee, pointing out that other states did not have so many on their management committees. He protested, "[I]t is not right for [the deaf] to be bossed as if they were children." Eaton also requested that there should be some deaf people on the Committee (there had been one in the past, but at that time, there were none). He pointed out that the Queensland Mission was the only one in Australia without any deaf people on its board or Committee. Three deaf people were duly nominated, but none of them were elected. The meeting concluded with the retiring president (Midson) lamenting that it was "very distressing on my last night to find the deaf people engaging in personal remarks."[49]

The Bradbury Report

Bradbury's report was released on August 19, 1931.[50] He found that, in general, funds had been carefully supervised and accounts well kept, although the costs of collection were high and salaries and wages "excessive." He supported the industrial training scheme and said, "Critics of the scheme had very little foundation for their objections," but that the depot's costs were excessive and could not "justify its existence as at present conducted." His assessment of Paul and his work was that

The Superintendent has had a wide experience through his work among the deaf. He has, however, failed to grasp the true perspective of his position. He has evidently forgotten his obligations to the responsible controlling body of the Mission, in order to make himself popular with the Deaf.[51]

C. C. Garner later wrote in reply to this accusation

> Oh! Yes! I say he did make himself popular with the deaf, not . . .
> by calling us to him like "bawbees" and feeding us on lollies and
> candy. Oh! No! but by giving it to us "in the neck" to waken us up
> out of our slumbers, where we sinned we paid for it in full; and
> the . . . committee would have quailed before his wrath, when he
> shed it on us, The Deaf. For doing so he was not hated, but loved
> as a man who stood to moral right and sound principle.[52]

This description of Paul's approach is reminiscent of Herbert Hersee's
claim to his British Mission in 1922 that he "found it necessary to drop
a bomb, for you were all asleep."[53] It is an interesting indication of the
similarities between Paul's and Hersee's approaches to working with
deaf people—a refusal to cocoon them in a narrow world or to provide
excessive support, and a sometimes tough insistence that deaf people
be treated as much like hearing people as possible. Paul wrote his own
response to the Bradbury Report, although it does not appear to have
been published anywhere, and only a fragment of it survives among
his papers. In this response, he addressed the accusation that he had
lost the "perspective" of his position. He claimed that the position was
changed so often and arbitrarily, "to suit individual whims" and without his being notified, that ". . . 'perspective' would have been possible only to one of those creatures of ancient mythology who had eyes
before and behind."[54]

Bradbury wrote elsewhere in his report that, "Mr Paul . . . should
know that the usually suspicious nature, which is generally apparent
in the deaf, should not be inflamed or provoked."[55] If any Deaf people commented on this allegation about their "suspicious nature," their
responses have not survived. Paul, however, wrote about this "harmful
falsehood" in a letter to *The Deaf Advocate* the following year, giving
several sarcastic examples of why Deaf people should indeed have
been suspicious of the Mission's Committee, such as "when one of
these suspicious deaf sat before a man who blackguarded him verbally
to the hearing committee and had not the courage to spell [interpret] it
to the deaf man, why be suspicious?" He continued rhetorically,

> My deaf friends, it is of no use that you say you have proofs, evi-
> dence, first hand information, direct complaints. That according
> to the moral standards ruling among men of repute you are right.
> You are only the deaf and dumb, what is praiseworthy among

hearing people as a desire for justice, honourable conduct, the upholding of moral standards, the maintenance of common rights IS IN YOU, A SUSPICIOUS NATURE.[56]

The attribution of traits such as "suspicious" to deaf people has parallels with the tendency to see them as children, and this was reflected in some of the Queensland Mission's reporting during these years, as we have seen. (See chapter 7 for further examples of this in Victoria.) Given Bradbury's acknowledged lack of experience with deaf people, it is likely that he had been advised on their "nature" by some of the Committee members. The Mission's Management Committee felt that the Bradbury inquiry "completely vindicated" them, despite a clause stating that "the Committee is largely to blame for the present state of affairs. Members of the Committee individually have not in some instances adopted the proper course in their dealings between the Superintendent and the Deaf." [57] They decided that they had "no option but to dismiss Mr Paul for disloyalty."[58]

The Committee's decision to dismiss Paul was taken at a meeting on July 31st, after reading their advance copy of the Bradbury Report. However, they agreed to wait until he was away on holiday the following month before sending him a letter, giving him one week's notice. Meanwhile, they arranged for Alf Eaton to be appointed "attendant" at the Mission during Paul's absence.[59] As soon as Eaton was in place, earning his much-needed £3.10.0 per week, they approached him and offered him the job on a longer-term, temporary basis. When Eaton realized the job was available because Paul had been dismissed, he consulted with the Deaf community and informed the Committee that "as he was a deaf man he must take his instructions from the deaf and not from the Committee," and refused the offer. The Committee then approached Martha Overend Wilson, but she "made it clear that she would not stop without Mr. Paul, she too saying she must work for the deaf, not the Committee."[60]

A New Breakaway

There then followed what Wilson described as "the determined and orderly retreat of the Deaf from an intolerable and humiliating position, an open and official break-away."[61] Deaf leaders, along with Paul, Wilson, and many hearing subscribers, moved quickly to establish a new organization. Writing in the *Advocate* later, C. C. Garner said that the actions of the Mission Committee "inflame[d] the Deaf and provoked them to such extent that they caused us to break away and form a new and free body in which we could have a say in our own affairs."[62] The actions of Queensland deaf people immediately after Paul's dismissal were similar to those of the deaf people at the "angry meeting" in Sydney two years before and attracted similar interest from local newspapers.

Deaf and Dumb Act

Members of the Queensland Adult Deaf and Dumb Mission seceded from the organisation at a protest meeting held last night . . . .

The meeting . . . was attended by about 100 persons, most of whom were either deaf or dumb, or deaf mutes . . . . Convened by Messrs. C. C. Garner and A. Eaton, the meeting was held in the mission rooms, and Mr. G. D. Harrison (a deaf mute) acted as chairman. Consequently, all "speeches" by deaf and dumb members were interpreted by the former superintendent, Mr. Paul . . . .

The meeting had been convened, stated Mr. C. C. Garner, by the manual language of the deaf and dumb, as a protest against the dismissal of the superintendent. He had been dismissed and no reason for it given by the committee. They had no faith in the general committee, he said . . . .

The [Bradbury] inquiry was a farce, he declared . . . .

Mr. E. Mackenzie (a subscribers' representative) said that the committee was not working for the best interests of the subscribers of Queensland. The money was subscribed for certain privileges for the deaf and dumb, whereas the committee, he said, had not been giving those privileges. The money had been wasted . . . .

The meeting then decided to appoint a provisional committee of four speaking members and four deaf and dumb members, to be augmented later to eight of each. The committee chosen comprised: Messrs. E. Mackenzie, G. Merson, H. Clark, and A. Justin (speaking members), Messrs. A. Eaton, C. C. Garner, G. D. Harrison, and J. Allardice (deaf, dumb members). Mr. J. M. Paul was appointed superintendent, with Miss M. O. Wilson as assistant. It was decided to elect other ladies and well-known men as the other committee members later. The new name of the society was decided upon as the Queensland Deaf and Dumb Citizens Reformed Association.[63]

Paul's presence at the meeting seemed to be in the role of interpreter only, allowing the deaf people to speak for themselves and to have their statements reported fully in the newspaper. It is interesting to note that this account has no references to deaf people "gesticulating wildly" or "waving [their] arms in an effort to be understood," such as appeared in Sydney newspapers.[64] These Queensland deaf people were fully understood and their statements reported in a coherent way, giving a clear picture of their outrage, decisiveness, and control of the situation. Paul's skill as an interpreter would have contributed significantly, if unobtrusively, to this.

For at least the first year of their existence, the breakaway group was given free use of the premises of the Church of Christ Scientist on Tank Street (little more than a block from the Mission, which was on the corner of Turbot Street and North Quay) to meet, work, and conduct church services.[65] Later, they moved to rented premises in Fortitude Valley. As in NSW, the new body was usually referred to as the "Association," in contrast to the "Mission."

The Queensland breakaway group invited Hersee of the NSW Association, to visit Brisbane and conduct an investigation to counterbalance Bradbury's inquiry. Hersee claimed that he "was given the task of endeavouring to find out the causes of the trouble and also to try and suggest some means whereby a reconciliation might be possible."[66] This seems to have been the Mission's initial understanding also, as W. R. Kingwell, from the Mission's Committee said that Hersee was invited to "heal the breach."[67] Hersee arrived just a few days after the Bradbury Report was released, and he talked with many people on both sides of the dispute. He reported that he was "cordially received" by the Mission Committee, and he met with numerous others, such as Bradbury himself; former members of the Mission Committee; staff at the Queensland Blind, Deaf and Dumb Institution and the Brisbane Polytechnic, where the much-disputed training scheme was conducted; and of course (unlike Bradbury) deaf people themselves.

An account of Hersee's investigations and conclusions was printed in *The Deaf Advocate* soon after, detailing "an entire loss of confidence in the Committee by the Deaf and Dumb," "roll stuffing," "a lack of understanding of the Superintendent's duties," "serious dissatisfaction re the Training Scheme," and most tellingly, "[v]arious protests have been made by the Deaf and Dumb and ignored. The Deaf and Dumb resent being treated as intellectually inferior and incapable of managing their own affairs."[68] Hersee concluded with several recommendations for restructuring the Mission, such as a new constitution and a new Management Committee with equal representation of deaf and hearing people; however, no one seems to have acted on these recommendations, certainly not the Mission. Kingwell wrote in a letter to Alfred Lonsdale (of the NSW Society) that, "All Mr. Hersee did was to fan the flame of extremism" and that, "Our Committee here is convinced that there is a definite move by a few extremists to get control of the Deaf and Dumb Societies of the Commonwealth . . . . We were given to understand that Victoria is to be the next move."[69]

Indeed, some Victorians hoped so too. A number of anonymous "Melbourne sympathisers" wrote collectively to *The Deaf Advocate*, praising the actions of the Queenslanders and declaring, "The growth of exclusive ASSOCIATIONS for the Deaf out of the primitive biased societies . . . show brilliant signs of promise for the future of the deaf."[70] These Victorians obviously envied their northern friends the support and leadership of Hersee and Paul, and their letter contains barely suppressed hope that a similar savior might emerge in Victoria to "unconditionally free the deaf from the 'prussian' methods adopted by the prehistoric prejudiced 'hearing' Boards of all the Societies throughout the Commonwealth." The letter concluded, "Hats off again to the N.S.W.A. [sic] under Mr. Hersee, and the new Q.D.D.A. [sic] under Mr. Paul. Will the next move be in Victoria!!!!?"[71]

Kingwell would have found further justification for his suspicions in an editorial in *The Deaf Advocate* that could have been read as a "call to arms."

> Let us hope that the experiences in New South Wales and in Queensland will be the forerunner of strengthening the Deaf in other States to safeguard their interests and demand a recognition of their rights, so that they are no longer regarded as incapable of managing their own affairs. These prejudices against the Deaf must be swept away once and for all and co-operation, goodwill, and fellowship must be firmly established.[72]

In his letter to Lonsdale, written in October 1931, Kingwell dismissed the new Association in Queensland as providing only "a job for Mr. Paul and easy billets as Collectors for the extremist Deaf." In a comment very revealing of his criteria for a respectable organization, Kingwell scoffed, "[T]here is not one prominent citizen associated with it."[73] However, this was not the case for long. Within a year, the Association had secured the patronage of both the governor of Queensland and the Hon. Digby Denham, the former Premier of the state who had been president of the Mission Committee from its beginnings in 1903 until 1929.[74] Denham was not the only long-standing supporter of the Mission who switched his allegiance to the Association. Isaac Dickson (superintendent of the Blind, Deaf and Dumb Institute) had been at the original meeting, which established the Mission in 1902 and had remained on the Mission Committee until 1928, and E. J. T. Barton had been on the Mission Committee from 1907 until 1928, serving as secretary or vice president under Denham for many of those years. Both of these men joined Denham in accepting seats on the new Association's council.[75] The fact that these prominent stalwarts of the Mission took the radical step of publicly switching their support to the Association gives some indication that the Mission had departed from its original ideals, and that these were now better embodied in the Association.

The upheaval in Queensland drew the attention of Deaf communities around Australia and abroad. *The Deaf Advocate* in Sydney ran regular reports and served as a public forum for Paul, Garner, and others. The *British Deaf Times* reported on Hersee's visit to Queensland and concluded that "one thing seems paramount from the reports to hand and that is, the status of the deaf needs to be raised in Queensland, and a fuller appreciation of the rights of the deaf to manage their own affairs."[76]

Reports such as this indicate that Hersee and Paul were in regular contact with former colleagues in Britain. They also illustrate that the overriding theme of deaf people managing their own affairs was one that resonated broadly during the late 1920s and 1930s, not only within Australia but in Deaf communities in other countries as well.

Few records of the composition of the Association's council survive, but *The Deaf Advocate* reported that it had an equal number of deaf and hearing councilors.[77] A 1932 newspaper interview with Alderman Massey, one of the Association's hearing councillors, confirmed

> Our constitution secures to the deaf and dumb representation on the council and the management committee from among their own members . . . . Experience has proved the value of enlisting their sympathy and knowledge of the needs of their fellows in the Land of Silence.[78]

Among the many deaf people who moved to the Association were three of the Mission's four collectors and Martha Overend Wilson, who continued to hold the position of Paul's assistant superintendent in the Association. Her long-standing commitment to "unity" must have been sorely tried by these adversarial circumstances, especially because she had been involved with the Mission from its very first meeting in 1902. However, her support for the Association was prompt and whole-hearted. She was probably the deaf person mentioned in an article in the *Cairns Post*, which reported, "[O]ne of the deaf and dumb, who was one of the original founders of the Mission, immediately advanced a generous sum to enable the Association to begin its operations."[79] Her long involvement with the Queensland Mission was widely known, and the editors of the *Advocate* pointed out that "Miss. M. O. Wilson who has given such devoted service to the cause must now start her work of building up all over again."[80] Although there is no surviving account of how the Mission Committee felt about these defections, they hastened to make use of one of the clauses in their brand-new constitution and revoked all five of their existing life memberships (including those held by Wilson and Barton) after the breakaway.[81]

As in NSW, the existence of rival organizations created (or emphasized) splits within the Deaf community. Kingwell referred to tensions among the young deaf men studying at the Brisbane Polytechnic, saying "[S]ome boys at work [were] calling those who went to the Mission scabs."[82] The Mission allegedly adopted the tactics of bribery and intimidation to stop the deaf people they employed from going to the Association or to entice them back to the Mission. Paul wrote

> The payment of wages in the opinion of certain officers of the Mission entitles them to dictate in matters of sport, friendships, social life. The deaf concerned have expressed their contempt for the methods used but the pay envelope is a serious thing these days. Now one man has had to leave our team and his wife has had to withdraw from the circle of her friends as a result of pressure, and the fact that his wage will be kept down till she attends the social functions arranged by the Mission.[83]

Some deaf people managed to resist these tactics, although at personal cost to themselves. The editors of *The Deaf Advocate* described "the collectors who gave up their positions rather than be a party to such tyrrany [sic]: Mr. Eaton who refused a tempting bait to be disloyal to the deaf but who preferred poverty with honour rather than riches with dishonour."[84] Martha Overend Wilson also confirmed these tactics when she described "how the Deaf and Dumb stand together in spite of tempting baits held out by the old Society; all the world will be theirs if they will only go back without Mr. Paul."[85] John Paul described the alternatives more starkly: "The Deaf world now knows the fight is on— Fear or Freedom."[86]

* * *

The relationship between the Mission Committee and the staff of the Queensland Blind, Deaf and Dumb Institution (the school) became even stronger after the breakaway, with Paul indicating that several extra seats on the Committee were provided to teachers as a "reward" for their assistance to the Mission.[87] He alleged that this assistance included "getting school children to swell the attendances" at Mission functions and using the school's direct contact with parents to ensure that young school-leavers were directed to the Mission rather than to the Association. Hersee had, during his investigation, addressed the problems of teachers being on the Committee. He wrote in the *Advocate*

> The school authorities should co-operate with the adult deaf work to the greatest extent but that does not mean that they should put themselves into the position of managing the affairs of the adult deaf. The position in itself is rather one of contradiction: the teachers openly take credit for turning out deaf pupils fitted to take their place in the world on an equal footing with those who are not handicapped. Mr. Holle even states that the deaf children under him are "abnormally intelligent." Surely then with these facts in mind it is not too much to ask "are they not able then as grown men and women . . . to conduct their own affairs?" Yet Mr. Holle and two of his assistant teachers sit on the Mission Committee on which no deaf are allowed because the Committee consider the deaf are totally unable to manage their affairs. Apparently the school teachers need to express their own views more forcibly upon their fellow committee members and practise what they preach.[88]

Despite the Mission's efforts, it seems that (as in NSW), the majority of deaf people in Queensland supported the Association, at least in the early years. Hersee reported that when he visited in August 1931, just after the breakaway, the church services and functions of the Association were attended by at least 70 deaf people, whereas "I visited the Mission headquarters twice and saw two or three deaf and I also attended a Mission Service at which there were present 10 deaf and 8 hearing people."[89] The following September 1932 article in the *Cairns Post* claimed that approximately two-thirds of deaf people in the state were with the Association.

> According to the best information available, there are 194 deaf mutes in Queensland, of whom 117 are resident in the metropolitan area. Of the latter, 82 are members of the Association and 42 country deaf are with us, making a total of 124. The deaf membership is entirely voluntary and subject to no pressure, and the fact that a large majority of the people for whose benefit the public so generously subscribe, are with us, is noteworthy."[90]

Relationships with Other Organizations

Compared to the rather cavalier attitude of the New South Wales Association, the Queensland Association seems to have been more committed to trying to maintain good relations with other organizations, including the Deaf societies of other states. Paul and Wilson frequently sent messages and greetings to other organizations, even managing to have a New Year's message included in a 1932 issue of *The Victorian Deaf*, although this publication rarely allowed news of the unseemly breakaways in northern states to appear in its pages. They evidently counted on the residual feelings of goodwill toward John Paul among the Victorian Deaf people he had worked with from 1914 to 1918. The New Year's message read as follows:

Message From Queensland

The opportunity to send a message to the Deaf of Victoria is a gladsome thing. One of our objects is to "advance friendships and good feeling amongst all Deaf and Dumb." The interests of the Deaf are one, and we who are sacrificing greatly to stand for a higher conception of our true weal send to you all the wish that 1932 may be a year of worthy peace and progress toward our highest ideals. May mutual trust and friendship enrich your lives and service yield its golden harvest.

It can be no intrusion for me to add a personal greeting to the folk whose great kindliness and trust made my years among them a memory that still comforts and is held dear. I do sincerely wish you all that is good.[91]

The gleeful jibes at the Deaf Society that regularly appeared in the pages of *The Deaf Advocate* do not seem to have been echoed in Queensland, once the angry outbursts of the initial split had subsided. There was, nevertheless, no forgiveness. The Queensland breakaway was to prove a tougher survivor than its NSW counterpart.

Events in NSW and Queensland during the late 1920s and early 30s were good examples of the "small land wars" identified by Wrigley (1996) as an important focus of Deaf history, when deaf people resisted the control of hearing administrators, and when the success and relevance of the "institutions into which Hearing people put Deaf people" were significantly challenged.[92] In these stories of resistance to institutions, it is possible to see deaf identities being examined and redefined. From these points of view, the breakaways are very important to the Deaf history of Australia.

These events also suggest a gathering resolve and assertiveness within Deaf communities, not only in NSW and Queensland, but in other states as well. The new spirit of independence seemed to point to greater things, to larger spheres of managing their own affairs. As has been seen, there were widespread fears and hopes that "Victoria was to be the next move."

5

The More We Are Together

The more we are together, together, together,
The more we are together, the happier we will be.
For my friends are your friends,
And your friends are my friends,
The more we are together, the happier we will be.

THERE WAS LITTLE chance of a breakaway succeeding in Victoria. The hostilities and tensions described in chapter 2 continued to grow during the late 1920s and early 1930s, encouraged by the events in NSW and Queensland. But for every dissident who took the bold step of speaking out, there was a countermovement from Ernest Abraham and the many deaf and hearing people who were enlisted (willingly or not) on his side. His "magic Victorian rod" was still an effective weapon, however tarnished it may have appeared to many people. He continued to be a master of illusion, so that the events and personalities of the time seem, in retrospect, to be cloaked in an atmosphere of genial bonhomie, with people regularly linking arms and singing (in voice or sign) "the more we are together, the happier we will be."

Chapter 5's epigraph was a frequently used refrain at Deaf Society events in Melbourne in the early 1930s. For example, the words of this traditional folk song were displayed on the notice board of the Adult Deaf Club House during the 1931–32 Cricket Carnival in Melbourne. (See "Interstate Visit of Deaf Cricket and Tennis Teams," *The Victorian Deaf* 2, no. 6 [Jan/Feb 1932]: 8.) It was often signed during gatherings of deaf people at the Society. Abraham used it in his Christmas greeting to readers of the *Victorian Deaf News* in December 1933.

This facade is only penetrated by close examination of the records. If Queensland's story is difficult to recover because of missing and fragmentary sources, Victoria's is difficult for the opposite reason. The records there are extensive, with volumes of effusive newsletters and well-ordered meeting records, "daybooks," correspondence, frequent newspaper articles, and of course, John Patrick Bourke's prodigious output of booklets.[1] However, apart from Bourke's writings, the records often need to be read between the lines or "against the grain," to discern the pattern of conflict seething beneath the surface, what one commentator called the "deep, bitter thing" dividing the community.[2]

Why were Abraham and his allies so effective? The Deaf community in Melbourne was one of the largest and best educated in Australia. The Victorian Deaf and Dumb Institution (VDDI) and the Adult Deaf and Dumb Society of Victoria had been among the very first to be established and had had relatively stable histories. Melbourne had a long and venerable tradition of deaf pioneers, such as Frederick Rose, the Muir brothers, and Matthew Miller, whose achievements were remembered and celebrated. It would appear that Melbourne should have been one of the first places for deaf people to assert their independence and take a leading role in their organizations, and some interpretations of their history might say that this was, in fact, the case. There is no shortage of prominent deaf people from that time to be held up as examples of leadership. But most of these people were firmly controlled by Abraham. The more dangerous rebels were met with formidable (and usually successful) opposition.

Abraham used many tactics. He drew on the traditional role of missioner in British Deaf institutions for some of these; others he cultivated himself.[3] The most immediate was to isolate and punish the rebels, if possible, using other deaf people to administer the punishment, or presenting it as a decision of the board or the Deaf Committee. This could be a simple matter of removing an offender from a job or a role, denying them basic entitlements or special privileges, or (in one extreme case) debarring an individual from the Deaf Society premises. But it could usually be achieved more subtly and gradually by labelling people as "outsiders," "not really Deaf and Dumb," or "not one of us," or by wearing them down through humiliation and unacceptable conditions. As some commentators phrased it, "[Y]ou were put outside."[4] Abraham would arrange rallies or mass meetings to summon grand displays of loyalty and support, making dissenting voices appear irrelevant, disloyal, and unrepresentative. Some of the most lavish and enjoyable festivities in the community were arranged around his birthday or the anniversary of his arrival in Melbourne, cleverly linking his role with images of munificence and generosity.

If a new and threatening organization or publication emerged, Abraham would often present a more dazzling and enticing alternative to whatever the dissidents were attempting to establish, making their efforts seem amateurish and irrelevant. He also used preventive strategies to discourage or frighten the "waverers" within the community. He would make use of their shared history, remind them that they were a "little band of pioneers" who had come through hard times together and were marching forward to greater things. Because he had been in Victoria for almost thirty years at that stage, he was able to tacitly remind many of them that he had dandled them as babies, known their parents, and interpreted at their weddings. It is impossible to know if Abraham made tactical use of his alleged sexual relationships within the Deaf community, but they never seemed to have held him back and possibly provided him with an additional hold over certain people. Abraham cultivated an almost literally paternal relationship to many deaf people and their families, which would have made it complicated for them to take sides in the acrimonious events of these times. When deaf people moved interstate, Abraham's connections moved with them.[5]

Abraham's most visible and powerful weapon was his eloquence in using sign language. He was widely acknowledged as a master, an "artist," and his style of signing (particularly interpreting) was emulated and admired by a generation of younger people.

> Well he was an artist, he was an artist, his language of gesture was beautiful to watch, it really was, it was in many ways so simple that it could be fully understood by hearing people and he had many gestures that he added into the language which [were] not at that time used and he enlarged it, he enhanced it.[6]

Calling this skill a "weapon" may seem strange, as fluency in sign language is usually highly valued by Deaf communities. Herbert Hersee and John Paul were also acknowledged as fluent signers and charismatic leaders, but neither was considered to use this skill in a manipulative way. However, it is possible to use language skill (especially minority language skill) as a way of infiltrating communities, accessing private information, and making those who use the language feel exposed

Ernest Abraham, 1930s.
Victorian Deaf Society Collection, State Library
of Victoria.

and vulnerable. Such privileged knowledge can, in the wrong hands, become a tool of oppression, a weapon—and Abraham provides a good case study of this process.

Abraham had also mastered the nuances of what we would call today "Deaf culture." As well as knowing the language, he was able to demonstrate the behaviors, idioms, and attitudes of deaf people with great fluency. As one newspaper article at the time struggled to express it, "He can assume deaf mutisms so well that strange deaf folk will not believe that he is not like themselves."[7] Abraham had acquired and cultivated this familiarity from his earliest years living and working with deaf people in England.[8] Being familiar with Deaf culture also meant that he understood the Deaf worldview, their perceptions and interpretations of things, and this was part of what made him a successful missioner. However, he could also manipulate this knowledge to his own advantage, and as he became older, his attitude to deaf people seemed to become more cynical. As another newspaper article declared, he was "a man with . . . intimate knowledge of . . . every twist and turn of deaf mute character."[9]

In Victoria, those who rebelled tended to be late-deafened or oral deaf people, several of them migrants from England or Scotland.[10] This contrasted with NSW and Queensland, where many or most of the activists were long-standing members of the Deaf community. These Victorian dissidents were less susceptible to Abraham's charisma and hypnotic signing style, and, being already somewhat marginal to the community, they had less to lose by his sanctions. But for the culturally deaf people who had grown up within the Melbourne Deaf community, whose social, sporting, and personal lives were closely tied to this community and its central meeting place, to rebel was to risk all that they most valued. Abraham was quite simply able to make the stakes too high for them.

During the 1920s and 30s, groups and individuals (most of them deaf, but some hearing) attempted to establish an independent voice for Victorian deaf people. As in NSW and Queensland, this activism initially took the form of criticizing the workings of the Deaf Society and its figurehead, Abraham. In Victoria, however, the critics were met with much stronger and more sophisticated opposition. The resulting repression and divisiveness within the Victorian Deaf community were to be replayed on a national scale soon afterwards, when deaf people attempted to form an independent Australia-wide organization (see chapter 6).

Going Public

In September 1928, before the breakaways in NSW and Queensland, the board of the Deaf Society in Victoria recorded their concern about the appearance of a paper or booklet called the *Commonwealth Silent Courier*. They resolved that "the Collectors be notified that the Board cannot agree to them, while being employees of the Society, also selling copies of a paper which reflects upon the Society."[11] The *Commonwealth Silent Courier* was the official organ of an obscure and short-lived group called the "Deaf Welfare Association." Bourke referred to them as "a section of the deaf," who "controlled and financed [the magazine] by themselves."[12] The honorary editors were A. F. Hull and E. Johnson, and the honorary Secretary was Mrs. E. Gladman. Although Bourke wrote of them with approval, he does not seem to have been involved. The magazine's title and contents showed aspirations to a national readership, and it was professionally typeset and printed. It ran to seventeen pages, and the contents included a brief roundup of news from around Australia, and many short pieces reprinted from American magazines. It contained advertisements from local Melbourne businesses, which may have supported the printing costs. The content was largely innocuous, except for some bold statements in the opening pages. When describing events in other states, the editors declared that the deaf people of Queensland and NSW were "fortunate" to have John Paul and Herbert Hersee as their superintendents. Hersee, in particular, was praised as someone who "welcomes constructive criticism" and had "many new methods." But when the editors came to Victoria, they stated:

> Melbourne deaf are not so happy like other States. There is something radically wrong with the whole Society.
>
> Several hearing business men on the Board resigned after 10 years' service. It was understood they resigned through lack of confidence in the superintendent.[13]

The Commonwealth Silent Courier, 1928.
State Library of Victoria.

The editors also criticized the old Australasian Deaf and Dumb Association (ADDA)—"once a mighty army, where is it now? Is it suffering from senile decay?"[14] Such public comments were unprecedented (*The Deaf Advocate* would not be published for another two years), and the deaf people behind them showed considerable daring.

This first issue was ambitiously numbered volume 1, number 1, but no subsequent issues have been found or were ever referred to by the board or by Bourke. It appears that no further issues were ever printed. As Bourke wrote later:

> Here were the deaf writing against Abraham and running a paper which he was not allowed to control! He was not going to have it and in his crafty and treacherous way he set out to use all the resources of the Society including the deaf and dumb to smash up the "Courier."[15]

Because the magazine was being distributed by the collectors, a subcommittee of the board investigated the performance of each collector, and they later recommended that two of them be dismissed. One of these was Robert Luff, who, apart from having unsatisfactory collections, "is apparently not acting in the best interests of the Society."[16] Luff was evidently one of the collectors distributing the *Commonwealth Silent Courier*. He had been a stalwart of the ADDA and an earlier supporter of Abraham, but had obviously become disillusioned and willing to join other dissidents. The dismissal of these collectors would have served as a warning to those involved in the *Courier* venture— transgressors would be punished.

Abraham used his own resources to present an attractive alternative to the *Courier*—a magazine called *Our Deaf Mute Citizens*. This was a cut and paste of older magazine pieces he had published in his more energetic journalistic days, from *The Gesture* and other pamphlets and magazines. It included many photographs of deaf people's signs, the fingerspelling alphabet, sporting teams, and "statuary," and was promoted as a way of helping unemployed deaf people.[17] Bourke attacked the magazine and the fact that it was printed by the firm of printers owned by E. R. Peacock (the president of the board) in a series of letters to the police commissioner, the Premier, and the board of the Deaf Society.[18] The magazine seems to have been discontinued after just two issues (possibly because of Bourke's complaints). However, it would have made the point that any magazine deaf people tried to put out could easily be bettered by Abraham.

Complaints to the Government

More than one deaf person in Victoria tried to take formal action against the Deaf Society by writing to their members of Parliament and state government departments. Bourke later claimed that he had been writing to the Charities Board (which he compared to the "Circumlocution Office" in Dickens' *Little Dorrit*) since 1925, but that whenever the Charities Board approached Abraham about the complaints, they always believed Abraham's denials.[19] There were, however, occasional supporters in Parliament who tried to keep deaf people's concerns on the agenda. Between July and September 1929, Mr. Jackson MLA (member for Prahran—J. P. Bourke's local member), raised the issue of unresolved complaints against the Adult Deaf and Dumb Society in state parliament several times. On 24 July, Jackson stated,

> Three deaf mutes associated with the institute conducted by Mr. Abraham have written to me, and, I understand, to other members of Parliament, complaining about the treatment they have received at his hands. They have endeavoured to get their case brought before the Chief Secretary, as well as before the Charities Board, and before the public generally . . . . I have received so many letters in connexion with the matter that I want the whole subject ventilated, and if these men have a grievance, it should be remedied.[20]

When asked for details of the complaints, Jackson reported that the letter-writers alleged "[b]rutal treatment in some cases, and very harsh treatment in others."[21] He claimed that calls for an inquiry into the affairs of Society had been made since 1925 and possibly earlier. He quoted from a letter that the previous secretary of the Charities Board had sent to one of the complainants in 1928, promising a full inquiry.[22] This letter had, in fact, been sent to Bourke, who also quoted from it in his writings.[23]

Jackson raised the matter again on August 28, saying that he had had no response from the chief secretary's department and promising not to rest until the "inmates" had been given "a fair hearing."[24] Another politician, Mr. Tunnecliffe MLA (member for Collingwood), followed up on Jackson's complaint the next day.[25] The chief secretary did not consider it a matter for his department, dismissing it as an issue for the Charities Board, which was administered by the treasurer.[26] More than once, Bourke deplored the disagreement and confusion over who was the appropriate authority.[27]

The Deaf Society's board showed some alarm at these developments. At their September 1929 board meeting, they passed a resolution "to arrange for the Committee to view the papers re statements made by Mr Jackson M.L.A.," and also to "arrange for parliamentary representation in both Houses."[28] The Hon. Herbert Brooks MLA subsequently agreed to represent the Society in Parliament.[29]

At the October board meeting, president E. R. Peacock reported "interviews with the Charities Board." Taking action to limit possible damage, the board stressed "the necessity of the Deaf being loyal to the Staff and the Society," and the two deaf representatives on the board, Mr. Paterson and Mr. F. E. Frewin, "assured the Chairman that the Society had their hearty support."[30] A report from the Charities Board, dated October 14, was forwarded to the Society on November 8, and (although no copy seems to survive) it evidently exonerated the Society from any wrongdoing.[31] The board resolved to send a copy of the letter accompanying the report to "each of the persons Bourke had communicated with," singling him out as the person most responsible for visiting this embarrassing incident on them.[32]

From the point of view of Bourke (and presumably of his fellow complainants), "No inquiry was ever held."[33] His scathing assessment of the "inquiry" was as follows:

> The Government sent the Inspector of Charities down to the farm . . . to make an inquiry. This consisted of the Inspector strolling through the farm on Sunday afternoon, October 13, 1929 accompanied by the President of the Society with Abraham's Secretary as interpreter. The inspector reported:
>
> "Careful inquiry and personal investigation failed to reveal that other than proper consideration and sympathetic treatment is accorded the inmates. All those with whom I came in contact expressed themselves as happy, contented and well treated. The Home, in my opinion, is a credit to the Society."[34]

If the dates reported by Bourke and the board were both correct, the inspector wrote his report the day after this "stroll" around the farm.

The Banning of Bourke

The ramifications of "banning" a deaf person from a Deaf society may be difficult for modern readers to comprehend. But during these decades, the Deaf Society represented a great deal to a deaf person.

Not only was it the center and focus of almost all community activities, celebrations, sporting contests, religious services, and practical assistance with interpreting, employment, dealings with bureaucracy and other everyday issues, it was also a deaf person's only recourse to certain types of assistance. Many government agencies that later became part of the Australian welfare system did not yet exist, and their functions devolved on Deaf societies. An example of this is the Deaf societies' distribution of sustenance funds or "relief" to deaf people who were out of work, particularly during the Depression. It was not always possible for a deaf person, especially someone with limited proficiency in English, to arrange independent access to such services. So to ban or expel a deaf person from his or her state Deaf society was a punishment of such severe symbolic and practical proportions that it was almost never used.[35] Indeed, apart from occasional temporary restrictions on individuals because of drunkenness or destructive behavior, the only incidence of "banning" deaf people in these years seems to be the case of Bourke in Victoria, and later, general exclusions of breakaway Association members in NSW and Queensland. But the latter had access to support and community within their associations. Bourke had nothing except his pride, resourcefulness, and a few long-suffering friends.

According to Bourke, Abraham tried to persuade the Deaf Committee to expel him from the Society on two occasions in early 1929, but the Deaf Committee refused to do so.[36] It would have been unusual for Abraham not to get his way with the Deaf Committee, because he was the chairman and always had several of his deaf staff on the Committee. But Bourke claimed that the Deaf Committee was particularly strong that year: "There were as many as four Abraham haters on it. There were another four whom those could sway. The rest were made up of employees of the Society."[37] Abraham would, of course, have preferred it if deaf people could have been persuaded to expel Bourke; however, because he could not arrange that, he seized an opportunity at board level later that year. At its September meeting, the board received a copy of a particularly long and vitriolic letter Bourke had sent to the Premier about Abraham and the Deaf Society and resolved that it be "not read." They then passed the following resolution:

> "that J. P. Bourke be excluded from all privileges of the Society until such time as he writes a satisfactory letter of apology withdrawing all his misstatements and promising not to repeat them."[38]

This decision was initially disputed by the Deaf Committee. They insisted on forming a subcommittee of five members to interview Bourke. This subcommittee told Bourke to "take no notice of the Board's embargo, that the right to discipline members rested with the deaf committee alone."[39] Bourke's incidental descriptions of the Deaf Committee provide a rare glimpse of that group's own power struggles with Abraham and his board.[40] If this incident is an example, it would seem that the Deaf Committee was particularly protective of its role in managing the Deaf community.

On the urging of the subcommittee, Bourke cautiously attended the Society's premises for a meeting, then a social. At the social, James Johnston beckoned Bourke to the back of the hall, but Bourke refused to leave his seat in the audience. Bourke later told Johnston that he had "meant no offence to him personally," but Johnston informed him that the subcommittee "had no power to interfere in the matter of [his] expulsion."[41] He said he had communicated this to R. H. Lambert (a deaf Scotsman and one of Bourke's supporters on the Deaf Committee). Lambert, however, "had watched and guarded me all the evening—the act of a gentleman and a true friend."[42]

The next time Bourke tried to attend the Society was on one of the regular Saturday night gatherings, to which he usually brought a deaf-blind man. Abraham attempted to prevent his attendance by sending Johnston to escort the deaf-blind man instead, but the deaf-blind man opted to go with Bourke. When Bourke arrived (Johnston had "rushed back . . . to tell Abraham I was coming"), he was handed a note by the caretaker, saying, "I am requested by the Board of Management to ask you to leave the building." There were only three members of the Deaf Committee there, Johnston, Hull, and a third whom he described as "weak," and Bourke appealed to them for help. Only Hull stood by him. Johnston "told me that it was useless fighting Abraham; that he was too strong for the deaf; he told me not to be a fool . . . shake hands with Abraham and have done with it all."[43] A humiliated Bourke left the premises, accompanied by his friend Hull.

The tactic of using Johnston and the caretaker (who would have been deaf) to actually remove Bourke from the building was consistent with Abraham's practice of trying whenever possible to have troublesome deaf people denounced from within the Deaf community, rather than by himself. As Bourke wrote bitterly, "Abraham had kept out of it all, but was behind the scenes pulling all the strings."[44]

The minutes of the October board meeting reported perfunctorily, "John P. Bourke had presented himself at the Centre and been refused admission."[45] It would seem that they had accomplished their mission. But Abraham knew he should not rest there and continued to work on the Deaf Committee. He was able to produce, at the next board meeting, a resolution and statement from the Deaf Committee. The statement read as follows:

> Having had a letter of one J. P. Bourke read to us, in which he claims to speak for the Adult Deaf and Dumb, we beg to say that Mr. Bourke is not a member of the Society and the views he expresses are not ours, nor is he authorised to speak for us. We are the elected representatives of the Adult Deaf and Dumb members of the Society, and we believe that the work, as at present carried on, is in the best interest of the members.[46]

This statement was signed by six members of the Deaf Committee— Paterson, Newnham, Puddy, McLean, Mortimer, and Frewin. But there were at least four other members of the Deaf Committee who had NOT signed it, including Lambert, Hull, Crush, and—interestingly—Johnston. The meeting at which Abraham managed to elicit this statement from a divided Deaf Committee would have been an interesting one.

Bourke then resorted to legal action, an unprecedented step for a deaf person at that time. He claimed that his purpose was to "test the matter of my expulsion in court, and so bring Abraham and his Board out into the open and show them up to the public."[47] He managed to procure the services of L. S. Lazarus, whom he described as "one of Melbourne's most prominent legal men," who took up his case pro bono. Lazarus told Bourke to get a copy of the Deaf Society's constitution—a relatively straightforward matter that Bourke had great difficulty achieving.[48] Lazarus evidently found that the board had not acted within the constitution, because he wrote to them in January 1930, "threatening to issue a Supreme Court Writ to challenge the validity of its action in expelling [Bourke]."[49] The minutes of the board meeting that month recorded receiving Lazarus's letter and mentioned an "informal meeting" between Lazarus and the president of the board.[50] Abraham and the secretary of the board subsequently met with the Society's solicitor, Mr. Martin, and the board decided to instruct Martin to "obtain Counsel's opinion from R. G. Menzies."[51] Menzies was an even more prominent Melbourne solicitor, a King's

Counsel—and future prime minister of Australia—whom the Society used in times of special need. For example, a few months after this, they used Menzies to introduce a special deputation from the Deaf Society to the Premier, seeking financial assistance.[52] This incident achieved considerable favorable publicity for the Society, and the presence of Menzies would have been a factor in this.[53]

Lazarus's threats and Menzies' advice evidently combined to induce the board to reverse its ban on Bourke. In March 1930, the minutes recorded:

> THAT having reviewed the case of J. P. Bourke's exclusion, and his manifest desire to take advantage of the privileges which the Society wishes to afford to all deaf-mutes, and believing that he will endeavour to refrain from giving cause for complaint in future, at the request and on the motion of the deaf members of the Board of Management who originally proposed his exclusion, and on the recommendation of the Principal, the Board now lifts the embargo placed upon Mr. Bourke by the resolution of 16th September, 1929, excluding him from the privileges of the Society.[54]

Bourke, who was sent a copy of this "capitulation," claimed that the deaf representatives denied being the ones to originally propose his exclusion (no proposers are named for that resolution in the September 1929 minutes).[55] The motion reversing Bourke's embargo was declared "Carried Unanimously," but the word "Unanimously" was later crossed out and initialled. Nothing seems to have been unanimous in these contentious times!

Further evidence suggests that the Board reluctantly lifted the embargo for legal reasons, rather than for any belief that Bourke would "refrain from giving cause for complaint." At their April 1930 meeting, they received correspondence from their solicitors, Martin and Martin, with a "proposed resolution empowering the Committee to exclude from privileges of the Society."[56] This would indicate that Menzies and Martin had recommended they change their constitution (or memorandum and articles of association), so that they would be able to impose such bans again if necessary, without fear of legal challenge. They resolved that "each hearing member of the Committee" be sent a copy of the proposed resolution, along with the solicitors' letter and the memorandum and articles of association. The two deaf representatives from the Deaf Committee were present when this resolution was passed, so the decision to send these documents only to the hearing members is further evidence of the continuing exclusion of deaf people on the board.

Bourke might have been banned for six months, but he could not be gagged. He continued to write letters to the board, the Charities Board and the premier, and various other city and state officials. Many of these agencies sent copies of Bourke's letters to the Deaf Society, so he was mentioned constantly in the minutes of board meetings, usually with barely suppressed exasperation.[57]

The incident of Bourke's banning is a useful study of a strategy used by Abraham and the board to control deaf people, and also demonstrates that resistance met with occasional success. In this episode, Bourke was able to summon quite a lot of support from other deaf individuals. People like Lambert, Crush, Hull, and Mrs. H. Gladman actively championed his cause. Mrs. Gladman wrote to the board on his behalf.[58] He may even have had some oblique support from others, such as Johnston. His legal challenge to the Society forced them to reverse a significant decision and change their articles, probably incurring unwelcome legal costs in the process. Such small victories were all too rare, particularly in Victoria.

Excluding Deaf People from Power

The board meeting of June 1930, had as its heading, "Minutes of Meeting of Hearing Members of Committee." During this meeting, without any deaf representatives present, new arrangements were made for the composition of board committees and their meeting schedules:

(a) The General board to meet quarterly at 8.00 p.m. on third Monday.
(b) Executive Committee of Hearing Members to meet at Intermediate months to deal with all matters between General Board Meetings.
(c) Home and Farm Committee to meet at Blackburn monthly.
(d) Finance Committee to meet monthly.
(e) Business of assistance to indigent deaf etc. to be transferred to Deaf Committee for consideration and recommendation to Executive.[59]

Because it had already been agreed some years before that the "Farm and Finance Committee . . . consist of the hearing and speaking members of the Board," this new arrangement effectively limited the deaf representatives to attending four board meetings a year, instead of the monthly meetings that they had attended up until that time.[60] After this one incident, it was no longer necessary to specify that a meeting was for the "Hearing Members of Committee"; meetings were referred to as either "Executive" or "General Board," with the implicit understanding that all but the general board meetings were for hearing members only.

This, along with similar moves in NSW, South Australia, and Queensland, demonstrates the deepening distrust between hearing and deaf people involved in the Deaf societies and the overt and covert tactics adopted by boards of management to consolidate power in the hands of the hearing members.[61] Many of the arrangements put in place during this time were to remain in force until the 1970s or later, establishing deep gulfs between the Deaf community and the administration of the societies, often shrouding their affairs in mystery and rendering their decision-making processes inaccessible to deaf people.

Withholding Relief

By the early 1930s, the Depression was having an effect on the finances of the Society, as it was everywhere else. This caused considerable inconvenience to Abraham, forcing him and his family to leave the large suburban house they were then living in and relinquish the £200 annual "house allowance" he received in addition to his salary (which was also reduced). At the board's request, he and his family returned to live at the Blackburn Home, and his wife took up her former position as matron once again.[62]

However, these changed circumstances allowed for new variations on Abraham's strategies for controlling deaf people. With high levels of unemployment, deaf people were reliant on the Society for providing sustenance or relief money, and for occasional casual work, such as gardening. But this assistance had strings attached. Abraham's successor, Ernest Reynolds, remembered:

> And if you crossed his path, he had ways and means of making sure you knew he was boss. (Laughter). Oh yes . . .
>
> Well, if you argued with him and told him that he was wrong, you would find that next week he didn't have enough money for you on relief . . . .
>
> He'd have it for this fella and that fella, but it's run out.[63]

But, as Reynolds remembered, "yet if the family was having hardship he would be the first there with money to help them out. Not his, the Society's money, it was welfare."[64] This would have been an astute way to use the financial resources at his disposal. Being able to deny a deaf person the public assistance they were legitimately entitled to, probably in front of other deaf people, would have been a humiliating reminder of their powerlessness; but being there with "welfare" assistance in truly dire circumstances would have helped cement his image as a generous savior and reinforced to deaf people that they needed him.

Bourke managed to keep himself employed through this time, and so he did not find himself a victim of this particular brand of humiliation. Still, he saw in the Depression a metaphor for the condition of deaf people everywhere:

> The depression that has overtaken Australia is no new thing to the intelligent impotent deaf. The hopeless and worried lives being led by the hearing unemployed on sustenance and on employment relief is a measure of the lives the impotent deaf have had to lead from time immemorial. Thousands of them in all parts of the world have lived in the midst of such depressions from generation to generation all down the ages.[65]

The Victorian Deaf Magazine

Deaf people in Victoria had tried at least once to develop an independent voice, with the experiment of the *Commonwealth Silent Courier* in 1928. Although that attempt had been quickly suppressed, the desire for an autonomous publication continued. They tried again in late 1929, this time aiming for control of an existing magazine, *Our Monthly Letter*. Bourke wrote later that a number of deaf people were stirred into action by Abraham's disappointing performance in editing the *Letter* (by then a "bimonthly"), allowing it to become irregular and writing too many flattering articles about himself. Bourke claimed that in 1929, the Deaf Committee "put its foot down and forced Mr. Abraham to relinquish the editorship of the 'Letter.'"[66] The Deaf Committee took over the newsletter at the beginning of 1930 and changed its name to *The Victorian Deaf*. A. Hull (who had been one of the editors of the *Commonwealth Silent Courier*) was once again editor, and R. H. Lambert was manager. Bourke, who was involved in the group this time, wrote:

We deaf were all very proud to be allowed to run our paper . . . .
[I]t was written of the deaf, for the deaf, by the deaf and it
appeared regularly. The deaf were expected to finance it themselves, and Mr. Abraham did everything he could to discourage,
thwart and hamper Mr. Lambert . . . .

   Both Mr. Hull and Mr. Lambert, and later Mr. W. Crush—
worked hard and sacrificed their leisure to make our paper a
success. Although they had the right to be fearless, outspoken and
aggressive, the tone of "The Victorian Deaf" was temperate, calm
and manly. No one could object to one word of it.[67]

Lambert took over as editor during 1930 (Hull was killed in an accident in June), with H. Puddy as his assistant.[68] The "temperate" tone
of the magazine became bolder, and the Christmas issue included
several items indicating that the Victorians were making some radical

The Victorian Deaf, vol. 1, no. 2, 1930.
Victorian Deaf Society Collection, State
Library of Victoria.

alliances. One was a short piece by "Bananalander" (probably John Paul or R. F. Tunley of Queensland), criticizing the vocational training scheme operating in Brisbane.[69] Another was the following letter from Mrs. M. Gladman:

> Hearty congratulations on the latest issue of "The Victorian Deaf." You certainly have made it "Deaf for the Deaf." I enjoyed every page of it. It is time we Deaf woke up and demanded full liberty rights, and may "The Victorian Deaf" be the means of securing the object which deserves the support of all classes of the Deaf.[70]

But the most provocative item was a long "Christmas Message" from Herbert Hersee, superintendent of the new New South Wales Association of Deaf and Dumb Citizens. Hersee congratulated the Victorian Deaf community for successfully publishing their own magazine for a year and delivered a little sermon based on the words of Marcus Aurelius:

> "Seek the truth by which no man was ever injured." The Deaf of Australia have for too long allowed themselves to be governed by a few people who have been incapable of really understanding the needs and point of view of the Deaf. The Deaf have been regarded as incapable of thought, and incapable of expressing their opinion—merely a body of afflicted people in need of charitable relief and pity.
> . . . [I]t is a vital necessity for the Deaf "to seek the truth," especially of the management of their own affairs.[71]

Almost as an afterthought, Hersee warned the Victorians that "[t]he truth may make enemies, for it is often a bitter pill to swallow."[72]

Sure enough, in the next issue, Lambert's name had disappeared from the editor's space on the front page of *The Victorian Deaf*. There was a short notice on the second page reporting the new editorial arrangements—a "Magazine Committee" of E. J. D. Abraham (chairman), J. M. Johnston, Geo. Newnham, J. McLean, and H. Puddy (manager).[73] Abraham had, it seemed, got his magazine back again. Lambert confirmed this in a letter he sent to *The Deaf Advocate* in NSW:

> As Editor of "The Victorian Deaf"—last year's magazine, I respectfully beg to inform you that the Deaf Committee . . . decided to accept the proposal of Mr. Abraham that "The Victorian Deaf" be continued for another year on the old way, of which I did not approve, so I withdrew from the Editorship.[74]

According to Bourke, Abraham had objected to the inclusion of Hersee's article and their refusal to include "flattering paragraphs" about himself so, "claiming the right to choose our friends for us, he has taken our paper away from us." Bourke said that although Lambert had tried to reject the interference, "he was not strong enough for Mr. Abraham."[75]

In Abraham's first issue of the magazine for 1931, he included a "Message from our President," E. R. Peacock. Peacock gently chided the rebels:

> It is . . . quite understandable that some who now are reaping the benefits of the work of others should think that they can kick away the ladder which has enabled them to climb, and that they can manage by themselves. This is a serious mistake.[76]

Peacock also deplored the fact that "many of the deaf are easy victims to plausible agitators," a comment that foreshadowed the accusations of W. R. Kingwell in Queensland a few months later. Bourke expostulated, "Mr. Peacock admonishes us to be good little boys and girls and to beware of the company we keep."[77]

Although Lambert had resigned rather than been dismissed, he obviously felt himself to have been forced out of the role of editor, and the incident rankled with him. He sent another article to *The Deaf Advocate* in June 1931, comparing his experience on *The Victorian Deaf* magazine with his involvement in Deaf communities overseas (probably in Scotland and England), and concluded with an accurate (if awkwardly phrased) summary of the tactics used by Abraham and his associates:

> Since twenty year's harmonious association with the Over-sea Deaf, it is the first time here I ever learned this kind of "proved" experience, which is met very similarly by the local bolder spirits in their endeavour to right the wrongs of the deaf, who have been ruthlessly suppressed by gradually being worked out of their respective locality.[78]

Bourke and other "local bolder spirits" would have been quick to agree. If they had not already experienced these tactics, many of them would over the next several years.

An example of the dissidents "gradually being worked out," or publicly marginalized, was reported in the July-August issue of *The Victorian Deaf* magazine, which described a "mass meeting of the deaf and dumb people of Melbourne" in July, at which two resolutions were "unanimously adopted":

> "In view of misstatements that have from time to time appeared in certain publications above the signature of unauthorised persons purporting to be the opinions of the deaf and dumb community, we, the deaf of Melbourne, desire to put upon record that those views, opinions and statements are not authorised by nor do they represent the views and opinions of the deaf community."
>
> "That this meeting of deaf wish to place upon record their implicit confidence in the Deaf Committee as their elected and authorised representatives."[79]

The staging of such events, and the reporting of such "unanimous" resolutions, would have had the effect of placing the dissidents outside the community. They would also have served as an ominous warning to any waverers still within the community of their likely fate should they begin expressing "unauthorised" opinions.

At the beginning of 1932, the magazine was again taken over by a deaf editor—W. H. Crush. Crush was another migrant (from England) and like many of the Victorian activists, had not grown up under Abraham's benevolent shadow. He seems to have moved with some ease between deaf and hearing worlds and often wrote on behalf of the "hard of hearing" or those on the cusp of the two communities.[80] Crush moved around and changed jobs frequently, and it was a fortuitous coincidence that he lived in Melbourne during these critical years. He had worked for some years as a collector for the Victorian Deaf and Dumb Institute (the school for deaf children).

Although Crush's background was similar to Bourke's in some ways, he seems to have been accepted more readily by other deaf people, possibly because he had the sporting prowess so highly valued in Deaf communities (Bourke seems never to have set foot in a sporting arena). Crush was mentioned more often in the social and sporting pages of *Our Monthly Letter*—serving, for example, in the Cricket Club and the Lacrosse Club.[81] He had written for the *Commonwealth Silent Courier* and *The Victorian Deaf* under Lambert's editorship, and there is evidence that he privately despised Abraham, referring to him as an "unscrupulous schemer."[82] However, he seems to have maintained an acceptable reputation in all camps—the Deaf community, the small group of activists, the Society's board and Abraham. He had been on

William H. Crush.
Victorian Deaf Society Collection, State
Library of Victoria.

the Deaf Committee for some years and was elected as one of their representatives to the general board of the Deaf Society in August 1931.[83]

Crush was announced as the new editor for the magazine's first issue of 1932. The name was changed to *The Victorian Deaf News*. In his first editorial, he compared the need for deaf people to work together on the Deaf Committee to the teamwork needed in a successful sporting team, always an effective metaphor in the Deaf community.[84]

Not long after, a few bold statements began to find their way into the magazine again; although Lambert's fate may have taught Crush to be, at first, a little more cautious. In his second issue, he quoted an "appreciative letter" from a reader: "The June 'Vic. Deaf News' proved to be a real Deaf paper, and now may I venture to hope that the deaf will be permitted to express their own views in its columns in future."[85] However, this quote was carefully hidden in the middle of a paragraph.

The Deaf Advocate in Sydney, always alert to radical developments in other states, quickly hailed Crush as a "real" deaf editor of *The Victorian Deaf News*.[86] Crush traveled to NSW and Queensland later that year and was evidently impressed by events, organizations, and personalities in those states. 1932 was also the year that Deaf people formed a new national organization, the Australian Association for the Advancement of the Deaf (AAAD; see chapter 6), and Crush was elected chairman of the Victorian branch. In the final issue of the magazine for 1932, he wrote at length about his trip to NSW and Queensland, and looked forward with anticipation to seeing his interstate friends again that Christmas at a conference of the new AAAD. He ventured to praise and promote the AAAD in *The Victorian Deaf News*:

> The formation of the A.A.A.D. has created great enthusiasm in Australian deaf circles recently, as is evident by the increased membership, especially in New South Wales and Queensland. Of a total membership of about 400, Victorians number over 130 already. By uniting, the Australian deaf are merely following the example of, and coming into line with, the deaf of overseas, notably the "N.A.D." of U.S.A., and the "B.D.&D. Association" of Great Britain, and marks a progressive step forward in the history of the adult deaf of Australia.
>
> It is one other evidence that the deaf of Australia are **emerging from the limbo** in which they have existed for so long and are assuming a recognised place in the universal scheme of things.[87]

The Victorian Deaf News had not mentioned the AAAD before this point. Because 130 Victorians had already joined it and Crush was chairman of the state branch, the magazine's silence on the subject had been noticeable and had almost certainly been influenced by Abraham's and the Society's opposition to the AAAD. The fact that Crush boldly spoke out about it in this issue of the magazine suggested that his days as editor might be numbered.

The next issue was subdued, except for two short paragraphs reporting that Crush and Lambert had gone to the AAAD Conference in Sydney as delegates from Victoria. No further reports of the conference were included.[88] However, it was to be Crush's last issue as editor.

Melbourne was the scene of a pivotal public meeting on March 15, 1933 (see chapter 6 for a full description), at which conflicts between the national aspirations of the AAAD and the Deaf societies came to a spectacular climax. When Crush tried to speak on behalf of deaf people at this meeting, he was publicly humiliated by Deaf Society officials. The following day, March 16, 1933, Crush resigned from the Deaf Committee, the general board, the editorship of *The Victorian Deaf News*, and (it seems) the Lacrosse Committee and the Cricket Committee.[89] He left Melbourne later that year. Another "bolder spirit" had been "worked out."

The following issue of the magazine did not mention Crush as editor or indeed any editor or editorial committee.[90] The next issue reported on the annual meeting of the Deaf Committee—although Lambert and Crush had both been on the Deaf Committee the previous year, their names had vanished without comment from the new lineup.[91] This issue also announced that the newly elected honorary editor of *The Victorian Deaf News* was James Johnston. Abraham had evidently decided that he needed one of his own men in the job.

At the community rally in October that celebrated the anniversary of Abraham's arrival every year, F. E. Frewin, a deaf member of the Deaf Committee and an old stalwart of the Society, made a "very forceful speech," praising and congratulating Abraham for his many achievements, and castigating the rebels:

> He regretted to find that there were even a few in our midst who are still blind to [Abraham's] active goodness and achievements, preferring to find fault and magnify it. He appealed to them to show a friendly spirit and loyalty toward Mr. Abraham, concluding with the hope that the present happy harmony will continue.[92]

In the next issue, Abraham reprised the ditty, "The more we are together, the happier we will be" in his Christmas message to the Deaf community.[93] When viewed against the background of deaf people's struggles to assert an independent voice, his jolly assurances of "[f]or my friends are your friends, and your friends are my friends" have the appearance of a thinly veiled threat.

Taking Protests Across the State Border

The NSW breakaway Association's publication, *The Deaf Advocate*, provided an alternative forum for disgruntled Victorian deaf people to express their views on what was happening in their state. Because their own newsletter proved so difficult to wrest from the control of the Society, Victorians may have deemed it safer to send their more outspoken comments and articles interstate, rather than risk trying to publish them in *The Victorian Deaf News*, even when it was being edited by Lambert and Crush. Once the experiments with the *Commonwealth Silent Courier* and *The Victorian Deaf News* failed, no local outlet remained for their writings, and many Victorians became regular contributors to *The Deaf Advocate*. It is interesting to note that many (or most) of the Victorian correspondents in the *Advocate* would not sign their names to their letters or articles. Bourke, Lambert, and Crush signed their contributions, but most others used nom de plumes like "A Victorian Deaf Defender" or their initials, or they simply remained anonymous.[94] The most obvious explanation is that the writers feared reprisals against them if they put their names to criticisms of events in Victoria.

At first, the contributions from Victorians were merely congratulatory and focused on the achievements of the Association in New South Wales. In one early example, "Mrs. Gladman of Victoria has written to say how she appreciates the 'Advocate' with its policy of freedom of speech which is so different to what the Deaf have been used to for so many years past."[95] As the radical tone of the *Advocate* became more evident, Victorians saw its potential as an alternative outlet, and they began to send articles that commented on and criticized events in their own state.

Bourke wrote in February 1932, attacking Abraham's comments about deaf people in the Adult Deaf and Dumb Society of Victoria's annual report for 1931. Abraham had written:

> The deaf community, mainly of the artisan class, includes all sorts and conditions, and embraces all religious beliefs, all degrees of mentality and morality—the good, indifferent and viciously bad. With few exceptions, they are of the artisan class and the main avenue to mental development—hearing—being closed, it is not surprising that they are not as developed intellectually as normal people.[96]

This was deeply offensive to many deaf people, and was, in fact, quite different from the more positive comments Abraham had usually made about deaf people earlier in his career. The tensions and conflicts within the Victorian community during the 1920s and 30s were evidently souring his views. Bourke railed against the statement, using it to criticize Abraham and his kind: "As if some hearing people are not viciously bad and intellectually undeveloped."[97]

The *Advocate*'s willingness to print exposés of events, such as the Cricket Carnival held in Victoria at Christmas in 1931, and its refusal to allow Deaf cricketers from the NSW Association to participate (see chapter 3), also drew comment. An unnamed "Deaf Subscriber in Victoria" wrote in response to the Cricket Carnival article:

> The correspondence on the Xmas Carnival was an eye opener to many of us. Its [sic] a pity the light of day is not shed on many other subjects as well. There would be less suspicion and a better understanding all round then . . . . With grateful thanks from the many Victorians who have gained so much strength and courage from the pages of the Advocate.[98]

This and similar articles drew attention to the sharp contrast between the openness of information practiced by *The Deaf Advocate* and the NSW Association, and the climate of secrecy, suspicion, and fear that prevailed in sections of the Victorian Deaf community of the time. The *Advocate* editors seemed to relish their paper's opportunity to attack and mock the Victorian Society , especially Abraham's claims to grandeur. One article that wittily deconstructed Abraham's role as "uncrowned and unabashed King of the Deaf of Australia" referred back to the days when Abraham was editor of the *British Deaf Times* in the 1890s. The paper at that time had an anonymous "Special Commissioner" who praised Abraham regularly:

> One looks through old files of the "British Deaf Times" and finds that its "Special Commissioner" walking down the street meets Mr. Abraham by chance, and finds him the foremost of all his brethren in the work. Think of that tribute!! Half a hundred men, many of whom were respect [sic] and revered, and whose memory is still sweet today, whose work stands high because of the high character they put into it, and above and beyond them all "Our Special Commissioner" finds a place apart for Mr. Abraham. The mere fact that "Our Special Commissioner" IS Mr. Abraham should not be allowed to detract from the high tribute he has paid to himself, any more than these splendid articles by himself of eulogy and flattering references of himself in "Our Monthly Letter" . . . should create criticism. It is axiomatic in English Law that the King can do no wrong.[99]

In May 1932, an anonymous deaf person who claimed to have been "condemned as 'mentally unfit' by the so-called leader of the Victorian Society" wrote an article for the *Advocate*. In awkward English, he or

she attempted to describe the profound difference in the way deaf and
hearing people perceived deafness:

> In fact, there is practically nothing wrong with the . . . deaf except
> the physical difference—the trivial loss of hearing—. . . .
>   It is a matter of "astigmation" [sic] of the eye—the inability of
> a "hearing" person's eye to fathom and sound the meaning of the
> handicap of deafness.
>   The word "handicap" . . . has no mien [sic] upon the deaf . . . .[100]

This was an interesting expression of the ongoing historical tension
between deaf people and those who wished to control them. Like many
other deaf people before and since, this person declared that the problem lay not with their "trivial" lack of hearing, but with the deep-seated
"astigmatism" in the way hearing people viewed them.[101]

There were occasional references in the early 1930s to plans for establishing a new national magazine. R. H. Lambert wrote to the *Advocate*
in March 1931 of his "aim and endeavour to preserve the personality of
the deaf by means of a proposed new magazine."[102] A few months later,
the *Advocate* editors reported, "We hear that there is talk of establishing an independent magazine for the deaf of Australia. It is to be run
entirely by the deaf, that is to say it is to be both managed and edited by
them."[103] Once again, Lambert was named in connection with the proposal, and the *Advocate* promised its support in the venture. However,
nothing seems to have come of these aspirations, and *The Deaf Advocate*
remained the closest thing to a national magazine that Australian deaf
people had during these years.

"A House Divided"

Although there was never a formal breakaway in Victoria, clearly
a loosely connected group of disaffected people moved in and out of
various short-lived projects together. Ernest Reynolds, recalling this
group fifty years later, referred to them as a "breakaway" and a "deaf
association," but these terms were never used at the time. Reynolds
described the group as being "headed by a lot of the older deaf," especially Bourke. He also remembered Robert Luff and Mrs. Gladman as
regular members and said that they "got a lot of younger deaf in," such
as Crush. He recalled that they were "a little more highly intelligent
than the average deaf." Reynolds would not give an estimate of the size

of the group, but it seems to have been quite small—probably no more than twenty or thirty. The group did not have formal meeting rooms, usually meeting in the home of Mrs. Gladman in Prahran, but Reynolds recalled that they sometimes met at the VDDI premises, where the superintendent, W. J. McCaskill, was sympathetic to them. He described the group as being driven by a "personal bitter feud" against Abraham, a "battle of wills." The division created in the Victorian Deaf community was "a deep bitter thing, very deep and bitter."[104]

Political activism was not the only way deaf people expressed their opposition to conditions at the Deaf Society under Abraham. It was during these years that significant numbers of deaf people left the Society and their close-knit community and joined the Exclusive Brethren, a religious sect.[105] Some deaf people were also members of the Exclusive Brethren in Great Britain, and British deaf migrants may have initiated the relationship with the Melbourne Brethren.[106] Deaf people may initially have joined because some large Melbourne companies, such as the flour and biscuit factory McAlpin's, were owned by members of the Brethren at that time, and they gave deaf people work during the Depression. Many hearing members of the Brethren learned to communicate easily with deaf people through fingerspelling, an important factor that made deaf people comfortable joining and staying in the church. Reynolds claimed that these deaf people were "more intelligent" and "deep thinkers," and that they objected to Abraham's assuming the role of minister or chaplain to the Deaf community when he was not formally ordained.[107] Bourke also described them as people who "took their religion seriously" and said that once they had joined the Brethren, they "keep to themselves and will not come near the Centre."[108] Unlike the political dissidents, the deaf membership of the Brethren lasted throughout the rest of the twentieth century, with successive generations of some deaf families remaining within the "EB." They were an almost exclusively Melbourne phenomenon in the Australian Deaf community.

These political and religious dissenters were the two primary examples of collective opposition to Abraham and the Deaf Society. Victorian deaf people may not have come as close to managing their own affairs in these years as those in NSW and Queensland, but they faced and challenged a more wily and dangerous opponent. As in the other states, they paid a heavy price in the fragmentation of their community. But in Victoria, the divisions within the community were not as easily identified with separate organizations—instead they spread within what appeared to be a single, unified group. Bourke described the Victorian Deaf community of this time as being "a house divided against itself," and Reynolds called the rift a "deep, bitter thing."[109] This was the darker side of the cheerful choruses of "the more we are together, the happier we will be."

As we have seen, these events in Victoria overlapped with the beginnings of a movement to establish a national Australian organization of deaf people. Inevitably, such a move would be contested by the societies, and Victoria was to be the site of the most significant clashes on the national front. The tactics that had been developed by Abraham and his associates in their domestic conflicts were soon to be used again on a much larger scale.

6

Managing Their Own Affairs: The National Scene

The next generation of the deaf will not be unmindful of what you are doing now—and will benefit by it. By joining up as a member of the Australian Association you will help in putting down the barriers of blind ignorance and prejudices and further advancing a new era in the history of the deaf.

—FLETCHER BOOTH, "EDITORIAL"

THE UPHEAVALS OF the late 1920s and early 1930s were making many people feel the need for action on a national level. Deaf people from the breakaway associations in NSW and Queensland, and the struggling rebels in Victoria, were feeling emboldened and ready to emulate deaf people in other countries who had active national associations. Hearing people in charge of the Deaf societies, along with some of their deaf allies, were feeling that they needed stronger national networks to counter the new and threatening activism from deaf people. Both of these groups began to make national moves during the early 1930s.

These developments did not happen in isolation. The early 1930s were a time of widespread political activism in Australia as elsewhere. The effects of the Depression highlighted inequalities and social divisions, and gave impetus to the efforts of minority groups to articulate their needs and organize to protect their interests. Such groups wanted not only to better their socioeconomic conditions, but also to enjoy equality and autonomy and have their contributions to society recognized. The role of "citizen" was used to embody these rights and responsibilities. Parallel to deaf people's activism in Australia was that of Aboriginal people, who struggled against the state "protection" systems that controlled and restricted them, and moved to begin national organizations such as the Australian Aborigines' League in 1933 and the Aborigines' Progressive Association in 1937.[1] Such parallels were rarely commented on by those involved in the Deaf community—John Bourke was perhaps the only one to claim that "the problem of the aborigines and the problem of the deaf and dumb is almost identical in every respect (i.e., of making them good and happy citizens and an economic asset to the nation)."[2] He considered that deaf people were more disadvantaged.

The Australasian Deaf and Dumb Association's Last Appearance

The Australasian Deaf and Dumb Association (ADDA) had all but vanished from the scene by the late 1920s. During Herbert Hersee's brief time with the Adult Deaf and Dumb Society of New South Wales, he accompanied the NSW Deaf cricket team to the cricket carnival held at Hobart in December 1928, and found himself appointed secretary of another meeting called to discuss the future of the ADDA.[3] By that time, the only surviving branch of the ADDA was in Victoria, and Ernest Abraham seemed to be the lone voice calling for its revival, although he asked the meeting initially to "discuss the advisability of the formation of some Inter-State Organisation" and left the way open for a new organization to replace the ADDA.[4] The record of the meeting (prepared by Hersee) was cursory and carried little information about the contributions of those present, apart from that of Abraham. It mentioned that William Crush, from Victoria, suggested a referendum of "all the deaf." Another person, identified as preferring to leave the matter with "the Deaf and Dumb as a whole," was South Australia's new superintendent, Oliver Redman.[5]

Hersee recorded his own contribution, which was that,

> whilst he agreed in much that had been said, he did not think that those present had the authority or the power to definitely reform the A.D.D.A. or to form some new organisation. He was strongly in favour of there being some body that would unite the Deaf of this great Commonwealth, providing it was organized and conducted on straightforward lines.[6]

Hersee also moved the closing resolution that those present consult with the "Deaf and Dumb of their State" as to what sort of organization they wished to see at the national level. Once again, this resolution appears not to have been pursued, and there seems to be no further mention of the ADDA in Australian records, apart from historical references.

Two National Organizations Are Planned

In April 1931, a "circular letter" was distributed by Fletcher Booth and Ernest Quinnell (deaf councilors of the New South Wales Association of Deaf and Dumb Citizens), proposing a conference of "deaf and dumb representatives of each State." It was stressed that the conference should be "organised by the deaf independently . . . not . . . under the auspices of any organisation for the adult deaf." They also insisted that it was not to be "domineered in any way by any Superintendent: in fact it is not yet decided whether Superintendents should even be invited to attend." The conference was proposed because

> the time has evidently come for the deaf to get together to exchange ideas and to try and form a common policy for the recognition of their rights. The A.D.D.A. is obviously either dead or else has become a one State show, and there being no organisation in existence we felt we had no alternative but to send this letter to you in an attempt to start the ball rolling.[7]

This seems to have been the first call to deaf people of Australia to meet independently. Booth and Quinnell followed it up with an editorial in their new magazine, *The Deaf Advocate*, calling for "independent management" for "the whole of the Deaf community."[8] A preliminary meeting was held in Sydney in July 1931, where "a prominent worker consented to set the ball rolling," and it was agreed that a constitution be prepared by "tried friends of the Deaf, well fitted for the task."[9] These "friends of the Deaf" would almost certainly have included Hersee, and he may also have been the "prominent worker" referred to.

Deaf people were not the only ones setting balls rolling. In March 1930, the president of the board of the Adult Deaf and Dumb Society of Victoria, Mr. E. H. Peacock, had visited Sydney and held discussions with the president and members of the Adult Deaf and Dumb Society of NSW. After this visit, he wrote a letter to his board proposing that an Australian Council of hearing and speaking representatives of the Boards of Management of the different Incorporated Societies holding property should be created.

The idea is not to create a new governing body with authority but an honorary supervisory and consultative Council to protect the public and serve the Deaf and Dumb community in Australia.[10]

He introduced his proposal by saying, "It is recognised that the Adult Deaf and Dumb constitute an Australian problem and not simply a State interest." It is interesting to note that he considered that only "hearing and speaking representatives" of the societies should be chosen to deal with this "Australian problem." No longer was there any attempt to placate supporters of the dying ADDA by saying that deaf people could be involved in the proposed council. Among the objects of Peacock's proposed Council were:

... the drafting of a model constitution to protect the public who contribute money for the work, and secure the continuity of Policy and Administration.

... the training of Australian Leaders or Teachers for the work in the Commonwealth.[11]

Peacock suggested that "the President and Management of the Sydney Society be invited to take the initiative, with the assurance of the cordial support of the Melbourne Society."[12] Correspondence was duly exchanged, and by August that year, the Victorian Society was suggesting that a conference be held in Melbourne that Christmas (1930), at the same time as "the Festival" (sports carnival), and that representatives of the schools for deaf children also be invited to attend.[13] No record survives of such a conference, if it was held.

Little more seems to have been said on the subject until September 1931, when Henry Gladwin of the NSW Society wrote to the Victorian Society about the proposed council (referred to in the Victorian Society's minutes as the "Commonwealth Society"). The Victorian response was evasive, with the secretary being instructed to reply

that the General Board regarded the matter sympathetically, but they would like to have some information as to what the proposed constitution will be, how it is proposed to function the Interstate Committee, and what liability there would be, before they can come to a definite conclusion.[14]

Officials from the Victorian and NSW Deaf societies met during a sports carnival in Melbourne in December 1931 and evidently held further discussions about the proposed new organization. It was reported on cryptically in the NSW Deaf Society's magazine *The Silent Messenger* in January 1932: "The discussion will, no doubt, lead to a big forward movement in the course of a very short time."[15] The editors of *The Deaf Advocate* decried this "secret conference," suspecting that it was called to plan the formation of a council of Deaf societies, which was prompted by fear of the success of the NSW and Queensland breakaway associations.[16] As was noted in chapter 4, there were certainly some fears among Deaf Society boards after the Queensland breakaway the previous year, as evidenced by W. R. Kingwell's speculations about "a definite move by a few extremists to get control of the Deaf and Dumb Societies of the Commonwealth."[17]

So, there were *two* national organizations being independently proposed and discussed in Australia in late 1931 and early 1932—one by deaf people and their allies, and the other by Deaf Societies and Missions. In a country with such a small deaf population and such a recent history of deaf education and community organizing, these two proposals did not seem destined to be compatible.

The Australian Association for the Advancement of the Deaf

J. P. Bourke in Victoria also urged the establishment of a new national body of deaf people in a letter to the editors of *The Deaf Advocate* in February 1932. He was careful to distinguish his proposed new organization from the earlier ADDA, which he associated with Abraham.

> Let us form an Australian Deaf and Dumb Association composed entirely of the deaf themselves. An interstate Association that will champion the cause of the deaf, protect their rights, encourage and help the State Societies and Associations to uplift them spiritually and morally, and guard our less fortunate brothers from exploitation, is long overdue in Australia.
>
> . . . I ask the deaf not to be frightened by the Bogey of the old (so-called) A.D.D.A. This . . . was formed by Mr Abraham for propaganda purposes while he was building up the Victorian Society.

The Association I have in mind is to be as different as possible from the A.D.D.A.[18]

The editors of *The Deaf Advocate* were only too ready to join in criticizing Abraham and dismissing the ADDA. They described the ADDA as a "sickly and weak child," which had accomplished nothing useful and "died a natural death."[19] This contrasts with the statements of some of the previous generation of deaf people (see chapter 2), who claimed that the ADDA had achieved important results. The change in attitude suggests that the ADDA had become tainted by its association with Abraham and an older generation of deaf people.

The Australian Association for the Advancement of the Deaf (AAAD) was established at a meeting in Sydney on March 22 and 23, 1932, convened by Martha Overend Wilson from Queensland (it was unusual for such a momentous meeting to be convened by a woman). The meeting was attended by four people from Queensland, one from South Australia, and nine from NSW.[20] Although no Victorians attended, supportive messages were received from them and all of the other states.[21] Wilson was the only woman, and Herbert Hersee, John Paul, and R. F. Tunley the only hearing people present. Hersee and Paul were invited "because of their long standing knowledge of the Deaf in Great Britain and for the assistance it was known they could render in helping to draw up a satisfactory Constitution."[22] Martha Overend Wilson became the acting honorary secretary of the new AAAD, and wrote after this first meeting, "Preliminary ideas and strong feelings of the necessity of such an Association have been in the air for a long time and finally crystalized."[23] Fletcher Booth, who presided over the conference, wrote in the next edition of the *Advocate*:

> I hope you will give your unselfish co-operation to the new organisation because it will be the means of promoting your social and moral welfare and higher education. The next generation of the deaf will not be unmindful of what you are doing now—and will benefit by it. By joining up as a member of the Australian Association you will help in putting down the barriers of blind ignorance and prejudices and further advancing a new era in the history of the deaf.[24]

The founders had high hopes for the AAAD. They saw it not only as a vehicle for carrying out some of the aspirations of the breakaways and other reformists on a wider scale, but also as a way of transforming public attitudes toward deaf people and bringing Australia into the international community of national Deaf organizations.

The National Council of Deaf and Dumb Societies

Meanwhile, the organizers of the Deaf societies' proposed council were also becoming active. The honorary acting secretary, Henry Gladwin of the NSW Society, wrote to all Deaf societies in early 1932, describing plans to act on some of the aims of the Council. These aims were:

1. Co-operation and help between the Societies in each State.
2. The Training of Australian Welfare Officers and Teachers who would be available for work in any State as the need arose.
3. Research into and consideration of the best methods of providing Vocational training and employment of the Deaf.
4. Medical research with a view of exploring all possible avenues for the curing of Deafness.[25]

The proposed plan for training new welfare officers was to place recruits with Abraham in Melbourne for a period of instruction. There seems to have been some muted opposition to this, suggesting that deaf people were not the only ones who saw Abraham as self-aggrandizing and hypocritical. A staff member of the South Australian Deaf and Dumb Mission left some revealing notes in the margins of their copy of Gladwin's letter—beside the declaration that Abraham was the person best fitted to do this training, this person has written several exclamation marks and a note "thought so." He cryptically underlined words such as "spiritually," "morally," "great need for ladies," and "Christian ethics," and beside the proposal that societies pay an "annual quota" to cover the costs of this training scheme, he has added "For Mr. A."[26]

By the middle of that year, the organizers were formally inviting all Deaf societies, and even the hearing officials of the breakaway groups, to join up. John Paul retained a copy of the letter his Queensland Deaf and Dumb Citizens' Reformed Association received from Gladwin in June 1932, inviting them to become a member of the proposed National Council of Deaf and Dumb Societies in Australia:

Each affiliated body is permitted to forward the names and addresses of three delegates who must be hearing members of the Board.

No reflection of course is imputed upon non-hearing persons, but it is felt that the business of the Conference can be expedited between hearing delegates who must obviously know the points of view on all matters of their Deaf and Dumb colleagues.[27]

At this early stage, the proposed National Council clearly had no intentions to involve deaf people in its new organization. It is important to note this, because they were to change this plan abruptly several months later.

The AAAD Expands

The AAAD quickly established itself in the eastern states during 1932. Queensland formed the first branch, and by November, it had eight-one members.[28] In July, a branch was established in NSW (ninety-six members joined up on the first night), and in the same month, one began in Victoria with "well over 100" members.[29] Although other states did not establish branches, individual members joined the AAAD from all states, and there were indications of support from organizations, such as the Adult Deaf and Dumb Society of Western Australia, which sent "a kind letter of encouragement and congratulations on progress."[30]

Australian Association for the Advancement of the Deaf logo.
The Deaf Society.

The acting honorary secretary, Martha Overend Wilson, wrote the first of many letters to members of AAAD via *The Deaf Advocate* in its September 1932 issue, because "your very live paper reaches most Australian Deaf friends." She called for more members, "because numbers will carry weight in the eyes of the world," and exhorted, "There may be no Branch in your State or district, but there is always a post office."[31] *The Deaf Advocate* remained an important tool of mass communication to AAAD members, as the organization never established its own magazine or newsletter. The *Advocate* not only published AAAD publicity material sent to them by Wilson and some of the state branches, but frequently commented in its editorials on the progress of the AAAD and its importance to the deaf people of Australia, and urged their readers to become active members of it.

It proved to be particularly difficult to set up a branch of the AAAD in Victoria. Because the AAAD branches in Queensland and NSW had been facilitated by the breakaway associations in those states, some people immediately perceived the Victorian branch of the AAAD to be a de facto breakaway group. A Victorian "Deaf Defender" had written to *The Deaf Advocate* a few months previously, helping to create the climate for such assumptions.

> The "Powers that be" in Victoria are inciting the deaf . . . and will only have themselves to blame if a breakaway occurs here sooner or later and the example of Queensland and New South Wales followed by forming a new Association controlled by the deaf themselves.[32]

The editors of *The Deaf Advocate* warned of the opposition being faced by those in Victoria trying to set up a branch, describing how Abraham had vetoed their request to the Deaf Committee for use of the Deaf Society hall for the inaugural AAAD meeting. The editors also described Abraham using "coercion, intimidation, and even threats to prevent the Deaf from joining," and concluded, "we may be sure their Branch will be one of the most active of all, for having suffered as they have they recognise what a power for good this A.A.A.D. will be."[33]

The meeting that was eventually held to set up a branch of the AAAD in Victoria was held in July 1932 at the Central Hall, Collins Street. It was chaired by W. J. McCaskill, the superintendent of the Victorian Deaf and Dumb Institution (VDDI), and the school's headmaster also spoke at the meeting.[34] The suspicion that it was a breakaway continued to dog the new branch and made it difficult for it to gain support. William

Crush, the president of the new branch, was also on the Deaf Committee and was one of its representatives on the board of the Society. He was careful to deny that the AAAD branch planned a breakaway from the Society, describing such rumors as "nonsensical notions."[35]

The VDDI, although initially supportive, had some ambivalence about being publicly associated with the AAAD branch. McCaskill later wrote a letter to the editors of *The Deaf Advocate*, which distanced himself and his colleagues somewhat from the AAAD. He stressed that the school did not support the idea of a breakaway group in Victoria and stated their concern that their attendance at the meeting "might be misconstrued by some workers for the deaf."[36] Despite this public protestation, McCaskill remained supportive of the AAAD[37] and appears to have been a personal friend of Herbert Hersee's.[38] The *Advocate* editors praised McCaskill as "out solely to serve the deaf in whatever way he can." In a peculiarly contemporary tribute, they added, "we are sure the Victorian Deaf will readily agree that he is 'a white man.'"[39]

Martha Overend Wilson, in one of her regular bulletins to AAAD members, gave encouraging reports about the perseverance of the Victorian branch in the face of its many trials.

> The Victorian Branch has come through great difficulties treacheries and attacks in a wonderful way .... Freedom is the right that is being taken from the Deaf, always a great price has to be paid to win Freedom.[40]

Although she may have been speaking rhetorically at the time, she articulated the growing certainty that this new independence would come at a cost.

AAAD members met again in Sydney in December 1932 to ratify their constitution, elect a federal executive, and make further plans for their new organization. The conference was attended by five people from Queensland (Martha Overend Wilson, Jack Allardice, G. D. Harrison, F. Barstow, and John Paul), two from Victoria (William Crush and R. H. Lambert), and many Sydney members. During his official opening, Gordon Winn (a hearing vice-president of the NSW Association) said that "the deaf of Australia should be entirely free from the fetters of prejudice and given every encouragement to manage and use their voice upon their own welfare in the spirit of an ordinary hearing person's independence."[41]

Despite this, one of the more important items for discussion was the "co-option of hearing helpers," and it was agreed to give Hersee and

Paul "equal standing with other delegates and full voting powers."
Indeed, when office bearers were formally elected, Hersee was elected
as president. This may seem an odd decision for an organization that
was so concerned with hearing people's control over other organizations for deaf people; however, it seems the AAAD adopted the practices of the British Deaf and Dumb Association (BDDA), which had
traditionally had a hearing president and a deaf secretary.[42] The new
constitution specified that the secretary-treasurer must always be a
deaf member, and Wilson was appointed to fill this post. She defended
Hersee's election as president, saying that it gave the AAAD "a very
fine point of contact with the public . . . as well as providing a wise
leader of business deliberations."[43]

Delegates agreed to seek affiliation with the BDDA and the National
Association of the Deaf in the United States. A sports secretary was also

The Australian Association for the Advancement of the Deaf's first Executive
Council, 1932–1933. Standing (L to R): Ernest Quinnell (NSW), R. H. Lambert
(Vic), J. Allardice (Qld), John Paul (Qld), G. D. Harrison (Qld). Seated (L to R):
William Crush (Vic), Martha Overend Wilson (Qld), Herbert Hersee (NSW),
Fletcher Booth (NSW), Isabel Winn (NSW).
The Deaf Society.

appointed (Ernest Quinnell of NSW), and the AAAD proposed holding regular sports carnivals.[44] Their constitution was adopted, with the declared objective that the AAAD would "unite the Deaf and advance their interests in every possible way." Membership was open to "all Deaf persons in Australia," and this was clarified with an explanatory clause, "The term 'DEAF' in the Constitution includes those who are Hard of Hearing, Deaf, or Deaf and Dumb." It was also possible for hearing persons to become members, "subject to the approval of the Executive Committee."[45] However, they had to pay an annual subscription of five shillings instead of the one shilling paid by deaf members— probably a commentary on the greater earning power of most hearing people, and possibly an attempt to build in a deterrent to large numbers of hearing people joining.

In the next issue of *The Deaf Advocate*, an anonymous scribe offered a triumphant "Welcome to the New Federal Executive Council."

> Our "A.A.A.D." has come to stay:
> We care not what the Societies say,
> Let Alfred scoff, and Ernest sneer,
> We know their Council is full of fear,
> So Comrades all, lets give three cheers,
> And congratulate our Pioneers.[46]

The defiant tone of this piece indicates that the AAAD knew their arrival was not universally welcomed. By the end of 1932, they were acknowledging that the societies were working against them. Wilson referred to "influences at work which are calculated to hinder progress,"[47] and she and others made repeated calls for unity. William Crush, president of the Victorian branch, warned, "The A.A.A.D. was founded to unite, not split up the Deaf."[48] The AAAD's first report, describing the organization's beginnings, said, "An opposition organisation for the Deaf, controlled by hearing Committees, immediately came into the field."[49] The jocular ditty above made an unequivocal declaration that the AAAD was in opposition to the societies, symbolized by "Alfred" (Lonsdale) and "Ernest" (Abraham) and under no illusions about the struggle that was to come.

A Collision Course

Most of the Deaf societies viewed the formation of the AAAD with alarm, and they tried a variety of tactics to discredit and undermine it. In Melbourne, they refused AAAD branches the use of the Deaf Society's meeting rooms; in another (unnamed) state, the Deaf Society allegedly sent staff members to visit parents of young deaf people, warning them against the AAAD.[50] The societies pointed out perceived inconsistencies in the AAAD's practices, such as their having a hearing president despite their proclamations of Deaf independence. The editors of *The Deaf Advocate* complained, "In an attempt to injure the Association these people are trying to discredit it because it has a hearing President . . . The Association makes no apology for having a hearing President."[51] The editors reiterated the example of the BDDA, which they claimed had always had a hearing president and a deaf secretary.

But the Deaf societies' master stroke was to quickly transform their proposed National Council into an alternative national Deaf organization, which would undermine the AAAD's claim to be the only national body representing deaf people. Their earlier proposals that the National Council should be restricted to hearing representatives of the Deaf societies gave way to bold claims that deaf people would be at the forefront. *The Deaf Advocate* reported, "Mr Gladwin . . . referring to this so far non existant [sic] National Council said 'We will have deaf officials, the president will be deaf.'"[52]

The Deaf societies' plans were revealed at a climactic public meeting in Melbourne in March 1933. This meeting also provided the setting for the first public clash between the two organizations. In March 1933, Herbert Hersee planned a visit to Melbourne to see his wife and children, who were sailing to England for a visit, and whose ship would dock briefly in Melbourne en route. Local deaf people took the opportunity of inviting Hersee to address the fledgling Victorian branch of the AAAD, and a public meeting was arranged for March 16th. Abraham and the Deaf Society swung into action, seeing a chance to preempt the AAAD. They hastily sent a request for Henry Gladwin of the NSW Society, the honorary secretary-elect of the proposed National Council, to come to Melbourne at the same time. This was discussed at the NSW Society's Executive Committee meeting on March 6.

> A confidential letter from Mr. Abraham re Adult D & D Federation [sic]. It was decided to authorise Mr. Lonsdale to act on his suggested [sic] and if possible arrange for Mr Gladwin to go to Melbourne with regard to same.[53]

With the wheels in motion for a confrontation, Ernest Abraham could not resist dropping a few teasing hints to AAAD members. John Bourke described Abraham's behavior a week before the public meeting with Hersee.

Round about the 8th of March [Abraham] was going about amongst the deaf asking, "Are you still a member of the A.A.A.D.?" "Yes," he was told. "We shall see," said he triumphantly, and we knew that there was something in the wind.[54]

Abraham then placed advertisements in all the Melbourne newspapers, announcing a public meeting "to inaugurate a National Council comprised solely of Deaf members for the advancement of the interests of the deaf and dumb of Australia."[55] This meeting was called for March 15th, the night before Hersee was to address the Victorian branch of the AAAD.

Members of the AAAD branch attended this March 15th meeting, and several newspaper reporters were there in response to Abraham's publicity. The Age reported that the "feeling was high among deaf and dumb people last night when, not without opposition, the [Society] decided to affiliate with an Australian Council."[56] Gladwin presented the proposed new council to the meeting in glowing terms, and (according to The Deaf Advocate's reporters) lied about the overwhelming support of deaf people in NSW for it. He explained that there would be two councils—"one of hearing persons of the National Council of Societies and one of Deaf persons of the National Council of the Deaf and Dumb. They will meet in perfect harmony and the hearing will sponsor the Deaf where their views are in accord." As the Advocate's editors tartly pointed out later, "If there is to be that perfect harmony there can be no views which are not in accord."[57]

After Gladwin's talk, William Crush rose to address the meeting. He announced that such an organization already existed in the AAAD and opposed the motion to form a National Council. According to reports in The Deaf Advocate, Crush was "hurriedly gagged," and "assisted off the platform" (as his views were so blatantly not "in accord"). Bourke claimed that Gladwin "kept trying to push [Crush] off the platform."[58] Local newspapers commented too—The Age reported, "In opposing the motion, Mr. W. Crush said an organisation similar to the proposed one was already in existence. After a show of hands, the motion was declared carried, amidst uproar."[59] Bourke claimed that these newspaper reports embarrassed Deaf Society officials, although this may have been wishful thinking on his part. He was exultant that some Victorian deaf people had finally "show[n] the same spirit as our brethren of the associations in New South Wales and Queensland" and triumphantly (though prematurely) declared, "And so the Victorian branch of the A.A.A.D. stormed the enemy's stronghold, and won a great victory!" [60]

Up until this time, William Crush had doggedly retained his seat on the Board of Management of the Deaf Society (as one of its two elected representatives from the Deaf Committee) and was also editor of *The Victorian Deaf News*. On March 16th, 1933, the day after he was hustled off the stage at the National Council meeting, Crush resigned from editorship of the magazine, the Deaf Committee, and the board of the Society.[61]

The Victorian Society's account of the meeting differed from *The Deaf Advocate*'s and also from the local newspapers' accounts. A report appeared in the next issue of *The Victorian Deaf News* (which Crush had edited until then), asserting that the meeting "was the outcome of a request from the Sydney Deaf, seeking the enlistment of support from the Deaf of Victoria." Rather than the strategically organized coup to preempt the AAAD's public meeting that Society records confirm it was, this article suggested that Henry Gladwin just happened to be visiting town: "As he was coming to Melbourne, the Sydney Deaf deputed Mr. Gladwin to seek our opinion and, if agreeable, to second their motion." As for Crush's intervention, the *News* reported disapprovingly of its erstwhile editor, "Mr. W. Crush dissented and spoke on subjects quite out of order to the aims of the meeting." The article also reported that, whatever "uproar" might have been observed by *The Age*, the motion to form the National Council was carried by 71 votes to 20.[62] The daily record book of the Deaf Society (probably kept by James Johnston) carried an almost identical account, adding that the interpreter for the meeting was Abraham. It also claimed that the motion to form the National Council was "carried with applaud [sic],"[63] in contrast to *The Age*, which had described it as being carried "amidst uproar."

The editors of *The Deaf Advocate* wrote at length about this infamous meeting—their most eloquent comment was another sardonic verse offered for "a little community singing."

> There is a home of pure delight,
> It's called "The Society":
> Where deaf and hearing never fight—
> They have such harmony!
> The hearing help the deaf along—

> When views are in accord.
> Could heaven possess a happier throng
> Than Alf's harmonic Board?[64]

They were clearly in no doubt that this new National Council of the Deaf and Dumb was merely the Deaf societies in another guise.

The following night, as originally planned, Hersee addressed the Victorian branch of the AAAD, denouncing the National Council of the Deaf and Dumb as a "sham and a mockery."[65] An anonymous correspondent for *The Deaf Advocate* pointed out that although Hersee had gone to hear Gladwin speak, Gladwin and his cohorts did not put in an appearance at the AAAD meeting. However, the *Advocate*'s correspondent revealed that the Deaf Society hired a professional shorthand writer to attend the AAAD meeting and prepare a transcript of the proceedings for them. No one was aware of this at the meeting, and the shorthand writer would probably have been mistaken for a newspaper reporter. The correspondent sent *The Deaf Advocate* a copy of the shorthand writer's bill (for four guineas) and demanded to know who had authorized all the expenditure (Gladwin's trip to Melbourne, the newspaper advertising for their meeting, and the shorthand writer) from "the funds of the deaf."[66]

Henry Gladwin himself provided an account of his Melbourne visit in a number of letters to W. R. Kingwell in Queensland. He adopted (or genuinely professed) an air of vagueness about the AAAD.

> I have to-day returned from Melbourne where some ten days have been spent in assisting the Victorian Society who are just now undergoing perplexing times owing to the presence there of Hersee who is trying to form a federal branch of a new Deaf Advancement Federation the purpose of which appears to be to make a split in Victoria.[67]

Because the AAAD had been active for a year in NSW and six months in Victoria, Gladwin was either unusually ignorant or deliberately disingenuous. In a more formal letter, sent a few weeks later and requesting the Queensland Mission to call a public meeting of their deaf members to support the formation of the National Council of the Deaf and Dumb, he elaborated,

> From details received anent another meeting held in Melbourne on the 16th March, and addressed by Mr. Hersee under the auspices

of a body unknown to me, named the Australian Association for Advancement of the Deaf, I conclude this new move was to be the disruptive instrument to create a split amongst the Victorian Deaf. Fortunately, the Society's National Council was able to frustrate these designs.[68]

Whether he was being deceptive or merely unworldly, Gladwin's letters indicate the depth of the Deaf Societies' fear of "splits" and breakaways, and the perceived importance of the new National Council as a strategy for "frustrating" the AAAD and protecting the Deaf societies.

The AAAD Resists

The AAAD members did not need this public confrontation to make them aware that their organization's role was contested by the Deaf societies. Their 1933 writings were full of references to "difficulties" and avowals of unity and determination in the face of opposition. Martha Overend Wilson wrote soon after the public clash in Melbourne, "The A.A.A.D. could have no greater tribute paid to its standing and spirit than the character and methods of the opposition."[69] John Bourke alleged, "The deaf of one of the States were favourable to the A.A.A.D. but one of its opponents got amongst them and tried to turn them against it."[70] William Crush attacked "unworthy outside criticism, founded on deliberate misrepresentation," although he insisted it had "unit[ed] us together more solidly and has increased our strength, faith and confidence."[71] There was recognition that they would be faced with continuing struggles—Wilson referred to their fundraising as filling "the war chest."[72] Doggedly optimistic, she wrote in mid-1933, "We have met with wonderful success in spite of difficulties. The ideals and spirit of our Association have taken a strong hold."[73]

Being forced to defend themselves so quickly seems also to have helped AAAD members define what made their organization different from the National Council of the Deaf and Dumb. Crush declared,

> The A.A.A.D. is an independent self-supporting organisation, founded and controlled by the deaf themselves, and is the only National Association in Australia in which the deaf have a full, free and unfettered right to advance their own interests.[74]

In another defining statement, *The Deaf Advocate* presented a laborious acrostic for the letters spelling "Australian Association for the

Advancement of the Deaf": "**A** United **S**incere **T**rustworthy **R**adiant **A**ssociation **L**ifting **I**nto **A** Natural . . . **A**nd **S**plendid **S**phere **O**ur Comrades' **I**n **A**dversity **T**his Institution **O**rganised **N**ationally . . . Forms **O**rderly **R**ules . . . **T**hat **H**elp **E**veryone . . . **A**nd **D**efies **V**ulgar **A**nd **N**oxious **C**ouncils **E**ngineering **M**ischief **E**xpounding **N**onsense **T**o . . . **O**ur Friends . . . **T**hat **H**elpfully **E**ncourage . . . **D**eaf **E**agerly **A**ttempting **F**reedom."[75]

Their attacks on the twin National Councils became more provocative, or possibly they seem this way, because so many were filtered through *The Deaf Advocate* and its fearless editors. In the July 1933 issue, the *Advocate* editors accused the National Council of Societies of being undemocratic in not consulting with deaf people about its plans, comparing its shadowy leaders to the emerging dictators of the era—Mussolini in Italy and Hitler in Germany.[76]

By April 1933, just one year after its establishment, the AAAD claimed more than 400 deaf members, and seemed confident and determined to forge ahead.[77] As Bourke declared,

> The A.A.A.D. was formed not by any hole and corner policy but out in the open and with clean hands . . . .
>
> Those who form the so-called hearing Council cannot be really interested in the deaf. If they were they would encourage the A.A.A.D. and not try to break it up. For who can object to the deaf forming an association to advance their interests? The deaf in every part of the world form similiar [sic] associations to help and protect one another . . . .
>
> We who formed the A.A.A.D. are in the right, and we are going straight ahead.[78]

The National Council of the Deaf and Dumb's First Year

After the March 1933 meeting in Melbourne, where the establishment of the National Council of Societies and the National Council of the Deaf and Dumb was voted on, Abraham used some of the regular Thursday night gatherings at the Victorian Society to further the cause. These gatherings usually started with a prayer meeting in the church, followed by a "lecturette" in the assembly hall, then other activities, such as games, small committee meetings, and supper. Just one week after the March 15th public meeting, on Thursday March 23rd, the daily record book noted that Abraham gave a lecturette on the "National

Council of the Deaf."[79] The record book also noted a meeting on May 7th to discuss a proposed conference of the National Council in Sydney that Christmas. A "provisional committee" met on May 18th and June 1st, but no other meetings related to the National Council of the Deaf and Dumb were recorded for that year.[80] As for the proposed National Council of Adult Deaf and Dumb Societies, there are no details about its actual formation—the societies seemed to be focused instead on the strategic establishment of the National Council of the Deaf and Dumb (NCDD).

A national sports carnival was scheduled in Sydney over the Christmas and New Year period at the end of 1933. Both the AAAD and the NCDD announced that they would hold conferences at this time too. The sports carnivals, which were enormously popular with deaf people, were controlled by the Deaf societies, and they made use of this "ownership" to debar teams from the breakaway associations in NSW and Queensland from participating. This would have meant that many of the younger and less politically inclined deaf people would have been drawn more easily to the conference of the NCDD than that of the AAAD, because its conference was connected with the busy sports and social program of the sports carnival.

The NCDD's conference was called a *congress* (in line with the congresses of the old ADDA) and was held at the premises of the Deaf Society on Elizabeth Street in central Sydney. Alfred Lonsdale presided at the opening, and a congress committee was elected, comprising the deaf representatives of each state with James Johnston (of Victoria) as chairman and Samuel Phillips (of NSW) as acting honorary secretary.[81] The evening was then given over to "the reading of a paper on 'A Survey of the Position of the Adulf [sic] Deaf,' by the Principal of the Victorian Adult Deaf and Dumb Society" (Abraham).[82]

The congress met only on two evenings (the days being taken up with sport), and on the final evening, a number of recommendations were presented and adopted. They confirmed that the preferred name for the organization was the National Council of the Deaf and Dumb. The then-current state representatives were to become a temporary council for the following year and be responsible for drawing up a draft constitution "on the lines of the extinct Adult Deaf and Dumb Association [sic]," to be approved at another congress the following Christmas. Unlike the AAAD, whose membership was open to "all Deaf persons in Australia," the National Council proposed to restrict membership to "deaf ex-pupils of Australian schools for the deaf"—a move that would have excluded migrants or late-deafened people, such as Bourke, Crush, Lambert, and Wilson. Associate membership was to be extended to "hearing sympathisers" and "the deafened" who had demonstrated their active involvement with the Deaf community; however, "any hearing benefactor officer of any Adult Deaf and Dumb Society" could become an active member on the advice of the NCDD (without paying the higher subscription fee that the AAAD required).[83] This would have ensured that hearing men, like Abraham and Lonsdale, could have become voting members if they so desired. But even if they preferred to wait on the sidelines, two other recommendations ensured that the NCDD would have to work with them.

> That the present Chairmen and Superintendents of Incorporated Adult Deaf & Dumb Societies of Australia be and are here elected Honorary Advisers to the National Council of the Deaf for a period of twelve months.
>   That this Council consults, co-operates, and acts with the National Council of the Adult Deaf and Dumb Societies upon all matters in relation to the work of Adult Deaf and Dumb Societies and the National well being of the Deaf.[84]

The congress also passed some resolutions, urging the NSW government to make education compulsory for deaf children as other states did, to work toward the development of vocational training for Deaf people, and most significantly

> That this Congress deplores the fact that other organisations for the Adult Deaf, with seemingly identical objectives as existing Societies, have been established in N.S.W. and Queensland, and strongly urges upon the Adult Deaf and Dumb Societies of New South Wales and Queensland to take such action as will bring to an end these detrimental conditions affecting the general well being of the Deaf.[85]

The AAAD Congress

The AAAD also held a congress in Sydney over the Christmas 1933 period, in the rooms of the NSW Association, away from the excitement of the sports carnival. Many more papers were read and discussed at this congress than at that of the NCDD—John Paul presented one on "Vocational Training for the Deaf," Alf Eaton on "The Deaf in their Own Association," Martha Overend Wilson on "Thirty Years Work for the Deaf," Fletcher Booth on "The Deaf Citizen," and Frank Martin on "Trades for the Deaf."[86] *The Deaf Advocate* noted that some South Australian members were in attendance and hoped to form a branch in their own state (although this does not seem to have happened).[87]

The paper presented by Alf Eaton, an active deaf member of the Queensland breakaway Association, was a remarkably prescient analysis of the problems facing the AAAD and the high standards of organization, conduct, fundraising, and public relations required to meet these challenges.[88] The influence of John Paul is evident throughout, particularly in the insistence that Australia needed to catch up with developments in other countries, and that the AAAD needed to be brought into "co-operation with, and knowledge of, the world wide deaf interests."[89] Eaton sternly called for deaf members to "back their Association with their money" by establishing a Foundation Fund, and warned against "sentimental appeals for unity" instead of genuine "unity of effort." He reminded members, "We set out to do this work. Opposition came into the field BECAUSE we took up the cause of the deaf." He considered this placed greater responsibility on them to succeed, because if they failed, they would be ceding control to a "clique" and a "dictatorship," and "[t]hat means the position is worse." Such responsibility meant there was no time to be wasted on "enmity and bitterness" (he could well have had Bourke in mind). The AAAD needed to work for all deaf people, not only its members. "Every difficulty, wrong, injustice, loss or harm that comes to any deaf person is the business of all of us . . . . We must be loyal to their interests, whether they are with us or not."[90]

* * *

Despite this inspiring call to action, or perhaps because of the enormity of the task it hinted at, things did not go smoothly for the AAAD in 1934. "Defections and other difficulties" were mentioned in *The Deaf Advocate* reports, probably due to the efforts of the Deaf societies and the NCDD.[91] A new Federal Executive Committee took over during that year, after some "objection to the methods used [by the old Executive] and the need to uphold the provisions of the Constitution."[92] Alf Eaton became the new president, with Jack Allardice, another Queenslander, replacing Martha Overend Wilson as honorary secretary. Wilson's chatty pieces for the *Advocate* ceased, although she continued her involvement with the Queensland branch. *The Deaf Advocate* itself changed—it became a bimonthly rather than a monthly magazine, and the two deaf editors moved on. Ernest Quinnell had become a collector, and Booth "relinquished the position, owing to his leaving Sydney to take up residence in the Mountains."[93] Hersee took on the role of editor in October 1934, but obviously had less time to devote to it—after that point, *The Deaf Advocate* relied more on reprinting articles from other sources and received fewer letters and news items from other states. It carried no further reports of the AAAD after the August-September issue in 1934.[94] It thus becomes more difficult to follow the AAAD's fortunes without this regular item written for a broad audience.

At the second annual general meeting of the Victorian branch of the AAAD that year, they were still being forced to defend and explain their role.

> The acting president (Mrs. M. Gladman) said the association was not, as many thought, a new club started in opposition to the Adult Deaf and Dumb Society, but had been founded by the deaf themselves to further the highest needs and aspirations of the deaf. It was not doing the work which the society was supposed to do, but, like a trades union, was intended to safeguard the interests of its members.[95]

At this meeting, their membership was seventy-two (compared to "well over a hundred" two years previously). Their accounts showed a deficit, largely due to the need to rent meeting rooms, because the Deaf Society still refused to let the organization meet in its premises.[96]

Another account of this meeting was published in *The Age* by a reporter who was more interested in the novelty of deaf people's rules of order than in the topics under discussion.

> Silence to visitors somewhat oppressive in its intensity prevailed throughout the annual meeting of the Association for the Advancement of the Deaf at 174 Collins-street last night. For the person possessing the faculty of hearing there was something at once poignant and inspiring in the cheerful and orderly conduct of the business by the brisk signs and facial expressions of the members. The lady president secured attention not by rapping the table, but by switching the lights off, and her audience could have been recognised as sufferers from grave disability only by the intent look customary to those who are unable to hear. They smiled cheerfully at jokes and applauded silently.[97]

But even this reporter noted that "the meeting revealed a rift between the two organisations striving to ameliorate the conditions of sufferers from deafness, a dispute which in the interests of all parties should be speedily settled." It seemed the Victorian branch of the AAAD was branded with an image of an organization that existed chiefly to oppose the Deaf Society. Bourke, whose campaign against Abraham and the Society continued, was probably in large part responsible for this.

A Grand Congress for the National Council of the Deaf and Dumb

The NCDD was sporadically active during 1934, mainly in Melbourne. Henry Gladwin followed up the Sydney congress by writing to all Deaf Society boards a few weeks later, informing them of the names of their state deaf representatives to the NCDD and advising them that these deaf representatives were required to "consult, co-operate and act with" the National Council. He warned that "the Council of the Deaf can only be kept alive by a stimulus from our own National Council."[98] The new chairman and secretary of the NCDD, James Johnston and Samuel Phillips, seemed to agree with this sentiment. They sent letters to the superintendents and chairmen of all the Deaf societies, inviting them to become honorary advisory officers to the NCDD and declaring

> We fully appreciate the magnificient [sic] work of the Adult Societies and are convinced that only by co-operation with these bodies can the real social status of the Deaf be advanced.[99]

Ironically, their new letterhead had a slogan at the bottom proclaiming "The only Australian organisation controlled by the Deaf." (Probably in response to this, the Queensland branch of the AAAD proclaimed in its annual report that year: "The A.A.A.D. is NOT controlled by or acting under any other Society, Mission or Federation. It is the Only Free Association for the Australian Deaf . . . . We are not compelled to accept officers of Societies or Missions to control our business.")[100]

The NSW Deaf Society's Executive Committee noted in February 1934 that deaf people there had formed a NCDD branch, but included no details about its composition or plans.[101] In March, a meeting was held at the Deaf Society in Melbourne, at which Johnston gave a report about the recent Sydney congress. At this meeting, they formed a Victorian branch of the NCDD and elected a committee of ten members.[102] This committee met in July and again in December, when they discussed the draft constitution and program for the forthcoming congress.[103] There is little or no information about NCDD activities in other states, although Johnston sent the draft constitution and Program to the various state representatives in September 1934.[104]

There was some anxiety among the Deaf societies about whether the Melbourne conference of the NCDD would actually happen, and the boards were urged to cover the costs of deaf representatives if necessary. An article in the NSW Society's magazine, *The Silent Messenger*, stressed, "Can we urge each State Board to make it possible for a number of their deaf to visit Melbourne."[105] Abraham used more forceful exhortations, writing to the Queensland Mission in October,

> I have received a letter from your Mr. Lack in which he says no Queensland deaf will be attending the Congress & Festivities to be held in Melbourne at Christmas. I hope this is not a definite decision. Under existing conditions in the deaf and dumb world it would be most unfortunate if your Mission is not represented at the National Council of the Deaf and its Congress. There are three Queensland representatives on this National Council & its in the best interests of the Queensland Mission that they be present at the Congress. Together with the members of the Council of other states, I understand, they are engaged in drawing up a Constitution to be submitted. We hope that your Mission will see your way to arrange for the representation of its organisation by the deaf.[106]

Abraham's letter made it clear that he considered the creation of the NCDD to be in the Deaf societies' best interests and the deaf representatives to be emissaries of the societies.

The Melbourne conference did proceed, along with an accompanying program of games and festivities held to celebrate Melbourne's centenary year in 1935. The conference was lifted out of the ordinary by being held at the Exhibition Building, one of Melbourne's grandest public buildings, which had been the site of Australia's first parliament after the country's federation in 1901. It is very likely that Abraham had worked to secure this venue, instead of following tradition and holding the event at the Deaf Society's premises, as a way to attract publicity and raise the profile of the NCDD—especially in relation to the AAAD, which held a small national meeting in Melbourne at the same time, in much humbler premises—Central House on Collins Street.[107]

The Exhibition Building in Melbourne, site of the National Council for the Deaf and Dumb conference in 1934–1935.
State Library of Victoria.

The NCDD seems to have adopted the proposed constitution that had been prepared and distributed in September (although no record of its adoption, or any amendments, survives). This constitution had modified the rules for membership developed at the previous congress, stating only that "membership . . . shall consist of deaf and dumb people domiciled in the Commonwealth of Australia who are ex-pupils of any school for the deaf and dumb."[108] The congress further determined, "Newcomers to Australia, from the British Empire only, shall be entitled to membership after twelve months' residence in Australia."[109] Although the draft constitution had used the name "The Commonwealth Association of the Deaf and Dumb," this name does not seem to have been adopted, and the organization was always referred to as the National Council of the Deaf and Dumb. The new constitution was very similar to that of the old ADDA, and was notable for its dense and legalistic language, especially compared to the more streamlined and accessible constitution of the AAAD.

The conference's only discussion of more general issues seems to have been in a presentation by a Victorian deaf man, E. Johnson (not J. M. Johnston), who addressed the gathering on the barriers deaf people faced in the workforce, such as their lack of access to technical training. He also suggested that deaf people should be exempted from joining trade unions and participating in strikes, as "with their disability in conversing and exchanging ideas with others, they were liable to be misled." Johnson also objected, like generations of deaf people before and after him, to the rise of oralism in the education of deaf children. He declared, "All deaf children should be taught the manual system. The oral system would never allow a deaf persons [sic] to understand a sermon or a lecture."[110]

The conference evidently discussed the AAAD and its annoying tirades against their Council, and passed a motion by Samuel Phillips of NSW, in which attendees "emphatically protested against published statements to the effect that the deaf people were 'brow-beaten and neglected' by the council," declaring that, "such statements came only from a small and discontented body of the Deaf."[111] The congress passed a resolution affirming that the NCDD was "composed of and controlled by deaf and dumb persons only."[112]

The conference was described in *The Age* each day, although one article was possibly by the same naïve reporter who had written about the AAAD branch's annual general meeting the previous June. This time, the reporter was so taken with the novelty of sign language that he neglected to say anything at all about the conference's content. At this "noiseless conference," he marvelled, "[T]here was scarcely a sound in the room," and "the speakers showed remarkable dexterity in making the requisite motions of the fingers and hands" as they went about their business.[113] Johnston, who had used his "vocal power" to interpret the proceedings for the reporter, must have felt that he had wasted his breath.

This conference, with its splendid venue and admiring press coverage, seems to have been the last real activity of the NCDD. No further correspondence has survived, no more national congresses or meetings of the Victorian state branch were listed in the daily record books of the Victorian Society (where its chairman, J. M. Johnston, worked), and no other state branches appear to have been active. Although the AAAD continued to refer to "opposition," and some further records may yet emerge, the National Council of the Deaf and Dumb seems to have effectively disappeared after December 1934, less than two years after its formation. Its work had largely been done—the AAAD was in disarray and on the defensive. As John Bourke wrote later of the Deaf societies, "[T]hey formed the Council for the purpose of drawing into it all the deaf who are under their influence, in order to prevent them joining up with the . . . Association."[114]

The AAAD Falters

The AAAD gathering that was held in Melbourne that Christmas found it hard to compete with its splendid rival. The few accounts of the gathering suggest that the organization was becoming isolated and defensive, and was struggling to retain its members. It was not an official conference, but rather a single meeting hosted by the Victorian branch of the AAAD, for visitors from around the country. Visitors attended from every state except Western Australia, but the papers were all presented by Victorians—Mrs. Gladman (the president of the Victorian branch), Bourke, Lambert, and one or two others.[115]

The Melbourne *Herald*, publishing an announcement of the meeting, said the following:

> Having dissociated itself from all other associations and organisations, the Australian Association for the Advancement of the Deaf (Victorian branch) will hold a special meeting at Central House, 174 Collins Street, tonight.
>
> Papers will be read by deaf members, and an explanation given of the difference between the aims of the association and those of other organisations for the deaf.[116]

This suggests that the AAAD was beginning to see itself solely in terms of its opposition to other organizations, and was losing its focus on a grand vision for uniting Australian deaf people. It is also possible that this view may only have been that of the more battle-weary Victorian branch, rather the whole organization. The honorary secretary of the Victorian branch later described the meeting as "a most encouraging gathering," which showed that with "a little more local support we would achieve our objective of forming a branch whose strength would benefit all."[117] The Victorian branch was still in existence, so this statement can probably be interpreted to mean that it was declining and struggling to reclaim relevance.

The backdrop to these competing gatherings of deaf people over Christmas 1934 was similar to that of a carnival, with a games program and social gatherings, as well as meetings of the rival bodies. At the New Year's Eve dinner for the combined National Councils, Abraham was making the most of being on his home turf. Not all guests, however, were happy to let him enjoy the limelight. An interpreter from the NSW contingent, Ella Doran, wrote,

> Each State's leader or captain spoke and Mr Abraham made most of the interpretation back and forth. Finally Mr Lonsdale rose to make his remarks for New South Wales. He didn't want Mr Abraham to sign for him and asked me to rise.
>
> I thought it wrong as we were guests and Mr Abraham was the official host, but I rose and began to pass on [interpret] Mr Lonsdale's talk. Mr Abraham interjected and said he was capable of better work then [sic] I was, anyway it was not women's work. "No lady would do such a thing." It was not the kind of situation that I wanted to occur over me, so I sat down with Mr Lonsdale breathing fire across my head. No-one was telling the deaf what was going on between them. After a few more remarks things settled down as Mr Abraham wanted. A few minutes later he asked his granddaughter to rise as he wished her to present the Cricketer's Shield with a few words on her hands. If I wasn't a lady, I didn't think his granddaughter was either; so I got up and walked out of the room . . . .
>
> Next morning Miss Empson, secretary to Mr Abraham, telephoned to say he would like me to come in and have morning tea with him so that I could see what he had meant the evening before. I refused.[118]

Abraham's disarming invitation to morning tea the next day is consistent with the strategies he used with people like Bourke—he had no qualms about humiliating people in public, but would make a point of trying to win them back to his fold afterwards.

Struggles and Setbacks

During the following two years, the AAAD continued to lose momentum. The NSW branch does not appear to have been very active, although the branches in Victoria and Queensland continued to meet and publish annual reports. The Federal Executive Committee seems to have been centred in Queensland, and Queensland was also the only state that contributed funds to the federal body.[119] As *The Deaf Advocate* became a quarterly (rather than bimonthly) magazine during 1935, the amount and quality of information about the AAAD declined.

The third annual report of the Victorian branch of the AAAD in 1935 showed an organization in difficulties. The honorary secretary, R. H. Lambert, described "two tremendous set-backs" for the branch during 1934–35—the "deliberate denial" to them of meeting rooms at the Deaf Society forcing them to pay for the hire of rooms for meetings and socials, and the "organisation of well-trained opposition formed particularly to mislead public opinion in respect to the A.A.A.D."[120] This obviously referred to the NCDD and their meetings during the conference and carnival the previous Christmas. These setbacks, combined with an "unfriendly atmosphere prevailing in Victoria . . . towards the A.A.A.D." meant that their membership had dropped from seventy-two to a mere twenty-six. Two of their meetings had to be adjourned because of the lack of a quorum.[121] They were determined to keep going, however, and continued to reject the tactics of the Society and its appeal to charity.

> Every set-back during the progress of the local A.A.A.D. is a spur to the higher endeavour of success which should be of certain help in building the A.A.A.D. its conspicious [sic] signpost of protection of the welfare of the deaf and dumb. The display of the affliction of the deaf before the public is <u>FATAL</u> to the welfare of the deaf.[122]

Lambert, like many others associated with the AAAD, placed his faith in the "educated deaf" and suggested that it was the "uneducated" who were most susceptible to the manipulations of the Deaf Society[123]

The Queensland branch's annual report that year also reported problems, although it was more optimistic.

> We believe that the difficulties which the Association has passed through during the last year have provided a splendid test as to the honesty of purpose, loyalty to the members' interests and rights, proper methods of management, and an intelligent carrying out of the work of the Association.
>
> The progress made during the year has proved that those who refused to desert the cause of the Deaf have every reason to be satisfied that loyalty has proved the better course . . . .[124]

The strong early voice of the AAAD, full of optimism and conviction, was becoming muffled and defensive. Members were obviously wearied by desertions, internal dissension, and lack of direction.

The establishment of these competing organizations can be seen as an outgrowth of earlier movements in Australian Deaf history. The Australasian Deaf and Dumb Association, begun in 1904, had established a precedent for a national organization in line with those of other countries. The growth of Deaf societies and the disaffection of some of their members, individual protests, small group opposition, and the successful establishment of breakaway organizations in two states had prepared the way for the Australian Association for the Advancement of the Deaf. The reactions of many people associated with the Deaf societies to the earlier conflicts, and the strategies they had developed to contain those protests, led to the National Councils and set the stage for the conflicts that ensued.

At the time, there were a variety of explanations for these rapid developments in the Australian Deaf community in the late 1920s and '30s. People in the Deaf societies downplayed the upheaval as the work of a few individual troublemakers, such as this commentator from the NSW Society:

> [Hersee] deliberately worked on the excitable nature of the D. & D. [Deaf and Dumb] to such an extent that after he had been with us for less than a year some of them thought that they should have practically full control . . . .[125]

This differed, of course, from the explanations of those who worked to establish the breakaways and the AAAD, who tended to explain the changes as organic and inevitable.

> Great changes for the better came to pass. These changes were not the work of rebellion against their own good as the societies are always telling the world; they are the natural result of the work done among the Deaf in the last forty years—natural results of the march of education with the light as natural as the tides of the sea, and as little subject to human control.[126]

Other commentators, such as John Paul, adopted a broader perspective, observing succinctly that "Totalitarianism . . . is always reflected in having no faith in the powers or possibilities of ordinary folk."[127]

There are many possible reasons for the limited success of these organizations, although reasons attributed retrospectively are usually colored by the ideological views of the time. Some may consider that deaf people were "not ready" for such national responsibilities; others may explain their difficulties solely in terms of the sophisticated opposition they received from the Deaf societies. Such explanations do not fully account for the complexities of these events; the many deaf people who demonstrated perception, commitment, and willingness to work toward greater autonomy; and their many hearing supporters and well-wishers. It seems reasonably clear that all of the newly formed organizations became too focused on their conflicts with each other and did not always keep sight of their original objectives or develop clear strategies for advancement. However, people such as Wilson, Eaton, Booth, Bourke, Paul, and Hersee, among many others, articulated a sustained vision for the Australian Deaf community and its future, and tried to bring it to fruition.

Reflecting the political events of the wider community, the early 1930s were some of the most fertile years of political activism in the history of the Australian Deaf community. Over the next few years, almost all of these new organizations—breakaways and national bodies—were to disappear.

7

All to No Purpose

*Every agent . . . has his tragic tale to tell you of his sad experience in the
Colonial Office.*

—THOMAS CARLYLE, "LATTER-DAY PAMPHLETS"

AS IN MANY western countries, there was a general climate of conserva-
tism and repression in Australia during the late 1930s and early 1940s,
and events in the Deaf community reflected this to a degree. The Australian government in the 1930s cracked down on dissident groups,
such as communists, limiting access to public meeting halls and street
gatherings and placing restrictions on the kinds of material that could
be sent through the mail.[1] Censorship was strict, and Australian writers
had difficulty publishing works dealing with controversial topics, such
as Aboriginal–white relationships.[2] Refugees from repressive regimes
in Europe were accepted with reluctance, and Jewish refugees had to
pay exorbitant landing fees. Australian government officials were not
averse to expressing their admiration for some of the fascist movements
in Europe and clamped down on groups, such as Italian anti-fascists in
Australia, who attempted to attack them.[3]

On the other hand, deaf people in many countries, including Australia, benefited from the labor shortages created by the Second World
War—like women, they were recruited to fill jobs left vacant by the men
who left home to fight. Unemployment and underemployment were
greatly reduced in Deaf communities in Australia during the 1940s.
The Deaf Society in NSW, for example, reported in 1942, "Before the
outbreak of the war large numbers were unemployed, but this year we
cannot place our hands on one unemployed deaf and dumb person
who is able to work. In every case those employed are receiving full

award wages."[4] These newly comfortable circumstances affected deaf people's involvement in the wider community and reduced their reliance on the services provided by Deaf societies.

Some of the decline in political activism in Australian Deaf communities during the late 1930s and beyond may be attributed to these wider influences, and some (such as the disappearance of the New South Wales Association of Deaf and Dumb Citizens) was triggered by changes in government legislation. It was also likely that the small Deaf communities in most Australian states were wearied by the energy required to maintain opposition to the Deaf societies and grew tired of the continuing negativity. One person who never tired of it was John Bourke.

Bourke's Continuing Campaign

Although Bourke was an enthusiastic supporter of Deaf community initiatives, such as the establishment of the Australian Association for the Advancement of the Deaf (AAAD) and the Deaf editorship of *The Victorian Deaf News*, during the 1930s he continued to wage his own campaign against the Adult Deaf and Dumb Society of Victoria and particularly against superintendent Ernest Abraham. Bourke kept the Society under the eye of government agencies, such as the Charities Board, but he also acquired a reputation as a crank. His campaign eventually damaged the AAAD and alienated him from many people he sought to influence.

Although Bourke had been a regular contributor to *The Deaf Advocate*, he also wrote more detailed information for a wider audience. He self-published a number of booklets during the 1930s and is also likely to have been responsible for the appearance of articles criticizing the Deaf Society in other newspapers, such as one in the Communist Party's paper *The Worker's Voice*.[5] This article described the Deaf Society as being run by "capitalists and their friends," and concluded,

> it is no wonder that considerable numbers of deaf people look upon it as a Society for their subjection not their protection, but then where is there ever a people suffering from affliction who are not taken advantage of by capitalists and their agents.[6]

Bourke acknowledged with disappointment that his booklets did not reach a large audience; in fact, he gave most of them away, and very few of the influential public figures he targeted made any significant response.[7] He had occasional successes, such as when humanitarian and politician Dr. W. R. Maloney, M.H.R., attended the Deaf Society's 1935 annual general meeting, brandishing one of Bourke's booklets and calling for an inquiry into the Society's management.[8] However, such successes were rare exceptions.

Bourke sought analogies from contemporary world affairs in his critiques of the Deaf Society. When he deplored the fact that the Society's board members were not elected, he compared the situation with that of colonized nations (anticipating some modern uses of colonialism in analysing deaf people's experiences): "[W]e adult deaf of Victoria, like the natives of India, Egypt, and South Africa do not elect those who govern us." He compared the Society's constitution with those of contemporary dictatorships: "If the Germans or the Italians have State Constitutions they must be something like this."[9] He regularly used such comparisons and references to literary texts, such as Dickens' novels, to highlight key themes of oppression and injustice in his writing.

The New South Wales Association of Deaf and Dumb Citizens

The New South Wales (NSW) government revised its Charitable Collections Act in 1934, making it virtually impossible for more than one organization to be registered to collect subscriptions from the public for a particular cause or group of people in need. The following year, they wrote to charitable organizations, informing them of the new definitions and inviting them to apply for registration or exemption under the Act.[10] Both the NSW Association of Deaf and Dumb Citizens and the Adult Deaf and Dumb Society applied for registration. They each received a reply from the Chief Secretary's Department, advising them of the other organization's application and of the department's wish to avoid "overlapping and duplication of effort." They were informed

> I am desired by the Minister to suggest that the governing bodies of both organisations should make an effort to effect a fusion or amalgamation as this is considered to be the best means of eliminating the possibility of duplication. Furthermore, such a fusion or amalgamation would be in the best interests of the deaf and dumb as well as charitably minded people on whom the institutions are largely dependent.[11]

This set the scene for a long-drawn-out process of amalgamation between the two organizations. After the request from the Chief Secretary's Department, a meeting was set up between the two organizations on February 13, 1936. The Deaf society sent board members Lake, Mortlock, and Dey as their representatives, and the Association's council appointed Alfred Winn, Gordon Winn, and the Reverend Edgar Potter as their delegates.[12] All of these men were hearing.

The Association proposed that both organizations be dissolved, and a new one established, with a provisional committee and an outside chairman. They stipulated that deaf members should have majority representation on this committee and the right to vote. These proposals were quite unacceptable to the Deaf Society, whose principal concern seemed to be that Herbert Hersee have no role in the new combined organization—which they assumed would be the Society, with the addition of the members and assets of the Association.[13]

The Deaf Society wrote to the chief secretary a few weeks later, setting out their objections to the Association's proposal. It is difficult not to see their arguments as those of wealthy and privileged hearing men alarmed at the prospect of losing their power. They considered that the public contributed money to the Society because of the "high standing in the community of those who comprise the Patrons, Officers, and members."[14] They described the Society's assets in detail and used these to strengthen their hand, declaring, "It is quite impossible for this Society to give equal representation to an organisation with only one-fiftieth part of the Society's Capital." (There was no acknowledgment of the fact that much of this capital had been raised by deaf collectors.) They also protested the impossibility of allowing deaf people to have a majority on any governing body, or of allowing deaf people to vote (because they would always form the majority of the organization's members).

> With our knowledge of world wide conditions, we are convinced that this Society must maintain it's [sic] present form of administration, and cannot be a party to forming an organisation to be controlled by a Council with a balance of power in favour of the Adult Deaf & Dumb.[15]

The Society insisted that the split between the two organizations was due only to a dispute with their former welfare officer (Hersee) and that "the adult deaf and dumb did not ask for any alteration in the management of this Society, nor have they made any such suggestion since."[16] This last statement is contradicted by almost any reading of the events of the time.

Due to this stalemate, a conference was arranged between three representatives of each organization, chaired by a government representative (a Mr. Quigley), and held on May 25, 1936. The Deaf Society sent
Alfred Lonsdale (their general secretary and superintendent) and William Brooks (their president) to accompany Mr. Dey this time, and the
Association's representatives were the same. Once again, they were all
hearing men. A transcript of this conference survives and is a revealing
record of the participants' attitudes and tactics.[17]

Both organizations strenuously objected to being "swamped" by the
other, rather than amalgamated. However, the Association's representatives seem to have accepted that their preferred option of forming a
new organization was not realistic, and that their task was to argue for
the best deal they could get before the inevitable re-absorption of their
Association into the Deaf Society. The debate centered on the accom-
modations the Society should make in the process. One issue was the
number of Association representatives who should be given places on
the Society's council and Executive Committee. They eventually nego-
tiated it down to six Association members on the Society's council (out
of a total of sixteen)—three deaf and three hearing. The Society was
willing to accept three hearing people from the Association on its Executive Committee (out of a total of nine) —but no deaf people. Although
the Association initially reacted to this offer with indignation, they
eventually accepted it.[18]

The Association insisted that deaf people should be eligible to be
voting members of the amalgamated organization and argued that they
should pay a lower subscription fee. This was strenuously resisted by
the Society—Lonsdale alleged that deaf people were not "clamouring
for a right to vote" and had never done so.[19] He considered that if they
allowed deaf people to vote, "You would hand the whole thing over to
the deaf."[20] Gordon Winn drew a distinction between the kind of charity that needed to be fully administered (which he compared to the Red
Cross) and one where the members retained their autonomy. The latter
he compared to the YMCA.

> The charitable public supply the building but the people don't sub-
> mit to charity by becoming members and I think that applies to the
> deaf . . . The members are people who will decide for themselves
> whether they will belong to it and they are entitled to a vote.[21]

Winn maintained that it was reasonable for deaf people to expect to
vote in their organizations, "considering that three-fourths of them are

citizens who have a vote in the Government, who have a Municipal vote."[22]

Much discussion revolved around the perceived wealth of each organization. Although the Deaf Society used their buildings and other assets as bargaining chips, the Association tried to present a different model, with Reverend Potter maintaining, "[I]rrespective of buildings I suggest our organisation is as big as the Society and the charitable work we are doing is equal to the Society." Although the Society reiterated that they brought £38,000 worth of assets to the proposed amalgamation, A. Winn responded, "[T]hat belongs to the deaf." Potter agreed, pointing out, "[T]he £38,000 property was raised to a certain extent by our deaf" (i.e., deaf people then in the Association). Potter had evidently been giving this some thought, because he went on to insist, "Legally we have a claim. If you read up the case of the Wee Frees of Scotland—and they got it."[23] He was referring to a splinter group of the Free Church of Scotland. When this church amalgamated with another to form the United Free Church of Scotland in 1900, a disaffected portion of the original Free Church of Scotland broke away and were known as the "Wee Frees." This splinter group succeeded in making a legal claim for ownership of a proportion of the buildings of the United Free Church of Scotland, because they constituted part of its original membership.[24] Quigley, the government official, unfortunately cut short Potter's intriguing argument, and it was not pursued. This was a daring claim and a fundamental difference between the hearing men allied with the Deaf Society and the Association. The Society's men felt that the assets belonged to the organization and had been accumulated largely because of the status of men like themselves. The Association's men (although they were from the retail industry and the church) radically proposed that the assets belonged to the "workers" or those who had toiled to raise the money, and that the Society could not lay full claim to them. It would be interesting to know if this sentiment was shared by the deaf members of the Association and to contemplate what might have happened had they decided to pursue such a claim.

Although the participants in this conference seemed to try to maintain civility, there were occasional bursts of hostility. At one point, Potter, when asked to offer an "alternative suggestion" to the Deaf Society's proposals, snapped, "My alternative suggestion is that it is about time that the Society had a few modern ideas."[25] When Lonsdale declared once too often, "[T]he deaf cannot control the organisation," Gordon Winn replied, "We've had seven years to demonstrate that it is a workable plan."[26] The comments of the Association's representatives often defended the aspirations and achievements of their organization and demonstrate a palpable disappointment that it was all to disappear.

The Adult Deaf and Dumb Society was granted registration under the Charitable Collections Act in late 1936; however, it took several more months of letter-writing, meetings, and concessions from the Society before amalgamation took place in August 1937.[27] The Society finally agreed to reduce the membership fee for deaf people to five shillings, with full voting rights, and also promised to employ the Association's staff on a casual basis—with the exception of Hersee. Quigley had tried to persuade the Society to let bygones be bygones, that "the dead past should bury its dead," but they flatly refused to contemplate working with Hersee.[28] The Association's practice of having deaf people fill at least half of their council positions was not adopted and was not to happen again in Australian Deaf societies for more than fifty years.

Amid all the official letters and arguments between hearing men, the attitudes of the deaf people of NSW to the amalgamation are difficult to ascertain. The Deaf Society claimed that their deaf people were fully in favor of the amalgamation and did not wish to make significant changes to the way the Society was run. A few letters from the Society's Deaf Committee to the Chief Secretary survive, confirming this.[29] But no record survives of how the deaf members of the Association responded. The surviving papers of the Association during its final year or so are mostly brisk and official announcements of meetings to vote on the amalgamation proposals, "winding up" galas, the closing of banking services at the Association, and other such administrative matters. *The Deaf Advocate* ceased to appear, and the strong deaf voice of the early Association is almost impossible to discern.

Among the surviving Association correspondence are some terse letters to and from the Queensland Deaf and Dumb Citizens' Reformed Association.[30] John Paul wrote seeking confirmation that the NSW Association was about to close and requested that any correspondence from the Queensland Association be destroyed before papers were handed over to the Deaf Society. Hersee agreed on the condition that the Queensland Association also destroyed the NSW Association's correspondence. The letters convey no indication of their personal response to these events, other than that implicit in their agreement to keep their correspondence out of the Deaf Society's hands.

Alfred Lonsdale, notorious for his involvement in every aspect of the Deaf Society's affairs and satirized as "The Shadow" by *The Deaf Advocate*, absented himself from the final stages of the amalgamation negotiations. He went travelling in Europe from March to October 1937, leaving his brother E. J. Lonsdale (who had been on the Society's council for a few years) in charge during his absence. The tone of communications between the Society and the Association was more cordial during those months, and the final arrangements for the amalgamation seem to have been concluded amicably, suggesting that Alfred Lonsdale's absence reduced much of the friction. Indeed, the program for a "Unity Social" on August 6th included a tableau with a theatrical "proclamation" devised by the Reverend Potter.

> I do hereby proclaim, announce and certify that the deaf of this state, once divided into two kingdoms, though speaking the same language are now and from henceforth to be united into one great Empire, to be ruled over by one Monarch, whose name is "Harmony," whose laws shall be the laws of understanding and goodwill, forebearance and mutual friendship and whose citizens shall be accounted worthy to uphold the high traditions of that great brotherhood which is the foundation of all well being.[31]

During his visit to England that year, Alfred Lonsdale spent much of his time visiting Deaf missions, societies, and other centers, and he represented Australia at an International Congress of the Deaf and Dumb in Paris.[32] Undoubtedly one of the highlights of his visit would have been going to Buckingham Palace to be presented with a silver coronation medal "for his charitable work among the deaf mutes."[33] But he was home in time to join the early meetings of the newly amalgamated organization, and by January 1938 had resumed his position as general secretary and superintendent of the Deaf Society, with his brother chairman of the Executive Committee.[34] "The Shadow" had prevailed.

The rise and fall of the New South Wales Association for Deaf and Dumb Citizens offers a richly resourced case study of the articulation of Deaf independence, using the widely accepted model of "citizens." Their attempts were frustrated by the institutions of charity and government. A simple change in government legislation, easily reinforced by the socially accepted mores of charitable service, was able to shape the possibilities of Deaf communities and their organizations.

Hersee Departs

Herbert Hersee and his family sailed back to England after the amalgamation, their fares arranged by the Association before its closure. The Association members presented Hersee with an ornate certificate, recording their appreciation for his "splendid service" and "ready sympathy with the Deaf and Dumb" and giving him much of the credit for "the great success of our Association in securing fuller powers of self expression and more complete self-government for the Deaf and Dumb." They declared that they would "forever remain grateful" for his achievements with the Association, concluding,

> We . . . trust that your labours for the welfare of the Deaf and Dumb in another land may be crowned with that measure of success your skill and knowledge deserve.[35]

Hersee was never to work with deaf people again. He applied for positions with Deaf missions and societies when he returned to England, but could not secure one. J. W. Flynn, who met with an embittered Hersee in England in 1956, reported that Hersee believed Lonsdale had used his many visits to British Deaf centers in 1937 to turn people against him.[36] Although Hersee stayed in touch with some of the deaf people he had befriended in Sydney, he passed the rest of his career working for a church insurance company.[37]

The End of the AAAD

After the mid-1930s, the only active branches of the AAAD were in Queensland and Victoria, and they were faltering. The long-drawn out amalgamation of the NSW Association with the Society probably had a demoralizing effect on the AAAD. Not only did it deprive the AAAD of a public forum for its reports (with the disappearance of *The Deaf Advocate*), the amalgamation would also have highlighted the vulnerability of radical deaf movements in Australia and the seeming invincibility of their opponents.

The few remaining records do not present a cheerful picture. The Victorian branch's annual meeting for 1936 was reported in *The Age*, describing the branch's unsuccessful appeals to the Charities Board and the Premier's Department about the Adult Deaf and Dumb Society. The article also reported that the branch was calling on the Australian prime minister, Mr. Lyons, to emulate his British counterpart.

The British Prime Minister, in an appeal some years ago to the English public on behalf of the deaf and dumb, said: "I think it would be a good thing to investigate, in the light of modern circumstances, the whole condition of the deaf and dumb." The association would like to ask Mr. Lyons to make the same appeal to the public of the Commonwealth.[38]

There is a surviving copy of that newspaper article from among Abraham's papers, with his comments written in the margin. He noted in disgust,

> Extraordinary Attitude of "Age." . . . Practically the "Association" is dead. The only Officers are Bourke Woods Storey. The latter does not understand the objective of the Association and was talked into "office" against his wishes. I am of the opinion that there is not a dozen interested members and Bourke is only one capable of drawing up this "statement." Lambert dropped out. Others refused to take office.[39]

Apart from showing Abraham's attitude to the AAAD, these comments also indicate that the Victorian branch had declined significantly and had lost the support of previous stalwarts, such as Lambert. His comments, and the concerns described in the article in *The Age*, suggest that the Victorian branch was being commandeered by Bourke and his continuing campaign against the Deaf Society.

The Queensland branch's annual report for 1936 described "a year which has simply meant 'holding on.'" Not only was their own branch having great difficulties, they reported that "[s]erious breaks in the work of the Association as a whole have taken place . . . . There are those who wish to boss the Association and make it a machine for their own ends."[40] There can be little doubt that they were referring to J. P. Bourke in Victoria.

Bourke had become secretary-treasurer of the Victorian branch of the AAAD toward the end of 1935. Some of his familiar diatribes and letters about the Deaf Society and Abraham soon began to appear on AAAD branch letterhead, and he began to publicly define the AAAD in terms of its relationship to the Society: "Whereas an adult Deaf and Dumb Society is an organisation for looking after the welfare of the Adult Deaf; our Association is an instrument for seeing that this is properly attended to and the Society managed in an efficient manner."[41] This appropriation of the AAAD's role was not likely to be well received by other members of the organization, especially those in other states.

Martha Overend Wilson, around this time, sent an open letter to AAAD members. It may have been sent specifically to those in Victoria (possibly aimed at Bourke in particular), but it was a printed circular rather than a typed letter, so would seem to have been meant for wide distribution. She pleaded with members to show the "high idealism" of the early AAAD in their dealings with all deaf organizations, saying specifically, "This Association is not a tool which individuals can use to attack Societies." She urged people "not to combat individual wrong by bitterness and denunciations," or to "seek satisfaction for our own . . . personal quarrels, to the injury of the standing of our Association."[42] She characteristically called for many other virtues to be displayed as well, but her appeal was fundamentally similar to that of Alf Eaton in 1934, pointing out that the survival of the AAAD was dependent on members rising above petty arguments and demonstrating their commitment to the progress of the Deaf community as a whole.[43]

Wilson's appeal may have influenced some people, but it was not enough to save the Victorian branch of the AAAD. In its annual report for 1937, J. P. Bourke reported, "[W]e have to state that the most disheartening happening of 1937 was the closing of the branch by the Federal Executive of the Association. This was due, to use the words of the Executive, 'Because of continued unauthorised action of the branch.'"[44] Bourke was unrepentant, filling the rest of the annual report with another of his long spiels about the Deaf Society and its injustices and the valiant but unsuccessful efforts of the Victorian branch (of which he was probably the only active member by that stage) to seek justice. As Ernest Reynolds recalled later, the Victorian branch

> folded up, in my opinion, because it got too spiteful and J. P. Bourke got to the stage where he could not write a line without condemning the late E.J.D.A. [Abraham] or the Society . . . and I think that eventually it made a lot of the sensible deaf feel this is not what we want.[45]

Although the Deaf societies and their strategic National Council of the Deaf and Dumb may have done most of the damage to the AAAD, it is difficult to avoid the conclusion that Bourke, however unintentionally, dealt the final blow to the Victorian branch and by extension to the AAAD itself. Once the Victorian branch had been closed down, the only remaining branch was in Queensland, where most of the National Executive Committee also lived. Although the Executive Committee was still in existence in 1937 (because it acted to close down the Victorian branch), no reports survive from either the National Executive Committee or the Queensland branch after 1936. After a tumultuous existence of little more than five years, the AAAD quietly disappeared.

A New National Council

Once these rival Australian Deaf organizations had disintegrated, the Deaf societies took up their national activities again in 1938, as if recognizing that the way was now clear for the sort of council they had originally intended. At a conference held during the sports carnival in Hobart in December 1938, they established an Australian National Council of Adult Deaf and Dumb Societies.[46] The minutes of the four-day conference studiously avoided any mention of the earlier National Councils and their clashes with Deaf communities, or even of the old ADDA. Reverend Edgar Potter (formerly of the NSW breakaway Association, then of the NSW Society) was elected president, and Alfred Lonsdale honorary secretary. An article in the Hobart *Mercury* announced that "the object of the Council will be the advancement and well-being of the deaf and dumb throughout Australia, and it will meet at least once every two years."[47]

Although one deaf man was in attendance at the conference (E. R. Noble of Victoria) no mention was made of any commitment to having deaf people participate in the new National Council. Bourke wrote dismissively that it was, as usual, controlled by Abraham: "The others connected with it are like a string of camels tied nose to tail, and he leads the whole bunch."[48]

Contesting Public Images of Deaf People

The Deaf community's efforts to present themselves in a particular way have always risked being undermined by misguided public opinion, particularly its reflection in the media of the time. John Paul, of the Queensland breakaway Association, made this point in 1932.

After forty years among them there is one thing I cannot tell you about the deaf. That is whether the deafness itself or the propagation of fallacious and harmful statements about them really constitutes the greatest handicap in their social and industrial lives.[49]

The breakaways and dissidents of the late 1920s and early 30s tried to change the public image of deaf people from one of passive and childlike recipients of charity to one of capable citizens who could manage their own affairs. But their efforts had had limited success. A measure of how resilient the old stereotypes were can be seen in an article in the Melbourne newspaper *The Sun* in 1937, which temporarily stirred up further disputes within the Deaf community.

The article was called "Lives His Shuttered Life with Shakespeare" and appeared under the byline of R. L. Hoffmann. Even by the standards of the time, it was a mawkish and sentimental account of a deaf-blind man—"Old Thompson" (which was acknowledged not to be his real name) —living at the Blackburn home (the residence for aged and infirm deaf people run by the Deaf Society in Victoria), which was described as "the Adult Deaf and Dumb Society's idyllic little haven."[50] The article segued skilfully into a description of the Society's headquarters at Jolimont and yet another panegyric to Abraham. Abraham was described as having

> a sort of patriarchal authority over the large family. To him they bring their joys and their sorrows, their differences and perplexities. They even approach his advice on matters of romantic interest—should they marry, and if they marry, should they have children? . . . and all the whys and wherefores of this shuttered world of theirs.[51]

The article described silent bridge parties and tranquil deaf-mutes whose "anger mounts no further than [their] fingertips," even when provoked. Deaf people were referred to as children: "The Society assumes responsibility for its children—they are all children, whether 16 or 60—so soon as they leave school . . . in every way they are taught to adjust themselves to a world for which nature forgot to equip them."[52]

"Old Thompson" was described as having been born "deaf and muted," before "age brought blindness." He loved Shakespeare and had most of his plays and poems literally "at his fingertips." Abraham's son Douglas (who was then superintendent of the Blackburn home) was said to "have a special pride in him." The article concluded with a glowing description of the Blackburn home, describing it as "a lovely retreat set among great gardens and an orchard with a lake gleaming at the foot of a hill" that provided an idyllic background for "old Thompson."

And there along the promenade verandah gropes old Thompson, living in the world of Shakespeare's yesterdays . . . taking tea, perhaps, in a Veronese garden with the Capulets . . . or in the tap room of the Boar's Head tavern making merry passes with Bardolph, Pistol, Falstaff and the rest . . . . Who can tell?[53]

Of course, this article was like a red rag to a bull to J. P. Bourke, and it also provoked complaints from others, such as Mrs. M. Gladman.[54] In December of that year, Bourke produced another of his self-published booklets, *"Fiction and Fact"—A Pamphlet,* about the story. He contradicted Hoffmann's article on virtually every point, from the identity of "Old Thompson" to the type of card games deaf people preferred—"we (do) not hold bridge parties . . . . Mostly we play euchre, five hundred and whist." However, he declared at the start, "We do not blame Mr. Hoffmann. We know that he got his information from Mr. Abraham." He and others identified "Old Thompson" as E. Cork, who had not been born "deaf and muted," but had been blind from an early age and deaf since 30. He had been educated at the Institute for the Blind, and "[w]hat he knows he learnt long before he ever came under the control of the Abrahams." Bourke and others had arranged for the article in *The Sun* to be transcribed into braille for Cork and reported that he was "hurt and very indignant" about it.[55]

Bourke wrote that, "another deaf friend asked me to get up a protest, and induce the deaf, their relations and friends to sign it . . . . I asked about sixty of them to record a protest against the statements . . . but only seven of them would put their name to it." This he attributed to deaf people's resigned passivity in the face of Abraham's control. "The majority of the deaf and dumb resent the way he talks about them, but take all his lies as a matter of course."[56] He quoted one deaf man as writing to him, "I feel it would be no use to answer it, Mr. Abraham is too strong. He has made his seat secure with the Committee . . . . Every dog has his day, and Mr. Abraham has had his and will have to answer to God for it soon."[57]

This incident demonstrates the persuasive power of portraying deaf people as "children," usually living in supervised "havens" and dependent on a "patriarchal authority." The Deaf societies' reliance on charitable funding exerted a constant pull toward this type of publicity, with its reassurance to the public that their charitable contributions had tangible and heart-warming results. Although contested by some deaf people, these images were very resistant to change.

Bourke and the Deaf Community

Despite Bourke's unflagging efforts to improve the lot of deaf people, he always occupied an uneasy position in the Deaf community. His hearing background would have placed him at a disadvantage, and he did not seem to possess the talents that might have helped him overcome this—he was not a sportsman or a raconteur. He never married (other men with a similar background to Bourke were assimilated into the Deaf community more quickly when they married deaf women).[58] The small circle of supporters he had in the 1920s appeared to dwindle during the 1930s. But a more likely reason for his lack of support was that he was not fully in tune with deaf people's perceptions of themselves. Bourke insisted that

> The adult deaf and dumb of Australia are not a happy people . . . . Lack of knowledge of them and their problems, needs, difficulties and helplessness on the part of the public is one of the chief reasons for the unhappy conditions that prevail amongst them.[59]

But was this supported by the majority of deaf people? Deaf people have generally confounded observers and reformers by their cheerfulness and acceptance of their condition—this was often remarked upon by newspaper reporters of this time. Although deaf people usually acknowledge frustrations and injustices and support those who fight to change them, in general, they enjoy the social and personal pleasures of their community, and they value its distinctive language and clear identity.

Bourke's insistence that all was misery, brutality, and unhappiness in the Deaf community would probably not have resonated with most of his peers and would have contributed to the seeming lack of support he received from them. The unrelenting bleakness of his writing contrasted with that of *The Deaf Advocate*, for example. Although the editors of the *Advocate* railed against the Deaf societies and injustice generally, large parts of their magazine simply celebrated the social life and everyday pleasures of a close-knit community.

As the 1930s wore on, it is probable that people became inured to Bourke's complaints and saw no point in them. As radical Deaf organizations and ventures crumbled around the country, most Victorian deaf people probably decided to stick even more closely to the devil they knew. Although he probably retained a few supporters, Bourke was generally regarded as a harbinger of pointless conflict, a "troublemaker."[60]

In the early 1930s, during the heyday of the AAAD and the break-aways in other states, Bourke could still summon enough support to organize a public meeting of Deaf people in Melbourne, as he did in April 1934, where a motion was carried calling yet again for a Royal Commission to inquire into the Deaf society.[61] His support had clearly dropped off by the late 1930s, although the Deaf Committee of the time may have been more conservative. In early 1938, he drafted a new Constitution for the Deaf Society and requested an opportunity to put it to a meeting of deaf people.[62] The Deaf Committee refused to hear him on the subject or to distribute his draft constitution, and it seems the proposal went no further.[63] Later that year, the Deaf Committee requested that the board of the Deaf Society reject Bourke's membership and return his subscription "in view of the harm he has done the Society."[64] After seeking legal advice, the board returned his annual subscription, in effect refusing him membership in the Society.[65] Bourke appears to have made no attempt to appeal the decision this time.

In 1939, the Deaf Society conducted a public appeal for funds with the permission of the Charities Board, and Bourke took the opportunity to distribute circulars criticizing the Society and attempting to undermine its appeal. The board of the Society acknowledged the "serious effect" his activities had on their appeal and recorded their view that "this person had done the greatest disservice to the deaf and dumb that it was possible for any person to do."[66] Bourke's activities in connection with the appeal also drew a sharp response from the Deaf Committee, which issued a letter dismissing Bourke's claims as "groundless and without any foundation of truth" and "a source of exasperation and annoyance to all of us." They dissociated themselves from Bourke, describing him as "not deaf and dumb in the generally accepted sense of the word" and assured readers that "Mr. Bourke speaks for himself alone and the Deaf Committee believes he has no support, sympathy or encouragement from amongst the deaf community of this State."[67]

All to No Purpose

By the late 1930s, Bourke began describing his quest as a doomed epic.

In his endeavour to expose conditions in the society and the treatment of the adult deaf and dumb, the writer has, for twelve years, been appealing to the governing powers, the Churches, Members of Parliament, public authorities, public bodies, public men, the Press, and to the hearing members of the society, but all to no purpose.[68]

He was bitter and scathing about the seeming indifference of the Victorian government to the concerns of deaf people—"The Victorian Government protects the aborigines, and kangaroos, koalas, and kookaburras, fish and wild duck, but not its adult deaf and dumb."[69] His endless railing against Abraham took on the character of a vendetta, an obsession—no matter what the declared topic of his writings, sooner or later each booklet, letter, or magazine descended into invective against Abraham, which unfortunately obscured some of his meticulously detailed work.

It would have been difficult for someone attracted to the Victorian social reformers, as Bourke was, not to cast his work in an epic light, and himself as a tragic hero. He quoted the *Latter-Day Pamphlets* of nineteenth-century Scottish satirist and social commentator Thomas Carlyle to summarize his experience with the Charities Board, the government, and "the Churches, Members of Parliament, public authorities, public bodies, public men, the Press, and . . . the hearing members of the society."

Every agent . . . has his tragic tale to tell you of his sad experiences in the Colonial Office; what blind obstructions, fatal indolences, pedantries, stupidities on the right hand and on the left he had to battle with; what a world-wide jungle of redtape, inhabited by doleful creatures, deaf or nearly so to human reason or entreaty, he had entered on; and how he paused in amazement, almost in despair; passionately appealing now to this doleful creature, now to that, and to the dead redtape jungle, and to the living Universe itself, and to the Voices and to the Silences;—and, on the whole, found that it was an adventure in sorrowful fact, equal to the fabulous ones by old Knights-errants against dragons and wizards in enchanted wildernesses and waste howling solitudes; not achievable except by nearly superhuman exercise of all the four cardinal virtues, and unexpected favour of the special blessing of Heaven.[70]

Despite the vivid imagery, it is unlikely that this gained him any extra sympathy from the Deaf community.

Bourke's Last Stand

In 1940, Bourke began a new magazine, *The Australian Deaf Citizen*, a quarterly magazine owned and edited by himself and "dedicated to the interests of the Deaf of Australia." Each issue consisted of a lengthy editorial, some local and national news items, quotes from a variety of sources, and an extract from Bourke's earlier booklet *The Story of a Deaf Drudge*, which he began to serialize in his new magazine. Although he used the terms *we* and *our* in his editorials, no evidence suggests that there were any other contributors. It is likely that Bourke could not continue to finance it, as it lasted for only six issues.[71]

Although the magazine may have met with little success at the time, the six copies were rediscovered in the State Library of Victoria more than forty years later by a deaf researcher, Michael Uniacke, who wrote about them for another fledgling Australian deaf magazine, *Sound Off*.[72] Uniacke was fascinated by these old accounts of deaf struggles for independence, commenting on how similar they were to the rhetoric of deaf activists in the late twentieth century. He also perceived the conflict between Bourke's high idealism and his extreme negativity.

> [The magazine] was too angry, too vitriolic, and this must surely have contributed to its downfall. Yet Bourke saw and felt what he believed was gross injustice. He was desperate to bring hearing people to account and to shake what he saw as apathy of deaf people around him.[73]

In *The Australian Deaf Citizen*, Bourke reported several times on the activities of a new Victorian group called the Past Pupils Association, which held social gatherings at the premises of VDDI, the school for the deaf. Bourke said the group was founded by the school superintendent, W. J. McCaskill; however, some of the names mentioned in connection with it (e.g., Robert Luff and Bourke himself) suggest that it may have included many of the dissidents of the 1920s and 30s and attempted to retain some of their ideals—an impression also suggested by modern informants.[74] Bourke described some hostility between this group and the Deaf Society, such as the Deaf Society organizing rival events whenever the Past Pupils Association had a social function.[75] There is no indication that the Past Pupils Association was politically active—Bourke's reports were of card parties and dances rather than of subversive magazines and public meetings. No other records of the group seem to have survived.

The End of Abraham's Rule

Ernest Abraham died on July 29, 1940, after almost forty years as superintendent of the Adult Deaf and Dumb Society of Victoria. Alfred Lonsdale, whatever his private opinions of Abraham had been, traveled down from Sydney to be a pallbearer at his funeral, along with James Johnston, E. R. Noble, M. Dyson, Edgar H. Peacock (secretary of the Society), and Sir Julius Bruche (president of the Society).[76]

Melbourne newspapers *The Argus* and *The Age* ran prominent obituaries, with *The Age* praising his "unique and extensive experience of educational and missionary work among the deaf and dumb, and his labours to ameliorate their condition [which] were rewarded with remarkable success."[77] A predictable counterpoint was provided by J. P. Bourke's magazine *The Australian Deaf Citizen,* which did not flinch from speaking ill of the dead, providing a final catalog of Abraham's sins and declaring bluntly, "The evil that he has done lives after him."[78]

Abraham's wife and daughter had died the previous year. His son Douglas continued as manager of the Blackburn farm and home, although he was bitterly disappointed that he did not inherit his father's job of Deaf Society superintendent. When Douglas Abraham died in 1949, his wife and son decided to change their surname to McLeod (his wife's maiden name), considering the name Abraham "too Jewish."[79]

Douglas Abraham destroyed most of his father's papers, although fragments remain in a collection of Deaf Society papers in the State Library of Victoria. Ernest Reynolds recalled remonstrating with Douglas as he burned "bags and bags and bags" of his father's life work, saying, "Doug, that would be history!" But Douglas was unmoved, replying, "Nobody's going to have them, they were my father's and now they are mine."[80] He thus ensured that Ernest Abraham, who poured his life into "instituting, organising, establishing, founding, manufacturing, and managing" is revealed chiefly through the words of others, not his own.[81]

A Supporter Topples

In 1941, one of the few long-standing allies of the Victorian dissidents had a spectacular fall from grace. The VDDI superintendent, W. J. McCaskill, the "white man" of the AAAD, was arrested for embezzling more than £25,000 from the school and subsequently sentenced to five years in prison. Although he was acknowledged to have "done a tremendous amount of honorary work for charitable and other organisations" and to be "held in high esteem," his trial caused a sensation and was featured in all of the Melbourne newspapers.[82] The school's directors were publicly criticized for their "laxity in the supervision of the accounts."[83] How Abraham would have relished it had he lived another year to see it!

McCaskill once sent a greeting to the NSW breakaway Association eight years before in the heady days of May 1933, when everything seemed possible.

I submit as a thought a few lines taken from an overseas paper, entitled "Ambition," which I think everyone can readily adapt to his own life.

I'd rather be a Could Be,
If I could not be an Are;
For a Could Be is a May Be,
With a chance of touching par.

I'd rather be a Has Been
Than a Might Have Been by far;
For a Might Have Been has never been,
But a Has was once an Are.[84]

In the becalmed state of the national Deaf community in the 1940s, quite a few people may have been reflecting on what "might have been."

The Passing of the Old Guard

John Paul

One renegade organization soldiered on amid the ruins. The Queensland Deaf and Dumb Citizens Reformed Association—with John Paul as its superintendent—continued until 1952. Anecdotal evidence suggests that membership declined during the 1940s, and it became an organization of "old men."[85] It appeared to be isolated both by its later location in Teneriffe—Paul observed that "The DD [Deaf and Dumb] just won't come out this distance despite the many comforts and benefits the place offers,"—and by Paul's strict principles, which seemed increasingly old fashioned in the more liberal post-war climate.[86] The Association encouraged local sports teams—indeed, its variety of sports was one of its attractions for many deaf men.[87] However, Paul dourly opposed national and international sports gatherings or carnivals, and the energy and resources that deaf people poured into them.[88] He lamented the prevalence of "Carnival romances" as a "serious symptom of a growing moral cancer" and was disgusted with the huge interest shown in the International Games for the Deaf in Brussels in 1953.[89]

> It is a shameful tragedy that when so much that is important to the Deaf is just dwindling away through neglect and lack of interest that so much time and money should be given to things like this. It is a serious reflection on our outlook. The work of every pioneer of the advancement of the Deaf will have been thrown away for a little hour of strutting in the arena with a small handful of a very small section of the community—and to no purpose.[90]

He seemed disappointed with the deaf people of the time, with their preoccupation with sport and their lack of interest in politics, and (he hints) their fickleness. He looked back nostalgically to the deaf people he had known at the beginning of his career: "I can say that the early years saw the DD at their pinnacle—a solid self respecting, happy, interested and interesting folk with lots of good will and loyalty."[91]

In 1952, Paul decided to retire and close down the Association. He "flatly refused to take the responsibility of bringing anyone into the work" or (evidently) to allow his board to replace him. Although he was saddened by the changes in the Deaf community that had led him to this decision, citing the "prosperity of the war years" and the development of other organizations, he had no regrets and concluded, "[M]y going will round off the 22 yrs work of [the Association] . . . . Yet it was a good venture."[92]

Martha Overend Wilson

Martha Overend Wilson died in 1945, after more than forty years working for Queensland and Australian Deaf organizations, most of it in a voluntary capacity. Her passing went unremarked by the Queensland Deaf Mission, and the papers of the Queensland breakaway Association, which would have been more likely to have honored her life, have not survived. At her request, her ashes were scattered over the rose bushes at the Mt. Thompson Crematorium in Brisbane. There is no memorial to her anywhere, and her name is little known in the modern Australian Deaf community.

She had seen much that she worked for disintegrate or go awry, but she remained endlessly optimistic and a believer in the power of unity. The conclusion of an article she wrote for *The Deaf Advocate* in 1934 seems an apt memorial.

> Though our work is not yet complete we can go on into the unknown future with sure hearts that the cause of the Deaf will by our united efforts be happier and brighter, and that the Deaf themselves will be regarded as a band of people worthy in every way to be looked upon as loyal citizens of Australia.[93]

James Johnston

James Johnston died in 1950. Although people like Bourke may have assessed his contributions rather astringently, Johnston is still remembered as someone who worked hard to build up the sports networks of the Australian Deaf community, particularly that of cricket. His most enduring legacy has been his descendants—his deaf daughter Dorothy Shaw was a long-time activist in the NSW Deaf community and became the first president of the Australian Association of the Deaf (AAD) when it was established in 1986. His many grandchildren, greatgrandchildren, and great-great-grandchildren are still prominent in the Australian Deaf community and include the author of the first dictionary of Australian Sign Language, Trevor Johnston.

Fletcher Booth

Fletcher Samuel Booth died in 1956 at the age of eighty-five. His death was reported in the Christmas 1956 issue of the Deaf Society's newsletter *The Silent Messenger*, and he was noted as being a "missioner" in the late nineteenth century before the Society started, a member of the first Organizing Committee of the Society, and for his work in gathering deaf people for meetings and church services.[94] His roles in the NSW Association for Deaf and Dumb Citizens, the Australian Association for the Advancement of the Deaf, and as editor of the pioneering *The Deaf Advocate* were not mentioned.

Alfred Lonsdale

Alfred Lambert Lonsdale died two years after Booth and received a more generous and fulsome obituary in *The Silent Messenger*. The growth of the Deaf Society during his long association with it was described in detail, and his "untiring energy and far-seeing initiative" were praised. Although he had retired from the Society five years previously, "The Shadow" had remained a "frequent visitor" to the premises. Deaf people were assured that they had "lost a friend who, more than anyone else, was responsible for the high standard of work being done for the deaf and the many amenities enjoyed by them today."[95]

John Bourke

John Bourke ended his association with the Deaf world where he had begun it—at the Blackburn home, this time as one of their "aged and infirm" residents. Some cryptic notes on the back of one of his record cards (on which the Deaf Society recorded details of their clients and residents) state that Bourke "met with an accident" on an unspecified date and could no longer keep his employment. He began receiving the old-age pension and was admitted to the Blackburn home in 1954.[96] He remained there until his death in 1960.

Bourke in his declining years does not disappoint posterity—he continued to write letters to the newspapers and authorities, complain, demand his rights, and try the patience of those around him right up until his death at the age of seventy six. When applying for admission to the home, he listed several "conditions" he wished to have met and was told unceremoniously that "he could only stay . . . providing he complied with the rules and regulations laid down for all inmates."[97] The minutes of the Deaf Society's Home Committee over the next six years regularly and resignedly referred to Bourke's letters to the newspapers, the Hospitals and Charities Commission, the Premier, the Pensioners' Association, the Brotherhood of St. Laurence, and other bodies, complaining about conditions at the home and the inadequate allowance he felt he received from his pension.[98] He also frequently requested improvements to the facilities at the home, such as heaters in the dining rooms and in his own room—some of which were granted.[99] One request, suggestive of failing eyesight, was for a "new magnifying glass."[100] He died in the nearby Box Hill Hospital on April 2, 1960, after a short illness.[101]

On the back of one of his record cards, a nostalgic staff member of the Deaf Society wrote, "Intelligent man. Deafened. Has been a stormy petrel in the deaf world."[102] It was an appropriate epitaph for John Patrick Bourke.

Moving On

Most deaf people who had participated in the upheavals of the 1920s and 1930s, whatever their feelings about those events, continued to participate with enthusiasm in Deaf community organizations and sporting clubs. Ernest Quinnell, who had been one of the editors of *The Deaf Advocate* and a collector for the NSW breakaway Association, was an example. After the amalgamation between the Association and the Deaf Society, he was actively involved in the Society's Deaf General Committee and sports clubs for another forty years. However, when family members were packing away his effects some years after his death, they discovered several immaculate "Collector's cards" for the NSW Association of Deaf and Dumb Citizens in the breast pocket of his Deaf Men's Bowling Club blazer.[103] Quinnell had retained these old mementos of his breakaway days, transferring them to the pockets of different jackets over the decades.

Some of the Victorian deaf activists seem to have retreated or withdrawn from the Deaf community, and others remained within the alternative community of the Exclusive Brethren. William Crush moved around rural Australia, regularly changing jobs. He stayed in touch

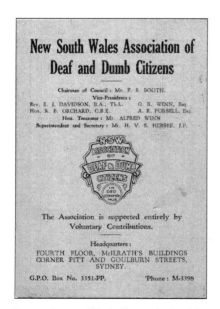

Ernest Quinnell's Collector's Card for the NSW Association of Deaf and Dumb Citizens.
Della Bampton.

with the Victorian and NSW Deaf communities, but seems to have taken no other active roles in community organizations. There were occasional mentions of Crush in *The Victorian Deaf News*, describing surprise visits by him, "looking the picture of health and quite tanned," with stories of his work "on motor transport all over northern New South Wales, Riverina, and northern Victoria" or "at Renmark transporting oranges for the New Zealand trade."[104] In 1936, he "[took] a selection up the Hawkesbury River way in New South Wales," enthusing over its isolated location, "completely cut off from the daily turmoil of civilisation."[105]

In the early 1980s, a welfare officer of the Victorian Deaf Society (formerly the Adult Deaf and Dumb Society) was summoned to attend to an elderly deaf man living in public housing in Melbourne. The man was in failing health, surrounded by piles of dusty papers, and obviously in need of assistance. But when it was made clear to him that his visitor was from the Victorian Deaf Society, the man ferociously resisted any suggestion of help. It was R. H. Lambert, another of the 1930s dissidents, and it seemed he had nursed his disillusionment with the Society for more than forty years. The young deaf welfare officer, sensing a story, persuaded Lambert to agree to an interview at a later date, but Lambert died before the interview could take place.[106]

Ernest Abraham and Alfred Lonsdale's names live on in Australian Deaf popular history, on sports trophies and buildings, and in folklore and photographs. But the deaf people described in this book have been largely forgotten.

Conclusion

Deaf political organizations may have disappeared, but important issues still demanded political responses. During the late 1940s and 50s, a new challenge emerged—Deaf education in Australia moved more decisively toward oralism, and signing was disallowed in most schools for deaf children. Although the move was being proposed in the late '40s, it is usually identified with a visit to Australia in 1950 by two prominent British educators of the deaf, Sir Alexander and Lady Irene Ewing. The Ewings visited Deaf schools in every state and gave detailed recommendations to state governments that Deaf education systems should adopt oral methods.[107]

This was when the Australian Deaf community needed a strong political voice—one of their most universally held values was under fire.

But there was little or no organized response by Deaf groups. Although Deaf community gatherings met the Ewings and debated their recommendations, only a few deaf individuals voiced the concerns of their community in public.[108] The lack of a national Deaf organization was felt, and it seems there was some discussion about trying to establish one again, although no records remain of any attempts. John Paul commented in 1947,

> The general tension created by the educational methods question has again led up to the idea of forming a National body of the Deaf to hold a watching brief in any interests that would be outside the ambit of the Societies' work. Previous bodies working under the aegis of the Societies failed.
>
> In a crisis such as the present which may result in the status of the Deaf being considerably depressed it can only be regretted that they have not banded themselves nationally and independently to maintain the general interest. Despite the need any move by any of the Societies just now could only result in failure. It should be a voluntary effort of the Deaf themselves completely independent of the Societies or their hearing officers for support.[109]

The lack of an organized political response does not necessarily mean that the deaf people of this time were indifferent to the political impact of changes such as the rise of oralism—it may just mean that their experiences in the 1920s and 30s had not encouraged them to persist with organized political activity or with opposition to the Deaf societies. The war years had brought them economic benefits and greater employment opportunities, and as often happens, it was difficult to maintain political activism in comfortable circumstances.

Over the following decades, the Australian Deaf community continued to grow and develop connections between states and with other countries. Although the organizations set up in the 1930s may not have survived, they reflected but one aspect of Deaf community life. Sport and its associated social activities, although deplored by people like John Paul, expanded and strengthened the community, providing another way of keeping it active and resilient. Christian church groups also provided an avenue for many deaf people to explore further dimensions of themselves and their lives within their community. The Exclusive Brethren continued to have a large deaf membership in Victoria, and other groups, such as the Deaf Christian Fellowship, became well established in some states and attracted some of those who had been active in the dissident groups, such as Isabel and Stan Winn in NSW.[110] Such groups sometimes provided outlets for deaf people to organize themselves and work toward more idealized communities—another form of managing their own affairs.

The rise of oralism in Deaf education in the late 1940s impacted Australian deaf people in ways that are outside the scope of this book, but the activities described here ensured that when young deaf people completed their schooling, a thriving community awaited them.

8

Epilogue

The idea of Australia as a land without history has proved remarkably resilient.

—Mark McKenna, "The History Anxiety"

Forty years after the demise of the Australian Association for the Advancement of the Deaf (AAD), a group of eighteen deaf people held a meeting during the triennial Australian Deaf Games (formerly the sports carnivals) in Adelaide in 1977. Most of these deaf people had leading roles in the sports organizations and Deaf committees of their respective states, and some were on the boards of their state Deaf societies, which at that time usually had only one or two deaf members. The purpose of the meeting was "to consider the formation of a national body of the Deaf."[1] During the discussion, no mention was made of the earlier national organizations—the Australasian Deaf and Dumb Association (ADDA), the Australian Association for the Advancement of the Deaf (AAAD), or the National Council of the Deaf and Dumb (NCDD)—and what they had achieved or why they had failed.

There was, however, frequent reference to the Australian Federation of Adult Deaf Societies (AFADS). The AFADS was the most recent version of the old National Council of Adult Deaf and Dumb Societies. After its brief revival in 1938, the council disappeared again until the early 1960s, and it was reformed in 1965 as AFADS.[2] In the absence of a national Deaf organization, the AFADS seemed to be the national advocate on Deaf issues in the 1970s, and it was the Australian member organization of the World Federation of the Deaf, to whose conferences it often sent a hearing representative.[3]

194

The deaf people present at this 1977 meeting perceived the AFADS to be a strong organization, and many of their comments revolved around concerns about possible conflicts between any new national body of deaf people and the AFADS. Almost all were against the formation of a new Deaf organization. A Queensland participant explained that, "the A.F.A.D.S. covered the ground sufficiently now and . . . there could be a conflict between the two bodies for affiliation with the W.F.D." A Victorian man agreed, saying, "[T]he A.F.A.D.S. had produced excellent results for the deaf of Australia and there was no reason for formation of a National Body if [it] was only going to duplicate the A.F.A.D.S." They warned each other that the AFADS might not recognize a new national body of Deaf people and that the federal government would probably recognize the AFADS rather than an organization of Deaf people. After general agreement that "the A.F.A.D.S. represented a great future for the Deaf of Australia," they passed a motion declaring that "it is inappropriate at present to form a national body of the Deaf in Australia."[4]

On a first reading of these minutes, it would appear that the struggles of the 1920s and '30s had vanished from the collective memory of the Australian Deaf community. These comments in 1977 seem little different from Fletcher Booth's 1922 declaration, "The best way is to leave our troubles and disputes and grievances to the hearing Board of Management, they will look after us very well" or John Bourke's early defense of the Adult Deaf and Dumb Society of Victoria: "Our Board consists of shrewd business men, and they know better than we deaf people what should be done."[5] However, on closer examination, it seems more likely that the deaf people who met in 1977 did have some subliminal awareness of the events that had transpired forty years previously.[6] Their comments suggest a shared belief that a national body of deaf people was likely to lead to "conflict" with the Deaf societies and that the Deaf societies would prevail in any such conflict. What is striking is the complete absence of any mention of these earlier organizations or events, or of the names of deaf people who had been associated with them.

The editors of *The Deaf Advocate* in the early 1930s had often pointed to the historical significance of the work their contemporaries were doing. When the AAAD was formed in 1932, its founding members were hailed as "advancing a new era in the history of the deaf" and assured that "the next generation of the deaf will not be unmindful of what you are doing now—and will benefit by it."[7] After the Queensland breakaway, the *Advocate* editors had praised deaf people, such as Martha Overend Wilson and Alf Eaton, who resisted financial lures from the Mission in order to remain loyal to deaf people, declaring, "their names will ever be cherished as loyal patriots when the history of the Deaf of Australia comes to be written."[8] This did not happen. Subsequent generations of deaf people may have retained a visceral memory of conflict and failure, but there was no commemoration of or homage to these events and pioneers.

Such episodes of silence and forgetfulness are, of course, not unknown in Australian history. In 1968, W. E. H. Stanner coined the term "the great Australian silence" to describe the suppression and absence of Aboriginal history in the national story.[9] It has now been widely acknowledged that this absence was not entirely accidental or innocent—Stanner claimed there was a "cult of disremembering," and Bain Attwood has suggested that the silence arose from "strategic forgetting."[10] In 2001, the centenary of the federation of Australian colonies into a single country, historians and government officials lamented the Australian people's general lack of knowledge of and interest in this historic event.

> All the people, events, and places that federalists declared would be historic never became so. The names of the convention delegates, the electoral battles of Barton against Reid, the landing place of the first Governor-General and the site of his swearing-in, the name of the first Prime Minister—all are forgotten.[11]

Re-examination and rewriting of neglected or "forgotten" areas of Australian history have been subject to controversy and sometimes officially rejected as too negative.[12] Perhaps, as a leading journalist wrote in the centenary of Federation year, "Australia is a nation consumed by amnesia."[13]

Strategic Forgetting

Was "strategic forgetting" part of the reason for the Deaf community's seeming lack of knowledge of the events of the 1920s and '30s (or unwillingness to make this knowledge explicit) during the latter part of the twentieth century? Information about the breakaways, the AAAD, and the conflicts of those years has certainly been left out of the official record on many occasions. A "short history" of the Adult Deaf and Dumb Society of New South Wales prepared for the organization's twenty-fifth anniversary in 1938 that seems to have been written by Fletcher Booth or the Reverend Edgar Potter, was judiciously edited by Alfred Lonsdale, who crossed out most of the section about the breakaway Association.[14] Booth's obituary in *The Silent Messenger* recorded only his work for the Deaf Society, not for the breakaway Association or *The Deaf Advocate*, and a pamphlet prepared for the NSW Society's move to a new building in 1975 included a brief history of the Society that made no mention of the breakaway.[15] There are many other examples of such omissions. Records and source material for the dissident groups, where they survive at all, are much less accessible than Deaf Society records. Bourke's books and magazines languish unread in a few state libraries and are unknown to most deaf people.

Other explanations may lie in the changes to deaf people's education after the late 1940s. Oral education was pervasive in the 1950s and '60s in Australia, and the mainstreaming of deaf children into small groups in regular schools spread during the 1970s. Mainstreaming weakens the transmission of sign language between and across generations of deaf people and delays or reduces the possibilities for learning cultural information and passing on shared history. Critics of these educational practices are quick to point out the connections—isolating deaf children from sign language and the company of other deaf people usually means that historical knowledge disappears too.[16] Although earlier educational practices may not have made this historical knowledge explicit either, they provided the conditions for deaf people to disseminate it among themselves, however imperfectly.

A National Organization Again

During the 1980s, conditions became more favorable for the reestablishment of a national organization. Recognition of Australian Sign Language (Auslan) as a community language made it possible to see Deaf people as a language minority as well as a disability group, and the discourses of multiculturalism, linguistic diversity, and disability rights provided new contexts for discussing Deaf communities.[17] Increasing international travel made Australian deaf people aware that they were unusual among developed countries in not having a national organization. After some years of discussion, the Australian Association of the Deaf (AAD) was established in 1986. Its founding president was Dorothy Shaw, whose father, James Johnston, had been president of the short-lived National Council of the Deaf and Dumb more than fifty years earlier. Despite this link, most members of the new AAD believed that it was Australia's first ever national organization of deaf people.

The AAD (now called Deaf Australia) continues to be an active national organization, and in 1999 hosted an international congress of the World Federation of the Deaf in Brisbane. Deaf societies are still in existence in all Australian states, but their practices and the social service environment they operate in are very different from those of their early twentieth-century antecedents. Most Deaf societies today have many deaf staff members and several are led by deaf people.

The collective memory of the breakaways still lingers in the Australian Deaf community, surfacing occasionally in asides and veiled comments. Families with several generations of deaf people may be more likely to retain such memories—one young deaf man from such a family recalled that when he went to work for the Deaf Society of NSW in the early twenty-first century, his father told him half-jokingly that he had "betrayed his grandfather" (his grandfather had been a member of the breakaway in the 1930s).[18]

But such memories are no longer the only repository of the national story. There has been a revival of interest in Australian Deaf history since the late 1980s, particularly in the lives of the deaf founders of early schools, such as Thomas Pattison, Frederick John Rose, and Sister Gabriel Hogan, and of early deaf convicts and settlers, such as Betty Steel and John Carmichael.[19] Although these stories seemed to satisfy, for a time, the need for deaf "pioneers," further work has explored more complex and multifaceted aspects of Australia's deaf past.[20] Deaf Society histories by John Flynn, Sue Wilson, and the Deaf Society of NSW have acknowledged the breakaways and the contributions of the people associated with them, and the Deaf Society of NSW recently named its board room after Fletcher Booth.[21]

Postmodern Citizens

Australian deaf people of the 1920s and 30s strove for the right to manage their own affairs, and to affirm their citizenship in the wider society and nation. The concept of citizenship has continued to prove a useful one for defining not only deaf people's place in their host country, but also the nature of national and transnational communities of deaf people. Owen Wrigley has suggested that these communities show that citizenship can transcend place, describing transnational gatherings of deaf people as evoking "a spontaneous sense of universal 'citizenry' that did not require a physical place. Like the link between speech and language, the connection between location and belonging suddenly was shown to be unnecessary."[22]

But for a citizenship without a place, the things that do bind people together—a living language and a shared history—are both more fragile and more vital. The history of deaf people in particular times and places, such as early twentieth-century Australia, contributes to both the multilayered histories of individual countries and to our understanding of how local and transnational Deaf communities evolve.

NOTES

Chapter 1

1. For example, Harlan Lane, *When the Mind Hears: A History of the Deaf* (New York: Random House, 1984); John Van Cleve and Barry Crouch, *A Place of Their Own: Creating the Deaf Community in America* (Washington, DC: Gallaudet University Press, 1989); Peter W. Jackson, *Britain's Deaf Heritage* (Edinburgh: The Pentland Press Ltd., 1990); Renate Fischer and Harlan Lane, eds. *Looking Back: A Reader on the History of Deaf Communities and Their Sign Languages* (Hamburg: Signum Press, 1993); Douglas C. Baynton, *Forbidden Signs: American Culture and the Campaign Against Sign Language* (Chicago: The University of Chicago Press, 1996); Lois Bragg, ed., *Deaf World: A Historical Reader and Primary Sourcebook* (New York: New York University Press, 2001); and a growing number of dissertations, edited collections, and conference proceedings.

2. Baynton, *Forbidden Signs*.

3. H.-D. L. Bauman and J. J. Murray, "Deaf Gain: An Introduction," in *Deaf Gain: Raising the Stakes for Human Diversity*, ed. H.-D. L. Bauman and J. J. Murray (Minneapolis: University of Minnesota Press, 2012), xv–xlii.

4. Pierre Desloges, "A Deaf Person's Observations about 'An Elementary Course of Education for the Deaf,'" in *The Deaf Experience: Classics in Language and Education*, edited by Harlan Lane, trans. Franklin Philip (Cambridge, MA: Harvard University Press, 1984), 28–48.

5. Owen Wrigley, *The Politics of Deafness* (Washington, DC: Gallaudet University Press, 1996), 50.

6. T. Johnston and A. Schembri, *Australian Sign Language: An Introduction to Sign Language Linguistics* (Cambridge: Cambridge University Press, 2007); Robert Adam, "Unimodal Bilingualism in the Deaf Community: Language Contact between Two Sign Languages in Australia and the United Kingdom" (PhD diss., University College London, London, 2016).

7. Martin Atherton, "Deserving of Charity or Deserving of Better? The Continuing Legacy of the 1834 Poor Law Amendment Act for Britain's Deaf Population," *Review of Disability Studies*, 7 (3 and 4) (2011): 18–25.

8. Paddy Ladd, *Understanding Deaf Culture: In Search of Deafhood* (Clevedon, England: Multilingual Matters Ltd., 2003), 334.

9. T. A. Froehlich, quoted in Van Cleve and Crouch, *A Place of Their Own*, 94.

10. Grant, *The Deaf Advance,* chapter 2.

11. Joseph J. Murray, "'One Touch of Nature Makes the Whole World Kin': The Transnational Lives of Deaf Americans, 1870–1924" (PhD diss., University of Iowa, 2007).

12. Martin Atherton, "Deaf Newspapers: A Cornerstone of the Deaf Community," (presentation, Disability Studies Association Conference, Lancaster University, September 2006).

13. Melissa Anderson and Breda Carty, "The Cosmopolitan Correspondence Club," in *Telling Deaf Lives: Agents of Change*, edited by Kristin Snoddon (Washington, DC: Gallaudet University Press, 2014), 148–62.

14. Adam Kendon, *Sign Languages of Aboriginal Australia: Cultural, Semiotic and Communicative Perspectives* (Cambridge: Cambridge University Press, 1988), 406–07. Kendon observed that deaf Aboriginal people usually communicate through "home sign" systems limited to some family members, rather than by appropriating existing tribal sign languages.

15. Michael Flynn, *The Second Fleet: Britain's Grim Convict Armada of 1790* (Sydney: Library of Australian History, 1993), 547–49.

16. Jan Branson and Don Miller, *The Story of Betty Steel: Deaf Convict and Pioneer* (Petersham, New South Wales: Deafness Resources Australia, 1995).

17. B. Carty and D. Thornton, "Deaf People in Colonial Australia," in *No History, No Future: Proceedings of the 7th DHI International Conference, Stockholm 2009*, ed. T. Hedberg (Solna, Sweden: Dixa, 2011), 148–55.

18. Breda Carty, "John Carmichael: Australian Deaf Pioneer," *Deaf History Journal* 3, no. 3 (April 2000): 24–36.

19. For example, a review of Carmichael's *Select Views of Sydney* (1829) in the *Australian* newspaper praised his taste and skill and added that the fact that "this young artist is not only deaf, but also dumb, should also interest the Public in his favour." Quoted in Richard Neville, "Printmakers in Colonial Sydney 1800–1850," (MA thesis, University of Sydney, 1988), 106; Andrew Houison, *History of the Post Office, Together with an Historical Account of the Issue of Postage Stamps in New South Wales Compiled Directly from the Records* (Sydney: Government Printer, 1890), 61.

20. Quoted in M. Cannon and I. MacFarlane, eds., *Historical Records of Victoria*, vol. 4 (Melbourne: Victorian Government Printing Office, 1985), 14–15. Some examples include: "I get another poor copper smith . . . . Thin copper cheap. No use map"; "I am now etching mountains, it will soon be finished. I will bring some proofs. I say hills is very much trouble etching &c."; "I know all printers in England never print size original. I was measure some maps at Surveyor printed in London, not size original . . ."

21. Joan Kerr, ed. *The Dictionary of Australian Artists: Painters, Sketchers, Photographers and Engravers to 1870* (Melbourne: Oxford University Press, 1992), 134–35.

22. Alexander, Atkinson. *Memoirs of My Youth* (Newcastle on Tyne: John Wilson Swanston, 1865), 192.

23. Travers Borrow, *The Hallett Family* (Adelaide: Pioneers' Association of South Australia, 1946); John Hallett, personal communication to author, 1993.

24. Penelope Hope, ed., *The Voyage of the Africaine: A Collection of Journals, Letters and Extracts from Contemporary Publications* (South Yarra: Heinemann Educational Australia Proprietary Ltd., 1968), 34.

25. Paul F. Cooper, "Thomas Pattison (1805–1899) Coach Painter and Founder of the Deaf and Dumb Institute, Sydney," *Philanthropy and Philanthropists in Australian Colonial History*, accessed August 27, 2014, https://phinaucohi.wordpress.com/2014/08/27/thomas-pattison-1805-1899/.

26. Paul F. Cooper, "Sherrington Alexander Gilder (1828–1902) and the Commencement of the Education of the Deaf in NSW," *Philanthropy and Philanthropists in Australian Colonial History*, accessed August 26, 2014, https://phinaucohi.wordpress.com/2014/08/26/sherrington-alexander-gilder/; Paul F. Cooper, "Thomas Pattison (1805–1899) Coach Painter and Founder of the Deaf and Dumb Institute, Sydney," *Philanthropy and Philanthropists in Australian Colonial History*, August 27, 2014, https://phinaucohi.wordpress.com/2014/08/27/thomas-pattison-1805-1899/.

27. Jackson, *A Pictorial History of Great Britain*, 63.

28. Cooper, "Thomas Pattison (1805–1899) Coach Painter and Founder of the Deaf and Dumb Institute, Sydney."

29. For example, Jan Branson and Don Miller, "Frederick John Rose: An Australian Pioneer," in *Collage: Works on International Deaf History*, ed. Renate Fischer and Tomas Vollhaber, 69–82.

30. Letters to the Editor, *The Argus,* February 14, 1859, 5; February 16, 1859, 5.

31. Supplement to *The Argus*, February 24, 1859, 1.

32. This school is, at time of publication, the only original Australian school for the deaf still operating. It has been on the site of 597 St Kilda Road in Melbourne since 1866.

33. Burchett, *Utmost for the Highest*, 108–9.

34. Flynn, *No Longer by Gaslight*, 3.

35. Lane, *When the Mind Hears*; Raymond Lee and John A. Hay, *Bermondsey 1792* (Feltham, Middlesex: National Union of the Deaf, 1993).

36. Burchett, *Utmost for the Highest*, 73.

37. Johnston and Schembri, *Australian Sign Language*.

38. Fitzgerald, *Open Minds, Open Hearts*, 53–58.

39. Adam, "Unimodal Bilingualism in the Deaf Community."

40. B. T. Wallis, *The Silent Book: A Deaf family and the Disappearing Australian-Irish Sign Language* (Melbourne, Victoria: Author, 2016).

41. For example, it was made compulsory in Victoria in 1910 (Burchett, *Utmost for the Highest*, 153); in Queensland in 1924, but in New South Wales not until the 1950s.

42. For example, in the *First Annual Report of the Adult Deaf Young Men's Mutual Improvement Society* in Adelaide in 1891, the rationale for its formation was given as "to prevent Deaf young men from wandering about the streets at night where they may meet with accidents, or fall in with bad company and be led astray. As Deaf young men cannot, by reason of their peculiar affliction avail themselves of the usual means of mental and moral improvement, this society was established, in order that they may have the same means of developing their mental powers and characters, as hearing young men do." Quoted in Rhonda Loades, "The Establishment and Maintenance of the the Deaf Community in South Australia," 32.

43. Flynn, *No Longer by Gaslight*; and *Post-School Organisations*.

44. Loades, "Deaf Community in South Australia," 36–47.

45. D. Thornton, S. Macready, and P. Levitzke-Gray, "Written into History: The Lives of Australian Deaf Leaders," in *Telling Deaf Lives: Agents of Change*, ed. K. Snoddon (Washington, DC: Gallaudet University Press, 2014) 93–101.

46. Fletcher S. Booth, "History of the N.S.W. Adult Deaf Society Organisation Work," undated manuscript, c. 1938. (File no. 0264, JWF Collection), 1.

47. Booth, "History of the N.S.W.," 1.

48. "The Rise of the Queensland Adult Deaf and Dumb Mission," *S.A. Deaf Monthly News*, January 1910, 7–9.

49. Sue Wilson, *The History of the Queensland Deaf Society: From Mission to Profession 1903–2003* (Brisbane: The Queensland Deaf Society, 2003).

50. Anne Bremner, "Deaf Sports in Australia." Master of Sign Language thesis, La Trobe University, 1996.

51. "Festivities in Connection with the Visit of New South Wales Deaf to Melbourne," *The British Deaf Mute* 5, no. 55 (March 1896): 122. Commentary ran over several issues and is quoted extensively in John W. Flynn, *Post-School Organisations*, 96–99.

52. Brian Greenwald, "Alexander Graham Bell Through the Lens of Eugenics, 1883-1922" (PhD diss., George Washington University, 2006).

Chapter 2

1. Bremner, "Deaf Sports in Australia," 27.

2. H. Dominic W. Stiles, "Editor, Journalist, Missioner—Ernest J. D. Abraham," blog post, accessed in 2014, http://blogs.ucl.ac.uk/library-rnid/2011/12/16/editor-journalist-missioner-having-having-previously-applied-for-and-been-rejected-as-missioner-ernest-j-d-abraham/.

3. Flynn, "Post-School Organisations," 36–38.

4. Joseph Hepworth, "Christmas at the Home of the B.D.M.," *The British Deaf-Mute* 5, no. 51 (Jan 1896): 89.

5. Quoted in Dominic Stiles, "Editor, Journalist, Missioner—Ernest J. D. Abraham," 2011.

6. Proceedings of the International Conference of Educators of the Deaf, Supplement to *American Annals of the Deaf*, 1893. Abraham's paper was not printed, as it was "withdrawn for revision, and, much to the editor's regret, [has] not been received for publication."

7. Hepworth, "Christmas at the Home of the B.D.M.," 91.

8. Flynn, *No Longer by Gaslight*, 24; Notes of the Victorian Deaf and Dumb Institution, Melbourne. From the Year 1898 to 1930. PROV, VA 02707 Charities Board of Victoria, VPRS 4523/P1, "Closed" Agency and General Correspondence Files, Unit 38, File No. 354. These notes state, in part, "[T]he fact that he was an applicant of the Superintendent's position some years previously is considered the reason for [Abraham's] prejudice [against the school]."

9. For example, Bourke, *The Story of a Deaf Drudge*, 18; Flynn, "Post-School Organisations," 37 and 58.

10. *The Gesture*, June 1907, quoted by Bourke, *Deaf Drudge*, 16–17.

11. Hepworth, "Christmas at the Home of the B.D.M.," 91.

12. "The Paradise of the Deaf," *The Gesture*, January 1913. Quoted by Bourke, *Deaf Drudge*, 17–18.

13. "A Pathetic Congress," *The Register* (January 4, 1904): 4; "Deaf and Dumb Congress," *The Argus* (December 30, 1903): 6.

14. Samuel Showell, Letter to the Editor, *The Age* (January 4, 1904): 5.

15. "A Pathetic Congress," 4.

16. "A Pathetic Congress," 4.

17. "Resolutions," *The Age* (December 30, 1903): 4.

18. "Resolutions," 4.

19. The term *Australasia* has usually referred to Australia and New Zealand combined.

20. Australasian Deaf and Dumb Association, *Rules*, n.d., 1-2. File No. 0431, JWF Collection.

21. *Our Monthly Letter* 8, no. 5 (January 1912): 4–5.

22. See Burch, *Signs of Resistance*, for a discussion of these issues in American Deaf communities between 1900 and 1940.

23. See Loades, "The Establishment and Maintenance of the Deaf Community in South Australia," chapter 4, for a discussion of these clashes.

24. "A Touch of Fellow Feeling," *The Advertiser*, August 16, 1902, 6; further discussion in Loades, *Deaf Community in South Australia*, 44.

25. Loades, *Deaf Community in South Australia*, 43–47.

26. Loades, *Deaf Community in South Australia*, 45.

27. QADDM, Second Annual Report, Year Ending 28 Feb 1905.

28. Flynn, "Post-School Organisations," 67. The Society's Committee was not happy with Abraham's action and resolved that "in future, [he] obtain the permission of the Committee before going away."

29. "Mr Abraham and N.S.W. Deaf," *Our Monthly Letter*, 10, no. 3 (November 1913): 1–4.

30. J. P. Bourke, *The After-School Problems of the Deaf and Dumb, No. I: The Problem of a Central Meeting Place for Them* (1933); *The After-School Problems of the Deaf and Dumb, No. II: The Problem of Ministering to Their Religious and Spiritual Needs* (1933); *The After-School Problems of the Deaf and Dumb, No. III: The Problem of the Impotent Deaf* (March 1935); *Benevolence and the Banned Baby* (May 1937); *"Fiction and Fact"—A Pamphlet* (December 1937); *Deaf Drudge* (1939), all published in Victoria by J. P.

Bourke; six issues of *The Australian Deaf Citizen,* were published between March 1940 and June 1941.

31. Bourke, *Deaf Drudge,* preface.

32. Bourke, "Brotherly Love!" *The Deaf Advocate* 3, no. 1 (January 1933).

33. Quoted in Bourke, *Deaf Drudge,* 15.

34. Bourke, *Deaf Drudge,* 1.

35. "Records of Members," Box No. 31, Victorian Deaf Society Collection.

36. J. O'Gorman, personal communication with author, November 5, 1992.

37. This has been described more recently as "dysconscious audism"—see Genie Gertz, "Dysconscious Audism: A Theoretical Proposition," in *Open Your Eyes: Deaf Studies Talking,* ed. H-D. Bauman (Minneapolis: University of Minnesota Press, 2008), 219–34.

38. Bourke, *Deaf Drudge,* 3.

39. Keri E. Iyall Smith and Patricia Leavy (eds.), *Hybrid Identities: Theoretical and Empirical Examinations* (Leiden: Brill, 2008).

40. Bourke, *"Fiction and Fact,"* 1, 10–11. Bourke included a quote from Garrison's "The Liberator" (1831) inside the front cover of all six issues of *The Australian Deaf Citizen.*

41. Arnold H. Payne, *King Silence: A Story* (London: Jarrolds Publishers, 1918).

42. Edna Edith Sayers, "B. H. and Arnold H. Payne: Early Champions of Sign Language in the United Kingdom," *Deaf History Review,* 5 (2007): 22–30.

43. Payne, *King Silence,* 203 (quoted in Bourke, *"Fiction and Fact,"* 13).

44. Payne, *King Silence,* 174 (quoted in Bourke, *Deaf Drudge,* title page).

45. Albert Ballin, *The Deaf Mute Howls* (Washington, DC: Gallaudet University Press. Reprint, 1998).

46. Ballin, *Howls,* 35. Emphasis in original.

47. Ballin, *Howls,* 1.

48. Farm & Home Committee Notes on John P. Bourke. File No. 668, JWF Collection.

49. Flynn, *No Longer by Gaslight: The First 100 Years of the Adult Deaf Society of Victoria,* Adult Deaf Society of Victoria, 47.

50. Bourke, *Deaf Drudge,* 28.

51. Bourke, *Deaf Drudge,* 21.

52. Bourke, *Deaf Drudge,* 26.

53. Bourke, *Deaf Drudge*, 19.

54. Bourke, *Deaf Drudge*, 20.

55. Bourke's salary commenced at ten shillings per week and rose to twenty shillings by the end of his term there. Farm & Home Committee Notes on John P. Bourke; Bourke, *Deaf Drudge*, 21.

56. Bourke, *Deaf Drudge*, 21.

57. Bourke, *Deaf Drudge*, 22.

58. Bourke, *Deaf Drudge*, 21.

59. Quoted in Bourke, *Deaf Drudge*, 21.

60. Bourke, *Deaf Drudge*, 22.

61. Bourke, *Deaf Drudge*, 22–23.

62. Bourke, *Deaf Drudge*, 23.

63. "Rose Day," *Our Monthly Letter* 21, no. 10, 11, and 12 (Oct./Nov./Dec. 1925).

64. Conference Notes: Australian [sic] Deaf & Dumb Association. October 5, 1922. File No. 253, JWF Collection. All subsequent quotes in this section are from this document.

65. Flynn, "Post-School Organisations," 80.

66. *The Herald*, February 2–9, 1923.

67. "Baby Banned. Father Loses His Job. 'Regretfully dispensed with,'" *The Herald*, February 2, 1923, 12.

68. For example, "Hearts Touched. Rescuing Young Couple. An Inspiring Response," *The Herald*, February 3, 1923, 1.

69. "Premises Sanitary. Fit for Family with Baby," *The Herald*, February 7, 1923, 1.

70. Bourke, *Deaf Drudge*, 23–24.

71. J. P. Bourke, "Shrewd Men" (Letter to the Editor), *The Herald*, February 6, 1923, 7.

72. Conference Notes: Australian (sic) Deaf & Dumb Association. October 5, 1922. File No. 253, JWF Collection.

73. Bourke, *Deaf Drudge*, 24.

74. E. A. Reynolds, interview by J. W. Flynn, March 26, 1981. Transcript in File No. 230, JWF Collection, 18–19.

75. Bourke, *Deaf Drudge*, 25–35.

76. Bourke, *Deaf Drudge*, 30.

77. Farm & Home Committee Notes on John P. Bourke.

78. Reg Hamilton, *The History of the Australian Minimum Wage*, Fair Work Commission, 2016. Accessed 1/10/17, https://www.fwc.gov.au/documents/documents/archives/exhibitions/minwage/exhibitionpaper-100yrsminwage.pdf

79. Bourke, *Deaf Drudge*, 29.

80. Farm & Home Committee Notes on John P. Bourke.

81. Bourke, *Deaf Drudge*, 29.

82. Bourke, *Deaf Drudge*, 34.

83. Farm & Home Committee Notes on John P. Bourke.

84. He still held this position at the time he wrote *The Story of a Deaf Drudge* in 1939.

85. Bourke, *Deaf Drudge*, 34.

86. "Our Late President, Mr. E. R. Peacock," *Victorian Deaf News* 3, no. 2 (July/Aug./Sept. 1932): 2; QADDM, Report for the Year Ending 28 Feb 1930, 13; Loades, *Deaf Community in South Australia*, 40; Extract from "Who's Who," File No. 855, JWF Collection.

87. QADDM, February 28, 1926.

88. "The Night of Nights at our Centre—Jolimont Square," *Our Monthly Letter* 22, no. 12 (December 1926).

89. *The Argus*, October 9, 1926, 33. See also *The Age*, (October 9, 1926): 19.

90. "Our Principal 'Resting,'" *Our Monthly Letter* 22, nos. 7 and 8 (July/August 1926).

91. "A Silent World. Memorable Week for the Deaf," *The Telegraph* (no date provided), quoted in *Our Monthly Letter* 22, nos. 7 and 8 (July/August 1926).

92. John Flynn describes them as having a "'distant' friendship." See Flynn, "Post School Organisations," 68.

93. "Our Principal 'Resting,'" *Our Monthly Letter* 22, nos. 7 and 8 (July/August 1926).

94. Bourke, *Deaf Drudge*, 37; "Men's Guild," *Our Monthly Letter* 21, nos. 4, 5, 6 (April/May/June 1925).

95. Bourke, *The After-School Problems, No. I*, 8.

96. Ladd, *Understanding Deaf Culture*, 332–33.

97. Bourke, *Deaf Drudge*, 8. This was Rule 2 of the Victorian Deaf Committee's constitution in the 1920s.

98. Abraham's practice of insinuating himself into and controlling all levels of the Society, from General Board to Deaf Committee (like Lonsdale in Sydney—See chapter 3) was similar to the way in which many British missioners operated at the time. See Ladd, *Understanding Deaf Culture*, 333–34.

99. Bourke, *Deaf Drudge*, 9.

100. For background on sectarian attitudes in Australia at this time, see Stephen Blyth, "A Historical Overview of Australian Religious

Sectarianism Accompanied by a Survey of Factors Contributing to Its Dissolution" *Integrity: A Journal of Australian Church History*, 1 (2012): 81–110.

101. Bourke, *Deaf Drudge*, 37.

102. Bourke, *Deaf Drudge*, 37–38.

103. Bourke, *Deaf Drudge*, 38.

104. "Men's Guild," *Our Monthly Letter* 22, no. 3 (March 1926).

105. Bourke, *Deaf Drudge*, 11–13.

106. Bourke, *Deaf Drudge*, 25.

107. Melby Dyson, interview by Michael Uniacke, July 15, 1982. Mr. Dyson was Abraham's chauffeur for many years.

108. Bourke, *Deaf Drudge*, 53.

109. Fred Sandon, interview by the author, June 28, 1995. Mr. Sandon also worked for a time as Abraham's chauffeur.

110. Bourke, *Deaf Drudge*, 53.

111. See Ladd, *Understanding Deaf Culture*, 377–78, for a description of similar practices in British missions. Ladd describes the role of the "Favoured Group."

112. The identity of "P. Clay" can be confirmed by some of the letters that Bourke reproduced and said were signed by Clay. In original newspaper copies, such as the one in *The Herald* on January 19, 1926; these letters are signed by J. M. Johnston.

113. Bourke, *Deaf Drudge*, 52–53.

114. Bourke, *Deaf Drudge*, 55.

115. Bourke, *Deaf Drudge*, 54.

116. Bourke, *Deaf Drudge*, 55.

117. Quoted in Bourke, *Deaf Drudge*, 39.

118. J. P. Bourke, Letter to the Editor, *The Herald*, January 18, 1926, 6.

119. J. M. Johnston, Letter to the Editor, *The Herald*, January 19, 1926, 4.

120. Bourke, *Deaf Drudge*, 40.

121. "Now—Lest We Forget," *Our Monthly Letter* 22, no. 2 (February 1926).

122. Bourke, *Deaf Drudge*, 39.

123. Bourke, *Deaf Drudge*, 40 (no date is given for the letter).

124. ADDSV, Minutes of General Board Meetings, July 27, 1926, and September 3, 1926.

125. Bourke, *Deaf Drudge*, 40–41.

126. Bourke, *Deaf Drudge*, 41.

127. Bourke, *Deaf Drudge*, 41.

128. Bourke, *Deaf Drudge*, 41. This letter, and other personal correspondence between Abraham and Bourke quoted in the next few pages, does not survive outside the pages of Bourke's book. Our acceptance of their authenticity must depend on the rigor Bourke shows elsewhere in his writing, where most of his information and quoted letters can be corroborated from other sources, and also on the authenticity of the "voice" in the letters.

129. Bourke, *Deaf Drudge*, 43.

130. J. P. Bourke, Letters to the Editor, *The Age*, May 7, 1927, 25; May 13, 1927, 11.

131. Quoted in Bourke, *Deaf Drudge*, 44.

132. J. P. Bourke, Letter to the Editor, *The Age*, May 31, 1927, 9.

133. J. M. Johnston, Letter to the Editor, *The Age*, June 1, 1927, 15.

134. Bourke, *Deaf Drudge*, 46.

135. Bourke, *Deaf Drudge*, 47.

136. E. J. D. Abraham, letter to J. P. Bourke, dated June 1, 1927, quoted in Bourke, *Deaf Drudge*, 46. The two instances of "(sic)" are by Bourke.

137. J. P. Bourke, letter to E. J. D. Abraham, dated June 1, 1927, quoted in Bourke, *Deaf Drudge*, 48–49.

138. Bourke, *Deaf Drudge*, 49.

Chapter 3

1. See Shurlee Swain, "Society and Welfare," in *The Cambridge History of Australia*, 2nd edition, Vol. 2, ed. Alison Bashford and Stuart Macintyre, 284–307 (Melbourne, Victoria: Cambridge University Press, 2013).

2. See Marilyn Lake, *Getting Equal: The History of Australian Feminism* (St. Leonards, New South Wales: Allen & Unwin, 1999), 50 and 140.

3. Lake, *Getting Equal*, 139.

4. Anna Haebich and Steve Kinnane, "Indigenous Australia," in *The Cambridge History of Australia*, Vol. 2, ed. Alison Bashford and Stuart Mcintyre (Port Melbourne, Cambridge University Press, 2013): 332–57.

5. ADDSNSW, Minutes of Executive Meeting, April 17, 1928.

6. "Portsmouth," *The British Deaf Times* XVII, no. 201–202 (September/October 1920): 79.

7. "Portsmouth," 79.

8. "Our Missioners. 2. Mr. H. V. S. Hersee, Portsmouth," *The British Deaf Times* XIX, no. 221–222 (May/June 1922): 39.

9. "Our Missioners. 2. Mr. H. V. S. Hersee, Portsmouth," 39.

10. Leila Altschwager, *The First Sixty Years: A History of Toc H in Australia from 1925 to 1985* (Adelaide: Toc H Australia, 1985), 6.

11. "The British Deaf and Dumb Association. Congress at Southampton," *The Deaf Quarterly News*, no. 83 (Oct./Nov./Dec. 1925): 1; *The Deaf Quarterly News*, no. 95 (Oct./Nov./Dec. 1928): 3.

12. M. Dyson, interview by Michael Uniacke, July 15, 1982.

13. ADDSNSW, Minutes of Executive Meeting, August 21, 1928.

14. ADDSNSW, August 21, 1928.

15. ADDSNSW, Minutes of Executive Meeting, September 4, 1928.

16. ADDSNSW, Minutes of Executive Meeting, September 18, 1928.

17. ADDSNSW, Minutes of Executive Meeting, October 9, 1928.

18. ADDSNSW, Minutes of Executive Meeting, October 23, 1928.

19. Ella Doran, *Hand in Hand with Time and Change: The Life of Ella Doran and Her Work with the Deaf in Australia* (Woden: Molonglo Press, 1998), 170.

20. ADDSNSW, Minutes of Executive Meeting, February 5, 1929.

21. ADDSNSW, Minutes of Executive Meeting, March 12, 1929; ADDSNSW, Minutes of Executive Meeting, March 26, 1929.

22. ADDSNSW, Minutes of Executive Meeting, March 26, 1929.

23. ADDSNSW, Minutes of Executive Meeting, March 26, 1929.

24. "Mr. Hersee's Dismissal: A Few Facts That Occurred in 1929," *Onward!* (August 1929): 6.

25. ADDSNSW, transcript of Special Meeting of Council held on April 8, 1929, 2–6. (File No. 0146, JWF Collection.)

26. ADDSNSW, Special Meeting of Council, 6–8.

27. ADDSNSW, Special Meeting of Council.

28. F. S. Booth, "Why the Association of Deaf and Dumb Citizens Was Formed," *Onward!* (January 1930): 8.

29. ADDSNSW, Minutes of Executive Meeting, April 16, 1929.

30. Booth, "Why the Association of Deaf and Dumb Citizens was Formed," 8.

31. ADDSNSW, Minutes of Executive Meeting, April 16, 1929.

32. Conference Notes: Australian (sic) Deaf & Dumb Association, October 5, 1922. File No. 253, JWF Collection.

33. See Stuart Macintyre, *The Oxford History of Australia Vol. 4: 1901-1942 The Succeeding Age* (Melbourne: Oxford University Press, 1986), 23454; Frank Bongiorno, "Search for a Solution, 1923-39," in *The Cambridge History of Australia*, 2nd edition, Vol. 2, ed. Alison Bashford and

Stuart Macintyre (Melbourne, Victoria: Cambridge University Press, 2013) 64–87.

34. Quoted in "Mr. Hersee's Dismissal," 6.

35. ADDSNSW, Minutes of Executive Meeting, May 3, 1929.

36. Quoted in "Mr. Hersee's Dismissal," 9.

37. ADDSNSW, Minutes of Executive Meeting, May 9, 1929.

38. Caption accompanying photo, *Sydney Morning Herald*, May 9, 1929, 12; Renate Fischer and Tomas Vollhaber, eds., *Collage: Works on International Deaf History* (Hamburg: Signum Press, 1996), 9.

39. "Deaf and Dumb. Angry Meeting," *Sydney Morning Herald*, May 9, 1929, 11.

40. "Deaf and Dumb. Angry Meeting," 11.

41. ADDSNSW, Minutes of Executive Meeting, May 9, 1929.

42. Deaf people's indignation at this particular decision echoed through their writings for several years afterwards. For example, on the occasion of the fifth anniversary of the breakaway, the editors of the Association's newspaper reminded readers of when "[Deaf people] were helpless when the doors of the Society were closed against them under instructions from the president. Locked out of their own home provided for them by a generous public!" *The Deaf Advocate* 4, no. 3 (May/June 1934): 2.

43. ADDSNSW, Minutes of Executive Meeting, May 14, 1929.

44. Doran, *Hand in Hand with Time and Change*, 45.

45. "Deaf and Dumb. New Society Formed," *Sydney Morning Herald*, May 11, 1929, 21.

46. Minutes of conference between representatives of the Adult Deaf and Dumb Society and the Association of Deaf and Dumb Citizens [sic], May 25, 1936. File No. 0144, JWF Collection.

47. "'Spoke' with Vehemence. Deaf and Dumb Form New Society," *Daily Telegraph Pictorial*, May 11, 1929, 5.

48. "Deaf and Dumb. New Society Formed," 12; "Deaf and Dumb Association," *Sydney Morning Herald*, June 19, 1929, 10.

49. For example, the New South Wales Attorney General, the Hon. H. E. Manning, K.C., M.L.C., spoke at the Association's third annual general meeting in 1932, declaring that the Association fulfilled the "obligations of citizenship"—self-respect, social intercourse, and mutual assistance. See the report in *The Deaf Advocate* 2, no. 8 (August 1932).

50. E. J. Davidson, "A Well-Wishing," *Onward!* (Aug 1929): 1.

51. ADDSNSW, Minutes of Executive Meeting, May 14, 1929.

52. "Deaf and Dumb. The Adult Society," *Sydney Morning Herald*, May 16, 1929, 13.

53. ADDSNSW, Minutes of Executive Meeting, May 21, 1929; ADDSNSW, Minutes of Executive Meeting, June 18, 1929; ADDSNSW, Minutes of Executive Meeting, July 16, 1929.

54. Booth, "Why the Association of Deaf and Dumb Citizens was Formed," 8.

55. ADDSNSW, Minutes of Executive Meeting, September 24, 1929.

56. "Editorial," *The Deaf Advocate* 1, no. 4 (April 1931): 1.

57. ADDSNSW, Minutes of Executive Meeting, May 21, 1929.

58. ADDSNSW, Minutes of Executive Meeting, May 21, 1929.

59. ADDSNSW, Minutes of Executive Meeting, June 18, 1929; ADDSNSW, Minutes of Executive Meeting, July 2, 1929.

60. Phillips, like Johnston in Victoria, could speak and lipread as well as sign, which probably made him seem ideal for both keeping an eye on deaf people and reporting to hearing employers. His speaking ability is mentioned in an interview with Alan Fairweather in Michael Clancy, ed., *Heritage in Our Hands: Stories of the Deaf Community of N.S.W.* (Sydney: Adult Education Centre for Deaf and Hearing Impaired Persons Inc., 1988), 129.

61. Gordon Winn, Letter to the Editor, *The Deaf Advocate* 2, no. 3 (March 1932).

62. Booth, "Why the Association of Deaf and Dumb Citizens was Formed," 9.

63. "Wild Meeting. Policemen Present," *News*, August 24, 1929. Quoted in *Onward!* (January 1930): 13–14.

64. ADDSNSW. Report for the Year Adopted at the Annual Meeting, August 23, 1929, 5.

65. Annual General Meeting of the Adult Deaf Society of New South Wales, Friday 23 August 1929. Transcript prepared by W. W. Lesslie, shorthand writer, 2. (File No. 0147, JWF Collection.)

66. "Wild Meeting," 13–14.

67. "Fooling the Deaf and Dumb! Lively Close to Annual Meeting," *Daily Telegraph Pictorial*, August 24, 1929, 3.

68. "Fooling the Deaf and Dumb!" 3.

69. Unnamed magazine (later *The Deaf Advocate*), December 1930, 4.

70. "Adult Deaf and Dumb Society Refuse all Mediation," *Onward!* (January 1930): 2–3.

71. "Resolutions Moved at a Publicly Convened Meeting of Adult Deaf and Dumb in the Adyar Hall, April 24th 1930." File No. 144, JWF Collection.

72. "Deaf and Dumb in Uproar," *The Daily Guardian*, April 25, 1930.

73. "Resolutions Moved at a Publicly Convened Meeting of Adult Deaf and Dumb in the Adyar Hall, April 24th 1930."

74. Lake, *Getting Equal*, 14.

75. ADDSNSW, Minutes of Executive Meeting, March 4, 1930.

76. Letter from President of the ADDSNSW to the Minister for Education, July 30, 1930. In File No. 0144, JWF Collection.

77. Letter from President of the ADDSNSW to the Minister for Education.

78. For example, in February 1933, nine of the fourteen councillors were deaf, and four of the five hearing councillors had deaf relatives. "Editorial," *The Deaf Advocate* 3, no. 2 (February 1933).

79. "Editorial," *The Deaf Advocate* 1, no. 3 (March 1931).

80. Letter from Walter Dickson & Co. to Fletcher S. Booth, April 30, 1931, reprinted in *The Deaf Advocate* 1, no. 6 (June 1931).

81. Letter from H. V. S. Hersee to Walter Dickson & Co., May 11, 1931, reprinted in *The Deaf Advocate* 1, No. 6 (June 1931).

82. Francis Gibson, in *The Frat* 1, no. 2 (March 1904). Quoted in Burch, *Signs of Resistance*, 107.

83. "The Deaf A R E Managing their Own Affairs."

84. *The Deaf Advocate* 3, no. 5 (May 1933).

85. "Fourth Annual Meeting of the New South Wales Association of Deaf and Dumb Citizens," *The Deaf Advocate* 3, no. 7 (July 1933).

86. "Noblesse Oblige," *The Deaf Advocate* 2, no. 4 (April 1932).

87. Lonsdale's practice of controlling all levels of the Society, from council to small club (like Abraham in Melbourne—See chapter 3) was similar to the way in which many British missioners operated at the time. See Ladd, *Understanding Deaf Culture*, 333–34.

88. "Fascism," *The Deaf Advocate* 2, no. 7 (July 1932).

89. "Good Bye to All That," *The Deaf Advocate* 2, no. 5 (May 1932).

90. "Good Bye to All That." Underlining and idiosyncratic punctuation in original.

91. "Fancy Dress Dance," *The Deaf Advocate* 4, no. 1 (Jan/Feb 1934): 8.

92. "Editorial," *The Deaf Advocate* 4, no. 4 (Aug/Sept 1934): 2–3.

93. "The Difference Between Sydney's Two Deaf Organisations," *The Deaf Advocate* 2, no. 4 (April 1932).

94. Doran, *Hand in Hand with Time and Change*, 45; "Fooling the Deaf and Dumb!" 3.

95. For example, Jenny Koschutzke, "The History of the Sydney Deaf Community's Boycott of the Adult Deaf and Dumb Society from 1929 to 1937 and the Establishment of their own Rival

Association of Deaf and Dumb Citizens." (MA thesis, University of Sydney, 1995).

96. Doran, *Hand in Hand with Time and Change*, 45.

97. Letter from President of the Adult Deaf and Dumb Society of NSW to the Minister for Education, July 30, 1930. File No. 0144, JWF Collection.

98. *The Silent Messenger* (January 1931).

99. "The Difference Between Sydney's Two Deaf Organisations," *The Deaf Advocate* 2, no. 4 (April 1932); "Christmas Dinner," *The Deaf Advocate* 3, No. 1 (Jan 1933).

100. Bob Herman, interview in Clancy, *Heritage in our Hands*, 117.

101. Bill Quinn, interview in Michael Clancy, ed., *Heritage in Our Hands*, 119.

102. For example, the NSW branch of the Australian Catholic Deaf Mutes' Association incorporated itself with the NSWADDC. "The Chairman's Message," *Onward!* (January 1930) 1.

103. "Editorial," unnamed magazine, (December 1931), 1. This unnamed magazine later became *The Deaf Advocate*.

104. *The Deaf Advocate* 1, no. 1 (January 1931).

105. Koschutzke, MA thesis, 28.

106. "The Adult Deaf and Dumb Society," *The Deaf Advocate* 1, no. 6 (June 1931).

107. "The Adult Deaf and Dumb Society."

108. "The Melbourne Cricket Carnival. Why the Association Was Not Represented. How Some Cricketers 'Play the Game,'"*The Deaf Advocate* 2, no. 2 (February 1932).

109. Letter to the Editor, *The Deaf Advocate* 2, no. 3 (March 1932).

110. Gordon Winn, Letter to the Editor, *The Deaf Advocate* 2, no. 3 (March 1932).

111. Gordon Winn, Christmas message, *The Deaf Advocate* 2, no. 12 (December 1932).

112. *The Deaf Advocate* 4, no. 4 (Aug/Sept 1934): 2.

Chapter 4

1. "Ayrshire Mission to the Deaf and Dumb," *British Deaf-Mute* V, no. 50 (December 1895): 42–43.

2. Flynn, *No Longer by Gaslight*, 43.

3. E. A. Reynolds, interview by Michael Uniacke., June 2, 1982.

4. E. A. Reynolds, interview by John W. Flynn, 16.

5. "Aberdeen," *The British Deaf Times* XVIII, no. 213–14 (Sept/Oct 1921): 79; "Aberdeen," *The British Deaf Times* XIX, no. 219–20 (March/ April 1922): 32.

6. Paul's papers are held in the John W. Flynn Collection, State Library of Victoria, MS13555. Paul's interest in the preservation of sign languages may have been influenced by the work of the National Association of the Deaf in the United States during the early decades of the twentieth century, when they made several films to preserve their language. See for example, George W. Veditz, "The Preservation of the Sign Language," in *Deaf World: A Historical Reader and Primary Sourcebook*, ed. L. Bragg (New York: New York University Press, 2001), 83–85.

7. Flynn, "Post-School Organisations," 85–89.

8. "Ian O'Marnoc," *Deaf Mutes Journal*, December 2, 1920; reprinted in full in Flynn, "Post-School Organisations," 88–89.

9. J. M. Paul, "Birthday Greetings," *The Deaf Advocate* 3, no. 5 (May 1933).

10. "Births," *Our Monthly Letter* 21, no. 10–12 (Oct/Nov/Dec 1925): 4; "Our Little World," *Our Monthly Letter* 22, no. 3 (March 1926): 5.

11. "Queenslands New Missioner," *Our Monthly News* 23, no. 3–5 (March/April/May 1927): 5.

12. For example, QADDM, *Report for the Year Ending 28 Feb, 1928*.

13. For example, QADDM, *Report for the Year Ending 28 Feb, 1925*; *Report for the Year Ending 28 Feb, 1933*, 17–18.

14. QADDM, *Report for the Year Ending 28 Feb, 1925*.

15. W. R. Kingwell (committee member of QADDM), letter to A. L. Lonsdale, dated October 26, 1931. File No. 0255, JWF Collection.

16. Paul, "Birthday Greetings."

17. For example, C. C. Garner, "Queensland Deaf and Vocational Training," *The Deaf Advocate* 2, no. 6 (June 1932).

18. Although Paul's name is not on the memorandum, the secretary of the Management Committee noted that it was from "a servant of the Mission," and Paul's style and philosophy are evident in it.

19. Queensland State Archives: Home Secretary's Office; Correspondence re blind deaf and dumb, general, 1900-1937; Extracts from Minute Book on Training Scheme Verified by & Initialled by Supt. Paul 23-2-31; RSI2383-1-21. [These documents were prepared for the Bradbury Inquiry, see following.] Stress in original.

20. QADDM, Minutes of Committee meeting held June 21, 1928.

21. QADDM, Minutes of Committee meeting held December 13, 1928.

22. QADDM, Minutes of Committee meeting held February 21, 1929.

23. QADDM, Report of Sub-Committee appointed to meet the Deaf-Mutes, attached to Minutes of Committee Meeting held June 5, 1930. There is some ambiguity about Tunley's status, with some records indicating that he was deaf himself; but this does not seem to be the case (Joe Conley, personal communication, May 14, 2003). It is possible that he may have been hard of hearing.

24. "Deaf and Dumb. Cost of Training. Deficit of £262," *The Daily Mail*, April 29, 1930, 12.

25. QADDM, Superintendent's Report for May, presented at committee meeting held June 5, 1930.

26. Queensland State Archives: Home Secretary's Office; Statement by President of Q. A. D & D. Mission (Incorp) at the Inquiry held by Mr Bradbury, Home Department 8-5-31; RSI2383-1-21, 35.

27. QADDM, *Report for the Year Ending 28 Feb 1931*, 9.

28. QADDM, *Report for the Year Ending 28 Feb 1931*, 11.

29. QADDM, *Report for the Year Ending 28 Feb 1931*, 9.

30. QADDM, *Report for the Year Ending 28 Feb 1931*, 11.

31. QADDM, *Report for the Year Ending 28 Feb 1931*, 11.

32. Queensland State Archives: Home Secretary's Office; Statement by President of Q. A. D & D. Mission (Incorp) at the Inquiry held by Mr Bradbury, Home Department 8-5-31; RSI2383-1-21, 24-25, 31.

33. QADDM, *Report for the Year Ending 28 Feb 1931*, 14.

34. QADDM. Minutes of Committee meeting held December 4, 1930.

35. J. M. Paul, "A call 'to think,'" *The Deaf Advocate* 2, no. 5 (May 1932).

36. Will Downem, Letter to the Editor, *The Deaf Advocate*, (Sept/Oct 1931). [This is likely to have been Paul writing under a pseudonym.] No volume or issue number—special issue on Queensland.

37. QADDM, Minutes of Committee meeting held January 22, 1931.

38. "Presentation to Mr. J. M. Paul," *The Deaf Advocate* 1, no. 4 (April 1931): 6.

39. "Presentation to Mr. J. M. Paul," 6.

40. QADDM, Minutes of Committee meeting held May 21, 1931.

41. Kingwell, letter to A. L. Lonsdale, dated October 26, 1931.

42. Queensland State Archives: Home Secretary's Office; Statement by President of Q. A. D & D. Mission (Incorp) at the Inquiry held by Mr Bradbury, Home Department 8-5-31; RSI2383-1-21, 38.

43. QADDM, Minutes of Special Meeting held February 10, 1931.

44. Benedict Arnold was a traitor during the American War of Independence.

45. Letter to the Editor, *The Deaf Advocate* 1, no. 3, March 1931.

46. QADDM, Minutes of Committee meeting held April 16, 1931.

47. QADDM, April 16, 1931.

48. "Definite Break. New Body Formed. Deaf and Dumb Act. Protest at Committee's Actions," *The Daily Mail*, August 19, 1931, 8.

49. QADDM, Minutes of annual general meeting, May 29, 1931.

50. W. Bradbury, "Inquiry into the Working of the Queensland Adult Deaf and Dumb Mission," 1931. File No. 0255 in JWF Collection.

51. Bradbury, "Inquiry." 14–15.

52. C. C. Garner, "To the Advocate," *The Deaf Advocate* 2, no. 3 (March 1932).

53. "Our Missioners. 2. Mr. H. V. S. Hersee, Portsmouth," *The British Deaf Times* XIX, no. 221–22 (May/June 1922): 39.

54. J. M. Paul, untitled fragment. File No. 0683 in JWF Collection.

55. Bradbury, "Inquiry."

56. J. M. Paul, "A letter from Queensland," *The Deaf Advocate* 2, no. 2 (February 1932). Capitals in original.

57. Kingwell, letter to A. L. Lonsdale, dated October 26, 1931; Bradbury, "Inquiry," 11–12.

58. Kingwell, letter to A. L. Lonsdale, dated October 26, 1931.

59. QADDM Finance, Property and Staff Committee. Minutes of Special Meeting, held July 31, 1931.

60. QADDM Finance, Property and Staff Committee. Minutes of Special Meetings, held August 14 and 17, 1931.

61. M. O. Wilson, "Queensland—A Lady's Point of View," *The Deaf Advocate*, (Sept/Oct 1931).

62. Garner, "To the Advocate."

63. "Definite Break," 8.

64. For example, reports in the *News*, August 24, 1929, quoted in *Onward!* (January 1930): 13–14; "Fooling the Deaf and Dumb! Lively Close to Annual Meeting," *Daily Telegraph Pictorial*, 24 Aug 1929, 3.

65. "Deaf and Dumb Citizens Reformed Association," *The Cairns Post*, September 1, 1932, 10.

66. H. V. S. Hersee, "Impressions of my Visit to Queensland," *The Deaf Advocate*, (Sept/Oct 1931).

67. Kingwell, letter to A. L. Lonsdale, dated October 26, 1931.

68. Hersee, "Visit to Queensland."

69. Kingwell, letter to A. L. Lonsdale, dated October 26, 1931.

70. "Hats off to Mr. J. M. Paul and Mr. H.V. S. Hersee!" *The Deaf Advocate*, (Sept/Oct 1931).

71. "Hats off to Mr. J. M. Paul and Mr. H.V. S. Hersee!"

72. "Editorial," *The Deaf Advocate*, (Sept/Oct 1931).

73. Kingwell, letter to A. L. Lonsdale, dated October 26, 1931.

74. "Deaf and Dumb Citizens Reformed Association," *The Cairns Post*, September 1, 1932, 10.

75. "Deaf and Dumb Citizens Reformed Association," *The Cairns Post*, September 1, 1932, 10.

76. "Overseas Page. Australia," *British Deaf Times* XXIX, no. 337–38 (Jan/Feb 1932): 3.

77. "Editorial," *The Deaf Advocate* 3, no. 2 (February 1933).

78. "Deaf and Dumb Citizens Reformed Association," *The Cairns Post*, 1 Sept 1932, 10.

79. "Deaf and Dumb Citizens Reformed Association," *The Cairns Post*, September 1 1932, 10.

80. "Editorial," *The Deaf Advocate*, (Sept/Oct 1931).

81. QADDM, Lists of Life Members in *Reports for the Year Ending 28 Feb 1931* and *29 Feb 1932*. See "Powers to Reject Members" under Clause 9 of Constitution, in *Report for the Year Ending 28 Feb 1931*, 11.

82. QADDM, Minutes of meeting held September 15, 1931.

83. J. M. Paul, "Queensland Deaf and Dumb Association News," *The Deaf Advocate* 2, no. 3 (March 1932).

84. "Editorial," *The Deaf Advocate*, (Sept/Oct 1931).

85. Wilson, "Queensland."

86. Paul, "Queensland Deaf and Dumb Association News."

87. J. M. Paul, "Self Advertisement by Insult," *The Deaf Advocate* 2, no. 6 (June 1932).

88. Hersee, "Visit to Queensland," stress in original.

89. Hersee, "Visit to Queensland."

90. "Deaf and Dumb Citizens Reformed Association," *The Cairns Post*, September 1, 1932, 10.

91. "Message from Queensland," *The Victorian Deaf*, (Jan/Feb 1932): 11–12.

92. Wrigley, *The Politics of Deafness*, 50.

Chapter 5

1. These resources are now relatively accessible, with most being preserved in two large collections in the State Library of Victoria—the

Victorian Deaf Society Collection (MS13362) and the J. W. Flynn Collection (MS13555). Some are held in the La Trobe University Library. Copies of J. P. Bourke's booklets are also held in the National Library of Australia, among other places.

2. Reynolds, interview by J. W. Flynn.

3. See Ladd, *Understanding Deaf Culture*, chapters 8 and 9, for an insightful analysis of the practices of British missioners.

4. E. A. Reynolds, interview by Michael Uniacke.

5. An example was Iris Boortz, a deaf daughter of deaf parents in Melbourne, who later moved to NSW and married A. D. Taylor—her husband was a collector for the NSWADDC, and Iris was active in the Association too. Abraham had known her all her life. At her twenty-first birthday party, he "made a very sincere speech for he had nursed Iris as a baby and watched her grow to girlhood, and now young womanhood, with much pride" (*Our Monthly Letter*, Jan/Feb/March 1925). He later interpreted for her wedding and proposed the toast to "The Bride and Bridegroom" (*Our Monthly Letter*, April/May/June 1925). Even after Iris joined the Association, Abraham would remind her of their shared history and once instructed her, while she was visiting her mother, to take back his "best wishes" to the Association in NSW. ["By the Way," *The Deaf Advocate* 1, no. 6 (June 1931).]

6. Reynolds, interview by J. W. Flynn, 34.

7. *The Age*, October 9, 1926, 19.

8. An article in the *British Deaf-Mute* had once praised him by saying rhetorically, "If all the superintendents mixed with their people, and **acted as though they were of them**, the deaf would certainly appreciate their efforts the more." [Hepworth, "Christmas at the Home of the B.D.M.," 91.]

9. Brisbane *Telegraph*, quoted in *Our Monthly Letter* 22, no. 7 and 8 (July/Aug 1926). (The *Telegraph* quote was undated.)

10. For example, W. H. Crush was English and spoke as well as signed, R. H. Lambert was Scottish, Bourke was late-deafened, and Mrs. M. Gladman had grown up in hearing schools rather than the state deaf school.

11. ADDSV, Minutes of General Board meeting, September 17, 1928.

12. Bourke, *Deaf Drudge*, 56.

13. *Commonwealth Silent Courier* 1, no. 1 (Sept 1928).

14. *Commonwealth Silent Courier* 1, no. 1 (Sept 1928).

15. Bourke, *Deaf Drudge*, 56.

16. ADDSV, Minutes of General Board Meeting, October 29, 1928, attachment.

17. *Our Deaf Mute Citizens*, n.d. (1928 handwritten on cover). File No. 0432, JWF Collection.

18. Bourke, *Deaf Drudge*, 56–58.

19. Bourke, *Deaf Drudge*, 70–71.

20. Supplementary Estimates [Assembly], July 24, 1929, *Hansard*, 430.

21. Supplementary Estimates [Assembly], July 24, 1929, *Hansard*, 430.

22. Supplementary Estimates [Assembly], July 24, 1929, *Hansard*, 430.

23. Bourke, *Deaf Drudge*, 71.

24. Supplementary Estimates [Assembly], August 28, 1929, *Hansard*, 1183.

25. Supplementary Estimates [Assembly], August 29, 1929, *Hansard*, 1237.

26. Supplementary Estimates [Assembly], August 28, 1929, *Hansard*, 1183, and 29 August 1929, 1237.

27. For example, in Bourke, *Banned Baby*, 1–2.

28. ADDSV, Minutes of General Board Meeting, September 16, 1929.

29. ADDSV, Minutes of General Board Meeting, October 20, 1929.

30. ADDSV, Minutes, October 20, 1929.

31. ADDSV, Minutes of General Board Meeting, November 25, 1929.

32. ADDSV, Minutes November 25, 1929.

33. Bourke, *Deaf Drudge*, 71.

34. Bourke, *Deaf Drudge*, 72–73.

35. See Ladd, *Understanding Deaf Culture*, 377, for a British comparison: "Given the vital importance of the club to Deaf people, the ability to ban someone for disagreeing with the missioner carried immense resonance, which served to keep other less bold souls quiescent."

36. Bourke, *Deaf Drudge*, 58.

37. Bourke, *Deaf Drudge*, 58.

38. ADDSV, Minutes of General Board Meeting, 16 September 16, 1929.

39. Bourke, *Deaf Drudge*, 61–62.

40. Bourke's account is particularly useful, as the only other surviving records of the Deaf Committee of the time seem to be some annual reports.

41. Bourke, *Deaf Drudge*, 62.

42. Bourke, *Deaf Drudge*, 62.

43. Bourke, *Deaf Drudge*, 63.

44. Bourke, *Deaf Drudge*, 63.

45. ADDSV, Minutes of General Board Meeting, 20 October 20, 1929.

46. Described in ADDSV, Minutes of General Board Meeting, November 25, 1929; actual statement is attached to minutes of February 17, 1930.

47. Bourke, *Deaf Drudge*, 61.

48. Bourke, *Deaf Drudge*, 64.

49. Bourke, *Deaf Drudge*, 65.

50. ADDSV, Minutes of General Board Meeting, January 20, 1930.

51. ADDSV, Minutes of General Board Meeting, February 17, 1930.

52. ADDSV, Minutes of General Board Meeting, March 21, 1930. Menzies was at that time the MLA for the state seat of Nunawading, which would have included the Blackburn farm and home. He was later to become Australia's longest-serving conservative prime minister, serving two terms from 1939 to 1941 and from 1949 to 1966. One of his proteges was to be Andrew Peacock, a relative of the then Deaf Society president, E. R. Peacock.

53. See, for example, "Deaf and Dumb Society: Government Guarantee Asked," *The Age*, March 15, 1930, 25.

54. ADDSV, Minutes of General Board Meeting, 21 March 21, 1930.

55. Bourke, *Deaf Drudge*, 65.

56. ADDSV, Minutes of General Board Meeting, April 28, 1930.

57. For example, ADDSV, Minutes of Executive Committee Meetings, August 13, 1930; September 15, 1930; December 16, 1930; February 24, 1931; and many others.

58. ADDSV, Minutes of General Board Meeting, 20 January 20, 1930.

59. ADDSV, Minutes of General Board Meeting, June 3, 1930.

60. ADDSV, Minutes of General Board Meeting, June 20, 1927.

61. See statement about separation of council and Executive Committee in NSW (Letter from President of the ADDSNSW to the Minister for Education, July 30, 1930. File No. 0144, JWF Collection); the South Australia Mission Committee's 1905 action to establish a separate Finance Committee of hearing members only to take over most of the administrative matters of the Mission, effectively disenfranchising the deaf members of the Mission Committee (Loades, *Deaf Community in South Australia*, 43); and Eaton's complaint that the Queensland Mission's Committee had no deaf members by 1931 (QADDM. Minutes of Annual General Meeting, held May 29, 1931).

62. ADDSV, Farm and Home Committee's recommendations, attached to Minutes of Executive Committee Meeting, October 21, 1931.

63. E. A. Reynolds, interview by Michael Uniacke.

64. E. A. Reynolds, interview by Michael Uniacke.

65. Bourke, *The After-School Problems of the Deaf and Dumb, No. III*, 20.

66. J. P. Bourke, "The Victorian Front," *The Deaf Advocate* 1, no. 4 (April 1931): 8.

67. Bourke, "The Victorian Front," 8–9.

68. Bourke, *Deaf Drudge*, 63.

69. "Vocational Training as It Is," *The Victorian Deaf* 1, no. 6 (Nov/Dec 1930): 14.

70. M. Gladman, "Letter," *The Victorian Deaf* 1, no. 6 (Nov/Dec 1930), 6.

71. H. V. S. Hersee, "Christmas Message," *The Victorian Deaf* 1, no. 6 (Nov/Dec 1930): 3–4.

72. Hersee, "Christmas Message," 4.

73. "Magazine Committee," *The Victorian Deaf* 2, no. 1 (February 1931): 2.

74. R. H. Lambert, Letter to the Editor, *The Deaf Advocate* 1, no. 3 (March 1931): 9.

75. Bourke, "Victorian Front," 9.

76. "A Message from Our President," *The Victorian Deaf* 2, no. 1 (February 1931): 2.

77. Kingwell, letter to A. L. Lonsdale, dated October 26, 1931; Bourke, "The Victorian Front," 9.

78. R. H. Lambert, "Why I Withdrew from the Editorship of 'The Victorian Deaf' Magazine," *The Deaf Advocate* 1, no. 6 (June 1931).

79. "Mass Meeting of the Deaf," *The Victorian Deaf* 2, no. 4 (July/Aug 1931): 8.

80. Records of Deaf people, n.d., Box 31, VDS Collection, SLV. Records stated that Crush was born and educated in England under the oral system, that he was a wood machinist, now collector, and was single.

81. *Victorian Deaf News*, 3, no. 2 (July/Aug/Sept 1932): 6 and 9.

82. Letter from Mr W. H. Crush to Mr. Adcock, superintendent of the Victorian Deaf and Dumb Institute), n.d. (but refers to imminent Charity Appeal in 1927). PROV, VA 02707 Charities Board of Victoria, VPRS 4523/P1, "Closed" Agency and General Correspondence Files, Unit 68, File 656.

83. ADDSV, Minutes of Executive Committee Meeting, August 17, 1931.

84. "Team Work," *The Victorian Deaf News* 3, no. 1 (April/May/June 1932).

85. *The Victorian Deaf News* 3, no. 2 (July/Aug/Sept 1932): 5.

86. "The Victorian Deaf News," *The Deaf Advocate* 2, no. 7 (July 1932).

87. "The Hon. Editor's Interstate Trip," *The Victorian Deaf News* 3, no. 3 (Oct/Nov/Dec 1932): 8–9. Emphasis in original.

88. *The Victorian Deaf News* 3, no. 4 (Jan/Feb/March 1933).

89. ADDSV, Minutes of General Board Meeting, March 27, 1933. Crush's resignation letter was dated March 16, 1933.

90. *The Victorian Deaf News* 4, no. 1 (April/May/June 1933).

91. *The Victorian Deaf News* 4, no. 2 (July/Aug/Sept 1933): 5.

92. *The Victorian Deaf News* 4, no. 3 (Oct/Nov 1933): 4.

93. "Xmas Greetings from our Principal," *Victorian Deaf News* 4, no. 4 (December 1933): 1.

94. A Victorian Deaf Defender, "A Victorian Disclaimer," *The Deaf Advocate* 2, no. 4 (April 1932).

95. "Association Jottings and Personal News," *The Deaf Advocate* 1, no. 6 (June 1931).

96. Quoted in "Two Opinions of the Deaf and Dumb—and Another," *The Deaf Advocate* 2, no. 2 (February 1932).

97. Quoted in "Two Opinions of the Deaf and Dumb." (The piece is unsigned, but has several Bourke trademarks, such as a quote from *King Silence*.)

98. Deaf subscriber in Victoria, Letter to the Editor, *The Deaf Advocate* 2, no. 3 (March 1932).

99. The Call Boy, "Brotherly Love," *The Deaf Advocate* 3, no. 2 (February 1933). The style of this article and the author's knowledge of the British scene suggest that John Paul was probably the author.

100. "What Is Wrong with the A. D. and D. S.?" *The Deaf Advocate* 2, no. 5 (May 1932).

101. For example, Pierre Desloges' claim in 1779 that "[n]ature has not been as cruel to us as is commonly assumed." (See chapter 2, n. 1.)

102. Lambert, Letter to the Editor, March 1931.

103. "An Independent Magazine for the Deaf," *The Deaf Advocate* 1, no. 5 (May 1931).

104. Reynolds, interview by J. W. Flynn, 18–21.

105. Andrew Wiltshire, personal communication with author, January 11, 2004.

106. Doreen E. Woodford, *Who's Interpreting on Sunday Morning? Stories About Deaf Exclusive Brethren.* British Deaf History Society, 2010.

107. Reynolds, interview by Michael Uniacke.

108. Bourke, *Deaf Drudge*, 83.

109. Bourke, *Deaf Drudge*, 75.

Chapter 6

1. Anna Haebich and Steve Kinnane, "Indigenous Australia," in *The Cambridge History of Australia*, 2nd edition, Vol. 2, ed. Alison Bashford and Stuart Macintyre (Melbourne, Victoria: Cambridge University Press, 2013), 332–57.

2. Bourke, *After-School Problems, No. I*, 24.

3. Minutes of a Meeting of the Deaf and Dumb at Hobart, December 27, 1928. File No. 254, JWF Collection.

4. Minutes of a Meeting of the Deaf and Dumb at Hobart, December 27, 1928.

5. Minutes of a Meeting of the Deaf and Dumb at Hobart, December 27, 1928.

6. Minutes of a Meeting of the Deaf and Dumb at Hobart, December 27, 1928.

7. "Circular Letter," reproduced in *The Deaf Advocate* 3, no. 10 (October 1933).

8. "Editorial," *The Deaf Advocate* 1, no. 6 (June 1931).

9. First Report, Australian Association for the Advancement of the Deaf, June 1936.

10. Letter from E. H. Peacock, dated March 27, 1930, attached to ADDSV, Minutes of General Board Meeting, April 28, 1930.

11. Letter from E. H. Peacock, dated March 27, 1930.

12. Letter from E. H. Peacock, dated March 27, 1930.

13. ADDSV, Minutes of Executive Committee Meeting, August 13, 1930.

14. ADDSV, Minutes of General Board Meeting, September 21, 1931.

15. Quoted in Bourke, *The After-School Problems, No. II*, 17.

16. "A Secret Conference Exposed. Plans to 'Rule' the Deaf," *The Deaf Advocate* 2, no. 2 (February 1932).

17. Kingwell, letter to A. L. Lonsdale, dated October 26, 1931.

18. J. P. Bourke, Letter to the Editor, *The Deaf Advocate* 2, no. 2 (February 1932).

19. "Editorial," *The Deaf Advocate* 2, no. 7 (July 1932).

20. Queensland: M. O. Wilson, C. C. Garner, R. F. Tunley, and J. M. Paul; South Australia: P. Smith; the Adult Deaf and Dumb Society of NSW: J. Sinclair; and the NSW Association of Deaf and Dumb Citizens: F. S. Booth, E. L. Quinnell, A. Hole, F. Sacker, A. Taylor, A. Power, A. O'Callaghan, and H. Hersee. See "Conference Notes," *The Deaf Advocate* 2, no. 4 (April 1932).

21. "Notes on the New Association for the Deaf of Australia," *The Deaf Advocate* 2, no. 4 (April 1932).

22. "Conference Notes," *The Deaf Advocate* 2, no. 4 (April 1932).

23. "Notes on the New Association for the Deaf of Australia."

24. "Editorial," *The Deaf Advocate* 2, no. 4 (April 1932).

25. Attachment to letter from H. Gladwin to Deaf societies (copy received by O. Redman of South Australia Deaf and Dumb Mission), March 21, 1932. File No. 0649, JWF Collection.

26. Attachment to letter from H. Gladwin to Deaf societies.

27. Letter from H. Gladwin to J. M. Paul, dated June 17, 1932, File No. 0258, JWF Collection.

28. "Editorial," *The Deaf Advocate* 2, no. 7 (July 1932); Editorial, *The Deaf Advocate* 2, no. 11 (November 1932).

29. "Australian Association for the Advancement of the Deaf," *The Deaf Advocate* 2, no. 7 (July 1932); "Editorial," *The Deaf Advocate* 2, no. 8 (Aug 1932).

30. "Australian Association for the Advancement of the Deaf. Federal Secretary's Bulletin for September," *The Deaf Advocate* 2, no. 11 (November 1932).

31. "Australian Association for the Advancement of the Deaf," *The Deaf Advocate* 2, no. 9 (Sept 1932).

32. A Victorian Deaf Defender, "A Victorian Disclaimer."

33. "Editorial," *The Deaf Advocate* 2, no. 7 (July 1932).

34. "Editorial," *The Deaf Advocate* 2, no. 8 (August 1932).

35. Letter to the Editor, *The Deaf Advocate* 2, no. 10 (October 1932).

36. Letter to the Editor, *The Deaf Advocate* 2, no. 9 (September 1932).

37. For example, the Victorian branch's third annual report stated, "The Victorian Deaf and Dumb Institution always open a warm heart towards the A.A.A.D., and by this happy manner it is a gem of encouragement." Australian Association for the Advancement of the Deaf (Victorian Branch). Third Annual Report, 1934–35. File No. 0856, JWF Collection.

38. This is suggested by the fact that Hersee usually stayed with the McCaskill family when he visited Melbourne.

39. "Editorial," *The Deaf Advocate* 2, no. 9 (September 1932); the *Macquarie Dictionary* (Australia's most comprehensive) has the following meaning for the colloquial/historical use of *white man*: "an honest, straightforward or reliable person."

40. "Australian Association for the Advancement of the Deaf. Bulletin for May 1933," *The Deaf Advocate* 3, no. 5 (May 1933).

41. R. H. Lambert, "A Conference Impression," *The Deaf Advocate* 3, no. 1 (January 1933).

42. "Editorial," *The Deaf Advocate* 3, no. 4 (April 1933).

43. "Australian Association for the Advancement of the Deaf. Official Report of the First Delegates Conference," *The Deaf Advocate* 3, no. 1 (January 1933).

44. "Australian Association for the Advancement of the Deaf. Bulletin for January and February, 1933," *The Deaf Advocate* 3, no. 2 (February 1933).

45. Australian Association for the Advancement of the Deaf, n.d., Constitution. File No. 0457, JWF Collection.

46. "The Australian Association for the Advancement of the Deaf. Welcome to the New Federal Executive Council," *The Deaf Advocate* 3, no. 1 (January 1933). It was possibly written by Alf Taylor, who wrote other satirical verses for the *Advocate* under the nom de plume "The Murrumbidgee Chap." He was the Association's collector for the southwest region of NSW, encompassing the Murrumbidgee River.

47. "Australian Association for the Advancement of the Deaf. Federal Secretary's Bulletin for August," *The Deaf Advocate* 2, no. 10 (October 1932).

48. "Australian Association for the Advancement of the Deaf," *The Deaf Advocate* 2, no. 11 (Nov. 1932).

49. Australian Association for the Advancement of the Deaf, First Report, June 1936.

50. Bourke, *After-School Problems, No. II*, 22.

51. "Editorial," *The Deaf Advocate* 3, no. 4 (April 1933).

52. "Editorial," *The Deaf Advocate* 3, no. 4 (April 1933).

53. ADDSV, Minutes of Executive Committee Meeting, March 6, 1933.

54. Bourke, "The Victorian Branch of the A.A.A.D. Advances," *The Deaf Advocate* 3, no. 4 (April 1933).

55. "The Farce of the Societies National Council," *The Deaf Advocate* 3, no. 4 (April 1933).

56. "Welfare of the Deaf. Move to Form Federal Council," *The Age*, March 16, 1933, 11.

57. "The Farce of the Societies National Council."

58. "The Farce of the Societies National Council."

59. "Welfare of the Deaf."

60. Bourke, "The Victorian Branch of the A.A.A.D. Advances."

61. ADDSV, Minutes of General Board Meeting, March 27, 1933. Crush's resignation letter was dated March 16, 1933.

62. "National Council of the Deaf," *Victorian Deaf News* 4, no. 1 (April/May/June 1933), 6–7.

63. ADDSV, "Daily Record Book 19 Oct 1931 to 14 July 1934," entry for March 16, 1933. Box 34, VDS Collection.

64. "The Farce of the Societies National Council."

65. Bourke, "The Victorian Branch of the A.A.A.D. Advances."

66. "Further Exposures on the Farcical National Council: Who Paid the Four Guinea Bill?" *The Deaf Advocate* 3, no. 5 (May 1933).

67. Letter from H. W. Gladwin to W. R. Kingwell, March 17, 1933. File No. 691 JWF Collection.

68. Letter from H. W. Gladwin to W. R. Kingwell, March 31, 1933. File No. 691 JWF Collection.

69. "Australian Association for the Advancement of the Deaf. Bulletin for April," *The Deaf Advocate* 3, no. 4 (April 1933).

70. J. P. Bourke, "The Parting of the Ways for the Deaf of Australia," *The Deaf Advocate* 3, no. 5 (May 1933).

71. W. H. Crush, "Australian Association for the Advancement of the Deaf. Victorian Branch. The State President's Message," *The Deaf Advocate* 3, no. 7 (July 1933).

72. M. Overend Wilson, "Australian Association for the Advancement of the Deaf. Bulletin for March," *The Deaf Advocate* 3, no. 3 (March 1933).

73. "Australian Association for the Advancement of the Deaf. Bulletin for June-July," *The Deaf Advocate* 3, no. 7 (July 1933).

74. W. H. Crush, "Australian Association for the Advancement of the Deaf. Victorian Branch. The State President's Message," *The Deaf Advocate* 3, no. 7 (July 1933).

75. "Can You Do Better Than This," *The Deaf Advocate* 3, no. 8 (August 1933). [Emphasis added.]

76. "Editorial," *The Deaf Advocate* 3, no. 7 (July 1933).

77. "Editorial," *The Deaf Advocate* 3, no. 4 (April 1933).

78. Bourke, "The Parting of Ways for the Deaf of Australia."

79. ADDSV, Daily Record Book, 19 October 1931 to 14 July 1934, entry for March 23, 1933. Box 34, VDS Collection.

80. ADDSV, Daily Record Book, entries for May 7, 1933, May 18, 1933, and June 1, 1933.

81. Others on the Congress Committee included Messrs. F. E. Frewin and A. Stephens, and Miss Rose Dow from Victoria; Messrs. G. S. Dunnet and W. A. Abbott, and Mrs. R. Medcalf from South Australia; Messrs. A. O. Flay and C. Beutel, and Mrs. P. Spranklin from Queensland; Messrs. W. Limbrick, F. Williams, and C. Webb from Tasmania; Messrs. C. Plunkett, J. Bircher from Western Australia; and Messrs. W. Molloy, H. L. Emerson, and C. H. Richards from NSW.

82. *The Victorian Deaf News* 4, no. 5 (Jan/Feb/March 1934): 2.

83. *The Silent Messenger* (Jan/Feb/March 1934).

84. *The Silent Messenger* (Jan/Feb/March 1934).

85. "Resolutions Passed at Congress of the Deaf, 29 Dec 1933." File No. 0691 in JWF Collection.

86. Australian Association for the Advancement of the Deaf, Report, (June 1936).

87. "A.A.A.D. News," *The Deaf Advocate* 4, no. 1 (Jan/Feb 1934), 8.

88. A. Eaton, "The Deaf in Their Own Association," File No. 0685, John W. Flynn Collection.

89. Eaton, "The Deaf in Their Own Association," 2.

90. Eaton, "The Deaf in Their Own Association," 2.

91. Australian Association for the Advancement of the Deaf, Report (June 1936).

92. Australian Association for the Advancement of the Deaf, Report (June 1936).

93. "Editorial," *The Deaf Advocate* 4, no. 5 (Oct/Nov 1934), 2.

94. It is possible that Hersee may have lost some enthusiasm for the AAAD when he was replaced as its president that year.

95. "Advancement of the Deaf: Association's Annual Meeting. Deaf and Dumb Society Criticised," *The Age*, June 23, 1934.

96. "Advancement of the Deaf," June 23, 1934.

97. "A Silent Meeting," *The Age*, June 23, 1934.

98. Letter from H. W. Gladwin to President of Queensland Adult Deaf and Dumb Mission, January 15, 1934. File No. 0691, JWF Collection.

99. Letter from J. M. Johnston and S. Phillips to Queensland Adult Deaf and Dumb Mission, February 20, 1934. File No. 0691, JWF Collection.

100. Queensland Branch of AAAD, Second Annual Report, June 30, 1934.

101. ADDSV, Minutes of Executive Committee Meeting, February 3, 1934.

102. ADDSV, Daily Record Book, 19 October 1931 to 14 July 1934, entry for March 8, 1934. Box 34, VDS Collection. The Committee was comprised of Messrs J. M. Johnston, A. Stephens, W. Ashby, F. Sandon, J. O'Gorman, and F. Rees, as well as Mrs. J. M. Johnston and Misses R. Dow, Elsie Stephens, and Alice Smith.

103. ADDSV, Daily Record Book, 14 July 1934 to 23 July 1936, entries for July 24, 1934 and December 18, 1934. Box 10, VDS Collection.

104. Letter from J. M. Johnston to undisclosed recipients, with draft congress program and constitution attached, September 20, 1934. File No. 0261, JWF Collection. Also in PROV, VA 02707 Charities Board of Victoria, VPRS4523/P1, "Closed" Agency and General Correspondence Files, Unit 68 File No. 656.

105. *The Silent Messenger* 6, no. 4 (Oct/Nov 1934): 5.

106. Letter from E. J. D. Abraham to Mr. Davies (QADDM), October 24, 1934. File No. 0691, JWF Collection.

107. "Affairs of the Deaf and Dumb," *The Age*, December 28, 1934, 9.

108. The Commonwealth Association of the Deaf and Dumb, constitution, n.d., PROV VPRS 4523/P1, Unit 68, File 656.

109. "Welfare of the Deaf. Their Part in Strikes. Deaf Council Debates Problems," *The Age*, December 29, 1934, 12.

110. "National Council of the Deaf," *The Victorian Deaf News* 5, nos. 3 and 4 (October 1934 to March 1935 - joint issue): 8.

111. "National Council of the Deaf." 9.

112. "Welfare of the Deaf." 12.

113. "A Noiseless Conference," *The Age*, December 28, 1934.

114. Bourke, *After-School Problems, No. I*, 21.

115. Australian Association for the Advancement of the Deaf (Victorian Branch). Third Annual Report: 1934–35. JWF, File No. 0856.

116. *The Herald*, December 27, 1934.

117. Third Annual Report: 1934–35.

118. Doran, *Hand in Hand with Time and Change*, 76–77.

119. J. M. Paul, letter to J. W. Flynn, n.d. (early 1952). File No. 0645, JWF Collection.

120. Australian Association for the Advancement of the Deaf (Victorian Branch). Third Annual Report: 1934–35.

121. Australian Association for the Advancement of the Deaf (Victorian Branch). Third Annual Report: 1934–35, 2.

122. Australian Association for the Advancement of the Deaf (Victorian Branch). Third Annual Report: 1934–35, 3.

123. Australian Association for the Advancement of the Deaf (Victorian Branch). Third Annual Report: 1934–35, covering letter.

124. Australian Association for the Advancement of the Deaf (Queensland Branch), Annual Report for the Year Ending June 30, 1935.

125. Report of Conference on February 13, 1936. Attached to ADDSNSW, Minutes of Executive Meeting, February 19, 1936.

126. M. O. Wilson, "Thirty Years Work with the Deaf and Dumb," *The Deaf Advocate* 4, no. 1 (Jan/Feb 1934): 2.

127. John Paul, handwritten notes on "Totalitarianism," n.d. File No. 0682, JWF Collection.

Chapter 7

1. For a description of Australian conformity and repression in the mid- to late 1930s, see Stuart Macintyre, *The Oxford History of Australia, Vol. 4: 1901-1942: The Succeeding Age* (Melbourne: Oxford University Press, 1993), 307–24.

2. For example, Katherine Susannah Pritchard's *Coonardoo* was rejected by the main Australian publishing house, Angus & Robertson. See Stuart Macintyre, *The Oxford History, Vol. 4*, 311–12.

3. See Macintyre, *The Oxford History, Vol. 4*, 308–09.

4. ADDSNSW, Annual Report, 1941–42, 5.

5. Bourke's booklets are listed in chapter 2, note 30.

6. Article by "Demos," *The Worker's Voice*, January 8, 1935. Copy in File No. 0381, JWF Collection.

7. Bourke, *Deaf Drudge*, 74.

8. "M. H. R. Suggests Inquiry. Control of Deaf and Dumb Society," *The Sun News-Pictorial*, July 19, 1935, 15.

9. Bourke, *"Fiction and Fact"—A Pamphlet*, 16.

10. For example, letter from E. B. Harkness, under secretary of Chief Secretary's Department, to ADDSNSW, June 11, 1935. State records NSW: colonial secretary; CGS905, main series of letters received, 1826–1982; items [12/7524 No. 1026 and No. 1085]. Copies of items also in File No. 0144, JWF Collection. (Subsequent references will use JWF Collection File number.)

11. Letter from E. B. Harkness, under secretary of Chief Secretary's Department, to ADDSNSW, December 12, 1935. File No. 0144, JWF Collection.

12. Miscellaneous letters from ADDSNSW and NSWADDC to E. B. Harkness, setting up meeting. File No. 0144, JWF Collection.

13. ADDSNSW, Minutes of Executive Committee, February 19, 1936.

14. Letter from Hon. Secretary, ADDSNSW, to Chief Secretary, March 5, 1936 (underlining in original). File No. 0144, JWF Collection.

15. Letter from Hon. Secretary, ADDSNSW, to Chief Secretary, March 5, 1936.

16. Letter from Hon. Secretary, ADDSNSW, to Chief Secretary, March 5, 1936.

17. Minutes of conference between representatives of the Adult Deaf and Dumb Society and the Association of Deaf and Dumb Citizens [sic], May 25, 1936. File No. 0144, JWF Collection.

18. Minutes of conference, May 25, 1936, 12.

19. Minutes of conference, May 25, 1936, 4.

20. Minutes of conference, May 25, 1936, 8.

21. Minutes of conference, May 25, 1936, 4.

22. Minutes of conference, May 25, 1936, 11.

23. Minutes of conference, May 25, 1936, 3, 9.

24. *General Assembly of the Free Church of Scotland v Overtoun* [1904] AC 515 (HL).

25. Minutes of conference, May 25, 1936, 3.

26. Minutes of conference, May 25, 1936, 11.

27. Minutes of General [Deaf] Committee meeting of ADDSNSW, November 4, 1936. File No. 0144, JWF Collection.

28. Minutes of conference, May 25, 1936, 5.

29. For example, letter from Adult Deaf and Dumb General Committee to Chief Secretary's Department, October 23, 1936. File No. 0144, JWF Collection.

30. Letters from J. M. Paul, July 22, 1937 and July 28, 1937; from H. V. S. Hersee August 2, 1937; from J. M. Paul August 4, 1937; and from an assistant secretary acting on Hersee's request, August 9, 1937. File No. 0144, JWF Collection.

31. "Programme for Unity Social," *Deaf Sports Notes* 1, no. 7 (August 6, 1937).

32. *Deaf Sports Notes* 1, no. 6 (July 30, 1937): 7.

33. *Deaf Sports Notes* 1, no. 6 (July 30, 1937): 5.

34. ADDSNSW, Minutes of Executive Committee Meeting, January 20, 1938.

35. Certificate, Branson/Miller Collection of Hersee Papers. Copy in File No. 0637, JWF Collection.

36. Flynn, "Post-School Organisations," 31.

37. For example, Stan and Isabel Winn's daughter Edena remembers receiving a sympathy card from Hersee when Stan died in 1959. Miss Edena Winn, personal communication to author, December 12, 2003.

38. "Society and the Deaf: Public Inquiry Suggested," *The Age*, 23 July 1936, 12.

39. File No. 0722, JWF Collection. Underlining in original.

40. Queensland Branch of the AAAD, Fourth Annual Report, June 30, 1936.

41. J. P. Bourke, "The Victorian Branch of the Australian Association for the Advancement of the Deaf" (pamphlet), October 9, 1936. PROV, VA 02707 Charities Board of Victoria, VPRS 4523/P1, "Closed" Agency and General Correspondence Files, Unit 51, File 477.

42. Wilson, untitled circular, n.d. File No. 0400, JWF Collection.

43. Eaton, "The Deaf in Their Own Association," File No. 0685, John W. Flynn Collection.

44. AAAD (Victorian Branch), Final Report of the Branch, April 1937. PROV, VA 02707 Charities Board of Victoria, VPRS 4523/P1, "Closed" Agency and General Correspondence Files, Unit 68, File 656.

45. E. A. Reynolds, interview by J. W. Flynn, 19.

46. Minutes, Conference of Adult Deaf and Dumb Societies and Missions of Australia. Copy attached to ADDSV, Minutes of General Board Meeting, January 24, 1939.

47. "News in Brief," *The Mercury*, December 28, 1938, 6.

48. J. P. Bourke, "Some Facts about the Deaf of Australia," *The Australian Deaf Citizen* no. 1, Jan/Feb/Mar 1940, 5.

49. J. M. Paul, "A letter from Queensland," *The Deaf Advocate* 2, no. 2 (February 1932).

50. R. L. Hoffmann, "Lives His Shuttered Life with Shakespeare," *The Sun News-Pictorial*, September 25, 1937, 49.

51. Hoffmann, "Lives His Shuttered Life with Shakespeare."

52. Hoffmann, "Lives His Shuttered Life with Shakespeare."

53. Hoffmann, "Lives His Shuttered Life with Shakespeare."

54. Mrs. Gladman wrote a letter to the *Sun*, protesting about the inaccuracies in the article. It was not published, but Bourke reproduced it in full in *"Fiction and Fact,"* 13.

55. Bourke, *"Fiction and Fact,"* 8.

56. Bourke, *"Fiction and Fact,"* 8 and 14.

57. Bourke, *"Fiction and Fact,"* 14.

58. For example, Alf Taylor of Sydney, who was deafened in the First World War and later married a Deaf woman, Iris Boortz.

59. Bourke, *"Fiction and Fact,"* 2.

60. J. O'Gorman, personal communication to author, November 12, 1992.

61. "Deaf and Dumb Society," *The Age*, May 12, 1934, 24.

62. Letter from J. P. Bourke to Hon. Secretary of Board of Management, ADDSV, January 4, 1938. (Confirmed in ADDSV, Minutes of Executive Committee Meeting, January 25, 1938.)

63. Letter from Deaf Committee to Hon. Secretary of Board, February 10, 1938. Receipt noted in ADDSV, Minutes of General Board Meeting, February 22, 1938.

64. Letter from E. R. Noble (Hon. Sec. to Deaf Committee) to General Board, July 17, 1938. Attached to ADDSV, Minutes of Executive Committee Meeting, July 25, 1938.

65. ADDSV, Minutes of Executive Committee Meetings, August 22 and September 26, 1939.

66. ADDSV, Minutes of General Board Meeting, July 25, 1939.

67. Letter from E. R. Noble (Hon. Sec. to Deaf Committee) to undisclosed recipients, July 11, 1939. Also signed by other members of the Deaf Committee: J. M. Johnston, W. A. Ross, J. N. McLaurin, Doris Hickey, Rose M. Dow, H. Puddy, H. Greensmith, W. Ashby, and Mrs A. Sutherland.

68. Bourke, *Banned Baby*, 1.

69. Bourke, *"Fiction and Fact,"* 1.

70. Carlyle, *Latter-Day Pamphlets*, 74. Quoted in Bourke, *Banned Baby*, 1–2.

71. Issue number 1 was dated January, February, March 1940, and it continued to appear every three months until issue number 6 in April/May/June 1941.

72. Michael Uniacke, "Anger in the '40s: 'The Australian Deaf Citizen,'" *Sound Off* 1 (June 1987): 2–4.

73. Uniacke, "Anger in the '40s," 4.

74. Bourke, "Some Facts," 5. Regarding the dissidents, see, for example, Cliff Ellwood, personal communication to author, June 2, 1995.

75. For example, "The Victorian Past Pulips [sic] Association," *The Australian Deaf Citizen* 2 (April/May/June 1940): 4; "The Blind Provide Music for Deaf Dancers," *The Australian Deaf Citizen* 3 (July/Aug/Sept 1940): 7–8.

76. Unidentified newspaper clipping, August 1, 1940. Scrapbook, Box 23, VDS Collection.

77. "Obituary: Mr. E. J. D. Abraham," *The Argus*, July 30, 1940, 2; "Obituary: Mr. E. J. D. Abraham," *The Age*, July 30, 1940, 8.

78. Editorial: "The Death of the Victorian Superintendent," *The Australian Deaf Citizen*, No. 3 (July/Aug/Sept 1940), 1.

79. E. A. Reynolds, interview by Michael Uniacke.

80. E. A. Reynolds, interview by Michael Uniacke.

81. Hepworth, "Christmas at the home of the B.D.M.," 89.

82. "5-Year Sentence for Theft of £25,670. Secretary Pleads Guilty," *The Herald*, October 13, 1941, 3.

83. "Deaf and Dumb Defrauded. Secretary Sentenced to Five Years," *The Age*, October 14, 1941, 6. See also "5 Years' Gaol for Secretary. Theft of £25, 670," *The Argus*, October 14, 1941, 2.

84. "Greeting," *The Deaf Advocate* 3, no. 5 (May 1933). [Underlining in original.]

85. Jeff Armstrong, Cliff Ellwood, and Fred Weber, personal communication to author, June 20, 1995.

86. J. M. Paul, letter to J. W. Flynn, February 6, 1953. In File No. 0645, JWF Collection.

87. Jeff Armstrong, personal communication to author, June 20, 1995. Armstrong joined the Association as a young man, because it had a deaf cricket team, whereas the Mission encouraged only tennis as a summer sport.

88. J. M. Paul, letter to J. W. Flynn, August 23, 1952. In File No. 0645, JWF Collection.

89. J. M. Paul, Superintendent's Report, QDDCRA, June 5, 1952. File No. 0645, JWF Collection.

90. J. M. Paul, letter to J. W. Flynn, n.d. (probably 1952). In File No. 0645, JWF Collection.

91. J. M. Paul, letter to J. W. Flynn, n.d.

92. J. M. Paul, letter to J. W. Flynn, n.d.

93. Wilson, "Thirty Years Work with the Deaf and Dumb," 2.

94. *The Silent Messenger*, Christmas 1956.

95. *The Silent Messenger*, August 1958.

96. Records of members, Box No. 31, VDS Collection.

97. ADDSV, Minutes of Home Committee meeting, May 9, 1954. Box No. 11, VDS Collection.

98. See, for example, ADDSV, Minutes of Home Committee Meetings, February 20, 1955; June 17, 1956; September 24, 1956; October 28, 1956; May 26, 1957; and July 27, 1958. Box No. 11, VDS Collection.

99. For example, ADDSV, Minutes of Home Committee Meetings, April 29, 1956; September 29, 1957; November 24, 1957; February 28, 1960. Box No. 11, VDS Collection.

100. ADDSV, Minutes of Home Committee Meeting, May 25, 1958. Box No. 11, VDS Collection.

101. ADDSV, "Home Report," Minutes of Home Committee Meeting, April 25, 1960. Box No. 11, VDS Collection.

102. Records of members, Box No. 31, VDS Collection. This comment was probably written by Ernest Reynolds, the then superintendent of the Society.

103. Della Bampton, personal communication to author, June 25, 2013.

104. *The Victorian Deaf News* 5, no. 2 (July/Aug/Sept 1934): 8.

105. *The Victorian Deaf News* 1 (New Series) (January 1936): 12.

106. Michael Uniacke, email communication to author, February 19, 2001.

107. National Archives of Australia: Commonwealth Office of Education; A1361, International Relations—Visits by Educationalists—Dr. and Mrs. Ewing; 4/15/10 Part 3, 1950–1953, accessed 11/25/2014 http://www.naa.gov.au/go.aspx?i=4788689.

108. For example, E. R. Noble in Victoria wrote a letter to the editor of *The Age,* criticizing the Ewings' recommendations and claiming, "The important thing [to hearing educators] is whether the ears work, not the brain in between them." See "Education for Deaf Children," Letter to the Editor, *The Age,* November 6, 1950, 2.

109. John Paul, QDDCRA Superintendent's Report, October 2, 1947. File No. 0685, JWF Collection.

110. For example, Isabel and Stan Winn of the NSW Association shifted their energies to the Deaf Christian Fellowship in the late 1930s (Miss Edena Winn, personal communication to author, December 12, 2003). Alf Eaton of the QDDCRA became active in the Catholic Deaf Association (Tony Doonan, personal communication to author, April 29, 1995).

Chapter 8

1. Minutes of the General Meeting held at the S.A. Deaf Centre on 1st January 1977 to Consider the Formation of a National Body of the Deaf. (Deaf Australia papers) The meeting minutes do not list the names of all eighteen attendees, but those who contributed to the meeting were Mr. B. Muller (SA), Mr. A. Mann (Vic.), Mr. J. Lovett (Vic.), Mr. I. McGregor (Qld.), Mrs. E. Girke (SA), Mr. B. Bernal (Vic.), Mr. D. Johnston (NSW), Mr. W. Cooper (WA), Miss D. Griffiths (NSW), Mr. B. Taylor (NSW), and Mrs D. Shaw (NSW).

2. Flynn, *Post-School Organisations,* 107.

3. The World Federation of the Deaf was founded in 1951 to represent Deaf people around the world. It holds a congress and general assembly every four years, inviting representatives from each member country.

4. Minutes of General Meeting to Consider Formation of a National Body of the Deaf, January 1, 1977.

5. Conference Notes: Australian [sic] Deaf & Dumb Association. October 5, 1922. Copy held in JWF Collection, File No. 253; J. P. Bourke, Letter to the Editor, *The Herald*, February 6, 1923, 7.

6. Among the participants in the 1977 meeting, Miss D. Griffiths had been a young employee of the NSWADDC when it amalgamated with the Society in 1937, and Mrs. D. Shaw was the daughter of J. M. Johnston.

7. "Editorial," *The Deaf Advocate* 2, no. 4 (April 1932).

8. "Editorial," *The Deaf Advocate* (Sept/Oct 1931).

9. W. E. H. Stanner, *The 1968 Boyer Lectures: After the Dreaming* (Sydney: Australian Broadcasting Commission, 1969), 25.

10. Stanner, *The 1968 Boyer Lectures*, 25; Bain Attwood, "Introduction," in *Power, Knowledge and Aborigines*, ed. Bain Attwood and John Arnold (Bundoora: La Trobe University Press in conjunction with the National Centre for Australian Studies, Monash University, 1992), x.

11. John Hirst, *The Sentimental Nation: The Making of the Australian Commonwealth* (Melbourne: Oxford University Press, 2000), 297.

12. See Stuart Macintyre and Anna Clark, *The History Wars* (Melbourne: Melbourne University Press, 2003) for a description of these debates.

13. Paul Kelly, "Jogging the Collective Memory." *The Weekend Australian*, April, 21–22, 2001, 29.

14. "A Short History of the Adult Deaf of New South Wales," n.d. File No. 0011, JWF Collection. John Flynn has identified the editor's handwriting as A. L. Lonsdale's.

15. *The Silent Messenger*, Christmas 1956; "Official Opening of the Deaf Centre," December 6, 1975. Pamphlet.

16. For example, Lane, *The Mask of Benevolence*. He points out that, "[p]aternalism deprives its beneficiaries of their history and therefore of the possible lives they can envision" (p. 39).

17. Auslan was first described as one of Australia's community languages in an early National Language Policy in 1987, after several years of lobbying. Its acceptance was formalized in the Department of Employment, Education and Training, *Australia's Language:*

The Australian Language and Literacy Policy, Companion Volume (Canberra: AGPS, 1991), 20.

18. Personal communication to author, Stephen Nicholson, September 3, 2004. Stephen's grandfather, Ludovic Nicholson, had been an active supporter of the NSWADDC during the 1930s.

19. See chapter 2, pages xx–xxx.

20. For example, the work of John Flynn, Rhonda Loades, Sarah Fitzgerald et. al., Melissa Anderson, Anne Bremner, Darlene Thornton, Susannah Macready, and Patricia Levitzke-Gray.

21. Flynn, "Post-School Organisations"; Sue Wilson, *The History of the Queensland Deaf Society*; and "Deaf in NSW: A Community History," accessed 1/20/2017, www.deafinnsw.com.

22. Wrigley, *The Politics of Deafness*, 102–3.

BIBLIOGRAPHY

Adam, Robert. "Unimodal Bilingualism in the Deaf Community: Language Contact Between Two Sign Languages in Australia and the United Kingdom." PhD diss., University College London, 2016.

Altschwager, Leila. *The First Sixty Years: A History of Toc H in Australia from 1925 to 1985.* Adelaide: Toc H Australia, 1985.

Anderson, Melissa. "Daisy Muir: A Remarkable Influence in the Deaf Community." MA of Education Research Essay, La Trobe University, 2001.

Anderson, Melissa, and Breda Carty. "The Cosmopolitan Correspondence Club." In *Telling Deaf Lives: Agents of Change,* edited by Kristin Snoddon, 148–62. Washington, DC: Gallaudet University Press, 2014.

Atherton, Martin. "Deserving of Charity or Deserving of Better? The Continuing Legacy of the 1834 Poor Law Amendment Act for Britain's Deaf Population. *Review of Disability Studies* 7 (3+4): 18–25.

Atherton, Martin. "Deaf Newspapers: A Cornerstone of the Deaf Community." Paper presented at the Disability Studies Association Conference, Lancaster University, September 2006.

Atkinson, Alexander. *Memoirs of My Youth.* Newcastle on Tyne: John Wilson Swanston, 1865.

Attwood, Bain, and John Arnold, eds. *Power, Knowledge and Aborigines.* Bundoora, Victoria: La Trobe University Press in conjunction with the National Centre for Australian Studies, Monash University, 1992.

Australian Department of Employment, Education and Training. *Australia's Language: The Australian Language and Literacy Policy, Companion Volume.* Canberra: Australian Government Publishing Service, 1991.

Ballin, Albert. *The Deaf Mute Howls.* Washington, DC: Gallaudet University Press. Reprint, 1998.

Bauman, H-Dirksen L., and Joseph J. Murray, eds., *Deaf Gain: Raising the Stakes for Human Diversity*. Minneapolis: University of Minnesota Press, 2014.

Baynton, Douglas C. *Forbidden Signs: American Culture and the Campaign against Sign Language*. Chicago: University of Chicago Press, 1996.

Blyth, Stephen. "A Historical Overview of Australian Religious Sectarianism Accompanied by a Survey of Factors Contributing to Its Dissolution." *Integrity: A Journal of Australian Church History* 1 (2012): 81–110.

Bongiorno, Frank. "Search for a Solution, 1923-39." In *The Cambridge History of Australia*, 2nd edition, Vol. 2, edited by Alison Bashford and Stuart Macintyre, 64–87. Melbourne, Victoria: Cambridge University Press, 2013.

Borrow, Travers. *The Hallett Family*. Adelaide: Pioneers' Association of South Australia, 1946.

Bourke, J. P. *The After-School Problems of the Deaf and Dumb, No. I: The Problem of a Central Meeting Place for Them*. Melbourne: J. P. Bourke, 1933.

———. *The After-School Problems of the Deaf and Dumb, No. II: The Problem of Ministering to Their Religious and Spiritual Needs*. Melbourne: J. P. Bourke, 1933.

———. *The After-School Problems of the Deaf and Dumb, No. III: The Problem of the Impotent Deaf*. Melbourne: J. P. Bourke, 1935.

———. *Benevolence and the Banned Baby*. Melbourne: J. P. Bourke, 1937.

———. *"Fiction and Fact"—a Pamphlet*. Melbourne: J. P. Bourke, 1937.

———. *The Story of a Deaf Drudge*. Melbourne: J. P. Bourke, 1939.

Bragg, Lois, ed. *Deaf World: A Historical Reader and Primary Sourcebook*. New York: New York University Press, 2001.

Branson, Jan, and Don Miller. *The Story of Betty Steel: Deaf Convict and Pioneer*. Petersham, New South Wales: Deafness Resources Australia Ltd., 1995.

Branson, Jan, and Don Miller. "Frederick John Rose: An Australian Pioneer." In *Collage: Works on International Deaf History*, edited by Renate Fischer and Tomas Vollhaber, 69–82. Hamburg: Signum, 1996.

Bremner, Anne. "Deaf Sports in Australia." Master of Sign Language thesis, La Trobe University, 1996.

Burch, Susan. *Signs of Resistance: American Deaf Cultural History, 1900 to World War II*. New York: New York University Press, 2002.

Burchett, J. H. *Utmost for the Highest: The Story of the Victorian School for Deaf Children*. Melbourne: Hall's Book Store Pty Ltd., 1964.

Cannon, Michael, and Ian MacFarlane, eds. *Historical Records of Victoria.* Vol. 4. Melbourne: Victorian Government Printing Office, 1985.

Carty, Breda. "John Carmichael: Australian Deaf Pioneer." *Deaf History Journal* 3, no. 3 (2000): 24–36.

Carty, Breda. "The 'Breakaways': Deaf Citizens' Groups in Australia in the 1920s and 1930s." In *In Our Own Hands: Essays in Deaf History 1780–1970*, edited by Brian H. Greenwald and Joseph J. Murray, 211–38. Washington, DC: Gallaudet University Press, 2016.

Carty, Breda, and Darlene Thornton. "Deaf People in Colonial Australia." In *No History, No Future: Proceedings of the 7th DHI International Conference, Stockholm 2009*, edited by Tomas Hedberg, 148–55. Solna: Dixa, 2011.

Clancy, Michael, ed. *Heritage in Our Hands: Stories of the Deaf Community of N.S.W.* Sydney: Adult Education Centre for Deaf and Hearing Impaired Persons Inc., 1988.

Cooper, Paul F. "Sherrington Alexander Gilder (1828–1902) and the Commencement of the Education of the Deaf in NSW." *Philanthropy and Philanthropists in Australian Colonial History*, August 26, 2014. Accessed October 6, 2017. https://phinaucohi.wordpress.com/2014/08/26/sherrington-alexander-gilder/.

Cooper, Paul F. "Thomas Pattison (1805–1899) Coach Painter and Founder of the Deaf and Dumb Institute, Sydney." *Philanthropy and Philanthropists in Australian Colonial History*, August 27, 2014. Accessed October 6, 2017. https://phinaucohi.wordpress.com/2014/08/27/thomas-pattison-1805-1899/.

Davidson, Alastair. *From Subject to Citizen: Australian Citizenship in the Twentieth Century.* Cambridge: Cambridge University Press, 1997.

"The Deaf A R E Managing their Own Affairs," *The Deaf Advocate* 2, no. 6 (June 1932).

Deaf Society. "Deaf in NSW: A Community History." Accessed October 6, 2017. deafinnsw.com.

Desloges, Pierre. "A Deaf Person's Observations About 'An Elementary Course of Education for the Deaf.'" In *The Deaf Experience: Classics in Language and Education*, edited by Harlan Lane. Translated by Franklin Philip, 28–48. Cambridge, MA: Harvard University Press. 1984.

Doran, Ella. *Hand in Hand with Time and Change: The Life of Ella Doran and Her Work with the Deaf in Australia.* Woden, ACT: Molonglo Press, 1998.

Fischer, Renate, and Harlan Lane, eds. *Looking Back: A Reader on the History of Deaf Communities and Their Sign Languages*. Hamburg: Signum Press, 1993.

Fischer, Renate, and Tomas Vollhaber, eds. *Collage: Works on International Deaf History*. Hamburg: Signum Press, 1996.

Fitzgerald, Sarah, narrated. *Open Minds Open Hearts: Stories of the Australian Catholic Deaf Community*. Lidcombe, New South Wales: CCOD, 1999.

Flynn, John. *No Longer by Gaslight: The First 100 Years of the Adult Deaf Society of Victoria*. East Melbourne: Adult Deaf Society of Victoria, 1984.

Flynn, John. "Some Aspects of the Development of Post-School Organisations of and for Deaf People in Australia." MA thesis, La Trobe University, 1999.

Flynn, Michael. *The Second Fleet: Britain's Grim Convict Armada of 1790*. Sydney: Library of Australian History, 1993.

Gertz, Genie. "Dysconscious Audism: A Theoretical Proposition." In *Open Your Eyes: Deaf Studies Talking*, edited by H-Dirksen L. Bauman, 219–34. Minneapolis: University of Minnesota Press, 2008.

Grant, Brian. *The Deaf Advance: A History of the British Deaf Association 1890–1990*. Edinburgh: The Pentland Press Ltd., 1990.

Greenwald, Brian. "Alexander Graham Bell Through the Lens of Eugenics, 1883-1922." PhD diss., George Washington University, 2006.

Haebich, Anna, and Steve Kinnane. "Indigenous Australia." In *The Cambridge History of Australia*, 2nd edition, Vol. 2, edited by Alison Bashford and Stuart Macintyre, 332–57. Melbourne, Victoria: Cambridge University Press, 2013.

Hamilton, Reg. "The History of the Australian Minimum Wage." Fair Work Commission, 2016. Accessed January 10, 2017. https://www.fwc.gov.au/documents/documents/archives/exhibitions/minwage/exhibitionpaper–100yrsminwage.pdf.

Hepworth, Joseph. "Christmas at the Home of the B.D.M." *The British Deaf-Mute* V, no. 51 (January 1896): 89.

Hirst, John. *The Sentimental Nation: The Making of the Australian Commonwealth*. Melbourne: Oxford University Press, 2000.

Hope, Penelope, ed. *The Voyage of the Africaine: A Collection of Journals, Letters and Extracts from Contemporary Publications*. South Yarra, Victoria: Heinemann Educational Australia Pty Ltd., 1968.

Houison, Andrew. *History of the Post Office, Together with an Historical Account of the Issue of Postage Stamps in New South Wales Compiled Directly from the Records*. Sydney: Government Printer, 1890.

Jackson, Peter. *Britain's Deaf Heritage*. Edinburgh: The Pentland Press Ltd., 1990.

―――. *A Pictorial History of Deaf Britain*. Winsford, Cheshire: Deafprint Winsford, 2001.

Johnston, Brian. *Memories of St Gabriel's: A History of St Gabriel's Deaf School, Castle Hill, NSW*. N.p.: New South Wales Government Printing Service, 2000.

Johnston, Trevor, and Adam Schembri. *Australian Sign Language: An Introduction to Sign Language Linguistics*. Cambridge: Cambridge University Press, 2007.

Kelly, Paul. "Jogging the Collective Memory." *The Weekend Australian*, April 2001, 21–22.

Kendon, Adam. *Sign Languages of Aboriginal Australia: Cultural, Semiotic and Communicative Perspectives*. Cambridge: Cambridge University Press, 1988.

Kerr, Joan, ed. *The Dictionary of Australian Artists: Painters, Sketchers, Photographers and Engravers to 1870*. Melbourne: Oxford University Press, 1992.

Koschutzke, Jenny. "The History of the Sydney Deaf Community's Boycott of the Adult Deaf and Dumb Society from 1929 to 1937 and the Establishment of Their Own Rival Association of Deaf and Dumb Citizens." MA thesis, University of Sydney, 1995.

Ladd, Paddy. *Understanding Deaf Culture: In Search of Deafhood*. Clevedon, England: Multilingual Matters Ltd., 2003.

Lake, Marilyn. *Getting Equal: The History of Australian Feminism*. St. Leonards, New South Wales: Allen & Unwin, 1999.

Lane, Harlan, ed. *The Deaf Experience: Classics in Language and Education*. Translated by Franklin Philip. Cambridge, MA: Harvard University Press, 1984.

―――. *The Mask of Benevolence: Disabling the Deaf Community*. New York: Alfred A. Knopf, 1992.

―――. *When the Mind Hears: A History of the Deaf*. New York: Random House, 1984.

Lee, Raymond, and John A. Hay. *Bermondsey 1792*. Feltham, Middlesex: National Union of the Deaf, 1993.

Loades, Rhonda. "The Establishment and Maintenance of the Deaf Community in South Australia." BA thesis, Flinders University, 1989.

Macintyre, Stuart. *The Oxford History of Australia, Vol. 4; 1901-1942: The Succeeding Age*. Melbourne: Oxford University Press, 1986.

Macintyre, Stuart, and Anna Clark. *The History Wars*. Melbourne: Melbourne University Press, 2003.

McKenna, Mark. "The History Anxiety." In *The Cambridge History of Australia*, 2nd edition, Vol. 2, edited by Alison Bashford and Stuart Macintyre, 561–80. Melbourne, Victoria: Cambridge University Press, 2013.

Murray, Joseph J. "'One Touch of Nature Makes the Whole World Kin': The Transnational Lives of Deaf Americans, 1870–1924." PhD diss., University of Iowa, 2007.

Neville, Richard. "Printmakers in Colonial Sydney 1800–1850." MA thesis, University of Sydney, 1988.

Payne, Arnold H. *King Silence: A Story.* London: Jarrolds Publishers, 1918.

Plann, Susan. *A Silent Minority: Deaf Education in Spain, 1550–1835.* Berkeley: University of California Press, 1997.

Proceedings of the International Conference of Educators of the Deaf, Supplement to *American Annals of the Deaf,* 1893.

Sayers, Edna Edith. "B. H. and Arnold H. Payne: Early Champions of Sign Language in the United Kingdom." *Deaf History Review,* 5 (2007), 22–30.

Stanner, William E. H. *The 1968 Boyer Lectures: After the Dreaming.* Sydney: Australian Broadcasting Commission, 1969.

Stiles, H. Dominic W. "Editor, Journalist, Missioner—Ernest J. D. Abraham." Accessed 2011. http://blogs.ucl.ac.uk/library-rnid/2011/12/16/editor-journalist-missioner-having-having-previously-applied-for-and-been-rejected-as-missioner-ernest-j-d-abraham/.

Swain, Shurlee. "Society and Welfare." In *The Cambridge History of Australia,* 2nd edition, Vol. 2, edited by Alison Bashford and Stuart Macintyre, 284–307. Melbourne, Victoria: Cambridge University Press, 2013.

Thornton, Darlene, Susannah Macready, and Patricia Levitzke-Gray. "Written into History: The Lives of Australian Deaf Leaders." In *Telling Deaf Lives: Agents of Change,* edited by Kristin Snoddon, 93–101. Washington, DC: Gallaudet University Press, 2014.

Uniacke, Michael. "Anger in the '40s: 'The Australian Deaf Citizen,'" *Sound Off* 1 (June 1987): 2–4.

Van Cleve, John V., and Barry A. Crouch. *A Place of Their Own: Creating the Deaf Community in America.* Washington, DC: Gallaudet University Press, 1989.

Veditz, George. "The Preservation of the Sign Language." Translated by Carol A. Padden and Eric Malzkuhn. In *Deaf World: A Historical*

Reader and Primary Sourcebook, edited by Lois Bragg, 83–85. New York: New York University Press. Reprint, 2001.

Wallis, Bernadette. *The Silent Book: A Deaf Family and the Disappearing Australian–Irish Sign Language*. Melbourne, Victoria: Author, 2016.

Wilson, Sue. *The History of the Queensland Deaf Society: From Mission to Profession 1903-2003*. Brisbane: The Queensland Deaf Society, 2003.

Wrigley, Owen. *The Politics of Deafness*. Washington, DC: Gallaudet University Press, 1996.

Archives

(a) Queensland State Archives

Home Secretary's Office; Correspondence re blind deaf and dumb, general, 1900–1937; Extracts from Minute Book on Training Scheme Verified and Initialed by Supt. Paul 23-2-31; RSI2383-1-21.

Home Secretary's Office; Statement by President of Q. A. D & D. Mission (Incorp) at the Inquiry held by Mr Bradbury, Home Department 8-5-31; RSI2383-1-21.

(b) State Records New South Wales

Colonial Secretary; CGS905, Main series of letters received, 1826–1982; items [12/7524 No. 1026 and No. 1085].

(c) Public Record Office, Victoria

PROV, VA 02707 Charities Board of Victoria, VPRS 4523/P1, "Closed" Agency and General Correspondence Files, Unit 38, File No. 354; Notes of the Victorian Deaf and Dumb Institution, Melbourne. From the Year 1898 to 1930.

PROV, VA 02707 Charities Board of Victoria, VPRS 4523/P1, "Closed" Agency and General Correspondence Files, Unit 51, File 477; J. P. Bourke, "The Victorian Branch of the Australian Association for the Advancement of the Deaf" (pamphlet), 9 October 1936.

PROV, VA 02707 Charities Board of Victoria, VPRS 4523/P1, "Closed" Agency and General Correspondence Files, Unit 68, File No. 656; Letter from Mr W. H. Crush to Mr Adcock Superintendent of the Victorian Deaf and Dumb Institute), n.d.

PROV, VA 02707 Charities Board of Victoria, VPRS 4523/P1, "Closed" Agency and General Correspondence Files, Unit 68, File 656; AAAD (Victorian Branch), Final Report of the Branch, April 1937.

PROV, VA 02707 Charities Board of Victoria, VPRS 4523/P1, "Closed" Agency and General Correspondence Files, Unit 68, File 656; The Commonwealth Association of the Deaf and Dumb, Constitution. (n.d.).

Legislation

Charitable Collections Act 1934 (No. 59) (NSW).

General Assembly of the Free Church of Scotland v Overtoun [1904] AC 515 (HL).

Other Official Sources

Victoria, Legislative Assembly, 1929, Supplementary Estimates.

Minutes, annual reports, constitutions, correspondence, and other records of Deaf-related organizations in Australia.

Periodicals

The Advertiser (SA), 1902.

The Age (Vic), 1903–1941.

The Argus (Vic), 1859–1941.

The Australian Deaf Citizen, 1940–41.

The British Deaf Mute, 1895–96.

The British Deaf Times, 1920–1932.

The Cairns Post, 1932.

Commonwealth Silent Courier, 1928.

The Daily Guardian (NSW), 1930.

The Daily Mail (Qld), 1930–1931.

The Daily Telegraph (NSW), 1929.

The Deaf Advocate, 1930–1937

Deaf Mutes Journal (USA), 1920.

The Deaf Quarterly News (UK), 1925–28.

Deaf Sports Notes (NSW), 1937.

The Herald (Vic), 1923–1941.

The Mercury (Tas), 1938.

Onward! (NSW) 1929–30.

Our Deaf Mute Citizens (Vic), n.d.

Our Monthly Letter (Vic), 1912–1930.

The News (NSW), 1929.

The Register (SA), 1904.
The Silent Messenger (NSW), 1907–1956.
Sound Off, 1987.
The South Australian Deaf Monthly News, 1910.
The Sun (Vic), 1903–1941.
The Sydney Morning Herald, 1929.
The Victorian Deaf, 1930–1932.
The Victorian Deaf News, 1932–1933.
The Weekend Australian, 2001.
The Worker's Voice, 1935.

INDEX

Page numbers in *italics* indicate illustrations.